THE QUEST
FOR
WILHELM
REICH

COLIN WILSON

THE QUEST FOR WILHELM REICH

ANCHOR PRESS/DOUBLEDAY
Garden City, New York 1981

The Anchor Press edition is the first publication of *The Quest for Wilhelm Reich*. Anchor Press edition: 1981

The author gratefully acknowledges permission to reprint material from *Me and the Orgone* by Orson Bean, copyright © 1971 by St. Martin's Press, Inc., Macmillan & Co., Ltd. Used by permission of the publisher.

ISBN: 0-385-01845-2
Library of Congress Catalog Card Number 78-22774

OCT 10 81

PREFATORY NOTE

In 1973, before I began to write this book on Wilhelm Reich, I wrote to both his English and American publishers—Vision Press, and Farrar, Straus & Giroux—to request permission to quote from his books. Farrar, Straus & Giroux granted it immediately; Vision Press agreed to a deal: they would grant permission if I would write an article on Emily Brontë, to be published in a symposium edited by Dr. Anne Smith. I wrote the article, which appeared in *The Art of Emily Brontë* in 1976, and that, as far as I was concerned, settled the problem of permission to quote.

I soon discovered I was mistaken. In the course of writing the book, I entered into correspondence with the authors of various other books on Reich, and learned that final permission to quote Reich had to be obtained from his executor, Mary Boyd Higgins. And this, apparently, was practically impossible to obtain if the book contained the slightest breath of criticism of Reich. One scholar remarked that it seemed ironical that Reich, who had gone to prison to defend intellectual freedom, should have left his work in the hands of someone who seemed to take the opposite view. I found myself unable to agree. I am sure Miss Higgins is behaving exactly as Reich would have wanted her to. He took the view that all critics of his work were motivated by malice and dishonesty, and would have been happy to see them suppressed.

Predictably, Miss Higgins reacted to my own book with indignation and denunciation. It was, she said, such a travesty of Reich that it left her no alternative except to refuse the required permission.

I have therefore made very few direct quotations from Reich—no more words, by way of criticism and fair comment, than is permitted by law. Whether this is fair to Reich is a question which I must leave to the individual reader. But the story seemed worth telling as a footnote to this study of a man whose attitude toward the truth about himself was always ambiguous.

ACKNOWLEDGMENTS

This book owes its existence to a suggestion of Bill Whitehead of Doubleday, who also commissioned it.

In the body of this book I have acknowledged my deep indebtedness to Robert Ollendorff, A. S. Neill, and Constance Rooth-Tracey, all, unfortunately, now dead. I also owe a debt of gratitude to: Kirstie Ollendorff, Ilse Ollendorff Reich, Peter Reich, David Boadella, Myron Sharaf, Ola Raknes, Charles Rycroft, Dr. Saul Lucas, Dr. Andrew Crawshaw, Dr. Raymond Pietroni and his wife Jennifer, Mrs. Suzanne Burford, Rudolph Nassauer, and Eileen Mackrory. I wish also to thank Orson Bean and his publisher St. Martin's Press for permission to quote a passage from *Me and the Orgone*. The London Library and Lewis's Medical Library have rendered invaluable assistance. Finally, my wife has patiently read this book as it came off the typewriter, and corrected spelling mistakes and grammatical and typing errors.

C.W.
Cornwall, Spring 1980

CONTENTS

PREFATORY NOTE   v

ACKNOWLEDGMENTS   vii

INTRODUCTION   1

The downfall of Wilhelm Reich. Reich's denunciations of his "enemies." Emotional plague. Reich's susceptibility to prejudice. Martin Gardner's ditto. Reich's vitalism; his views on cancer. Suppose he was right? Reich: the materialist who became a mystic. Reich's increasing paranoia. Van Vogt's "Right Man" theory. His pathological jealousy. Anticipations of Reich's orgone energy theory. Mesmer, Reichenbach, Fairfield, Féré, Harold Burr. Kirlian photography. I meet Robert Ollendorff. The orgone box. How Reich invented it. Ollendorff's career. Constance Rooth-Tracey. Reich's breathing therapy. I meet Ilse Reich. Why the marriage broke down. A. S. Neill on Reich. Reich on the murder of Jesus; loopholes in his theory. Reich's self-deception. The "Shakespearian tragedy" of his life. Human "personality" and "impersonality." Yin and yang. Beethoven. Poe. Reich's shrill self-assertion. Reich and Einstein. Reich's mistakes.

CHAPTER ONE   23

   *Austria under the Hapsburgs. The Badeni Ordinances.
The German-Austrian revolt. The beginning of the end of the em-
pire. Reich's childhood. His father and mother. His mother's
infidelity and suicide. Death of Reich's father. Loss of the farm.
Reich's army period. Student years in Vienna. Medical student.
The course in sexology. Hirschfeld and Havelock Ellis. Krafft-
Ebing. Sexual deviations. Reich's first reaction to Freudianism.
The "libido"—Reich's vitalism. Freud's pragmatism. Reich visits
Freud. Reich's later opinion of Freud: "not a genitally healthy
man."*

CHAPTER TWO   39

   *The history of psychoanalysis. Pre-Freudian views: "men-
tal diseases are brain diseases." Beard and "neurasthenia." The
Puységurs and hypnosis. Bernheim. Charcot and hypnosis. Axel
Munthe on Charcot. Freud studies with Charcot. Breuer and
Bertha Pappenheim. The power of the unconscious mind. Freud's
basic error: failure to recognize the "feedback mechanism." "The
ego is the puppet of the id." What is the unconscious? The mechanism of neurosis: the feedback effect. Freud and Maslow. Viktor
Frankl and the prisoners from Auschwitz. Powers of the unconscious: Coleridge and the illiterate who spoke Latin. Jean Houston
and the man who conversed with Socrates. Jung causes a "poltergeist effect." Freud abandons the libido and invents the death instinct. Reich's fundamental optimism. How the sexual theory
came about: Breuer and Anna O. The case of Little Hans. Freud
and the Wolf Man. What Freud suppressed in his paper. Freud's
paranoid bitterness about Adler. Freud and Jung. Freud and
Thomas Mann. Karl Kraus. Viktor Tausk. Tausk's suicide.*

CHAPTER THREE   69

*Reich on Freud. The Freud circle in Vienna. Federn,
Hitschmann, Nunberg, Rank, Silberer, Ferenczi. Suicide of Silberer. Reich's self-assurance. His unpopularity among Freud's
older followers. Reich's Peer Gynt paper; his denial of free will.
"The weakness that would destroy him." Reich casts himself as
the misunderstood martyr. Reich becomes a member of the
Vienna Psychoanalytic Society. Sadger's lack of tact. Federn begins to dislike Reich. "The aggressive, paranoid and ambitious
type." Why Reich broke off three "training analyses." Reich and
the sexual theory. Reich teaches his patients to masturbate. Case
of the impotent waiter. "Actual neurosis." The orgasm theory.
Reich marries. His work under Wagner-Jauregg. Reich's interest
in psychotic patients: "could they be right after all?" Reich's optimism. Freud invents the super-ego. Reich rejects it. The technical
seminar—designed to keep Reich out of mischief. Death of Reich's
brother Robert. Reich's first paper on genitality; its cool reception.
Reich's conviction that patients harbor hostility to the psychotherapist.* Function of the Orgasm: *Freud's lack of enthusiasm.
The problem of "resistance." Freud's disagreement. Freud as
Reich's father-substitute. Reich's loyalty to Freud. His ration-
alization of Freud's rejection. Freud refuses to psychoanalyze
Reich. Reich's breakdown. His "deterioration." Federn "slanders"
Reich. Reich's affairs with patients. Freud's narrow-mindedness.
Reich's return from the sanitarium.*

CHAPTER FOUR   97

*Was Reich's life-work based on a fallacy? Freud's theory
of neurosis. Neurasthenic patients. Frankl's law of reverse effort.
The evolutionary view of psychology. Freud's obsession with
being "scientific." Reich's cases of cardiac neurosis. Polanyi and
the problem of alienation. Split-brain research. The right and left
hemispheres. Sperry's work with epileptics. The "ego" as the left
hemisphere, the "id" as the right. Neurosis as failure of synchro-*

*nization between left and right. The feedback effect. The left is
always in a hurry. Stage fright. T. E. Lawrence as an example of
left-brain domination. Role of the right hemisphere: to add
"depth" to reality. Lady Chatterley and the orgasm. Reich's sexual
theory as a partial recognition of the truth about right and left.
The evolutionary possibilities of a closer cooperation of left and
right. Slowing down the left or speeding up the right? Reich's
variant of the sexual theory. Mechanism of neurosis.*

CHAPTER FIVE   113

*Reich's return to Vienna from Davos. The killings at
Schattendorff. The killers are acquitted; riots. Reich's sympathy
with the left. Reich's working-class patient. Reich's conversion to
Marxism. Psychoanalysis as "bourgeois thinking."* Dialectical Materialism and Psychoanalysis. *Reich joins the Communist Party.
The ideal society. The "compulsory sex morality." Malinowski's
Trobrianders. Are Reich's views borne out by modern "permissive
societies"? Human perverseness. "To be free is nothing; to become free is heavenly." Reich attempts to justify psychoanalysis to
the Marxists. Reich goes to Moscow. Increasing hostility of the
Freud circle. Freud's political views. Reich's lecture on "blockage." Freud's reaction:* Civilization and Its Discontents. *Freud
abandons the sexual theory; Reich disagrees. Reich and the defensive mechanism of patients. Methods to pinpoint "resistances."
Reich's new technique of character analysis. Provoking the patient's hostility. The impotent patient: Reich's analysis. How
would Maslow or Frankl have treated the case? Reich's psychoanalysis as a battle of wills. Another hostile patient. The "English
lord." Freud's increasing impatience. Reich as Communist agitator. He decides to go to Berlin. Initial success there. The Red
Block cell. Koestler's description of the cell. Reich's attempt to
combine sexual reform and Communism. Success of Association
for Sexual Politics. Why the Communists rejected Reich: their
feeling that he was "decadent." Reich's quarrel with Bischoff and
Schneider.* The Mass Psychology of Fascism. *Breakdown of his
marriage. The Reichstag fire. The German Communists are*

*suppressed. Reich is attacked in the Nazi press. He escapes back
to Vienna.*

CHAPTER SIX   147

    The quarrel with Freud; Freud refuses to publish Charac-
ter Analysis. *Federn forbids Reich to lecture. Reich decides to go
to Copenhagen. Reich's opportunism. Analysis of his miscalculations. His determination to compromise. Reich was basically
an authoritarian élitist. Arrival in Copenhagen; feelers to Rado in
New York. Publication of* Mass Psychology of Fascism. *Problems
with Danish authorities. Freud declines support. Move to Malmö.
Trip to London.* What Is Class Consciousness? *European tour. Expulsion from Sweden. Summer in Sletten. Thirteenth Psychoanalytical Congress: Reich's expulsion. The Oslo period. Electric
currents of the body. "Readiness potential." The "breakthrough
into the biological realm." Masochism: the desire to burst. Muscular armor. Orson Bean's description of treatment. Elsworth Baker:*
Man in the Trap. *Abreaction therapy: persuading patients to
relive experience. William Sargant. "The Freud of Oslo." Fenichel's defection. Rumors of Reich's insanity. The discovery of
bions. The T-bacilli. Bion research. Reich and Gerd Bergersen.
Reich's orgasm theories anger the Norwegians. Scandal. The attacks. SAPA bions and free orgone energy. Reich sails to New
York.*

CHAPTER SEVEN   181

    *The move to Long Island; marriage to Ilse Ollendorff.
Cure for cancer? The orgone box. The Maine camping trip: Reich
sees orgone energy in the sky. Invention of the accumulator. Experiments with mice. Cancer patients and the orgone accumulator.
The "Einstein episode." Einstein's rejection. "Freud's good old
doctrines." Reich's failure to recognize that the roots of psychological illness lie in the mind. The concept of "purpose." The rigidity of Reich's sexual doctrines. Reich's mistake in working
alone. Quarrel with Gertrude Gaasland. Hostility of neighbors.*

Briehl breaks with Reich: "not the same person he had known in Vienna." Reich's increasing success. Purchase of cabin on Mooselookmeguntic Lake. Photographing orgone energy. Experiment XX. Spontaneous creation of matter. Life at Orgonon. Birth of Peter. Increasing interest in child rearing. Listen, Little Man!—*a turning point in Reich's life. Emotional plague. The Mildred Brady "interview." "The Strange Case of Wilhelm Reich." The False Messiah problem. John Humphrey Noyes. The FDA sends an investigator. Dismissal of Reichian therapists. The 1948 Conference.*

CHAPTER EIGHT   207

Use of the Geiger counter to detect orgone energy. Reich's interest in atomic energy. The Oranur experiment. What happened? High radiation in the Rangeley area. Deadly Orgone Radiation. The cloudbuster. Weather control. Reich ends a drought. Ether, God and Devil *and* Cosmic Superimposition. The Murder of Christ. *The truth about Giordano Bruno. Modju. Reich's UFO phase. The cloudbuster versus the UFOs. The FDA's complaint. Reich's response. The Injunction. Reich causes snow to fall over the East Coast. Operation Emotional Plague. The attempt at intervention. The trip to Arizona. Orgone Energy Operation in the desert.* Contact with Space. *UFOs over Mount Catalina. "UFOs cause deserts." The Eas attack. Success of the desert experiment. Silvert sends accumulators to New York. The contempt proceedings. Reich arms his followers. Reich appears in court. The lawyers resign. Reich is arrested. The trial. Reich is fined and sentenced to prison. The appeal. Reich is transferred to Lewisburg. His death. The Reich revival.*

POSTSCRIPT   233

Was Reich a martyr? His self-centeredness. The bion experiments. Reich and flying saucers. Roerich's sighting. Jung's theory of "psychological projection." Poltergeist phenomena. Synchronicity. Kammerer and "seriality." Peter Fairley's experiences of synchronicity and second sight. Was Reich capable of producing "poltergeist effects"? Reich's masochism. His father fixation. Reich's loyalty to Freud. His denial of free will. His attempt to escape the cul-de-sac. Burr and life-fields. The "jelly mold." The retreat from psychology. Janet's psychology of tension. Janet and multiple personality. Léonie and Lucie. Irene. The "partial mind." Creative tension. Problem-solving: the evolutionary drive. The paradox of Reich. Reich's theory of "the Fall of man." "The deep experience of the self." The reaffirmation of free will.

NOTES   253

BIBLIOGRAPHY   257

INDEX   261

INTRODUCTION

It must have been some time in the mid-1960s when I came across a copy of Wilhelm Reich's *The Cancer Biopathy* in an Oxfam shop. Although the battered, blue-covered volume cost only a few pennies, I was of two minds as to whether or not to buy it. Reich had never interested me greatly. On the fringe of the anarchist movement in the early 1950s, I had often heard him praised as a "sexual liberator," but I could never understand why anybody under the age of seventy needed sexual liberating; that battle had surely been won by the mid-1920s? I could also recollect that Reich had held certain cranky views about medicine that had landed him in jail, where he died. I vaguely remember thinking that it served him right.

Still, I bought the book, and when I got home I tried to look up Reich in various encyclopedias; I couldn't locate even a reference. Then I remembered where I'd read about his downfall. It was in Martin Gardner's *Fads and Fallacies in the Name of Science*. I reread Gardner's chapter entitled "Orgonomy," and recalled why I'd felt hostile about Reich. It seemed that he had started off as an orthodox Freudian, contributing fairly respectable work on the sexual origin of neurosis, then joined the Communist Party; after his attempts to combine Freud and Marx offended both groups, he was rejected by both Freudians and Communists. Following a stay in Norway, he moved to America and announced his discovery of an unknown form of energy called orgone. This was supposed to be blue in color, and to cause the blueness of the sky. (It was also believed to cause the shimmering above roads and mountain tops that is sometimes "mistaken" for heat waves.) According to Reich, orgone energy permeates the universe; it is the basic element in the health in all living creatures, and lack of it causes disease. Reich devised a kind of greenhouse for trapping this energy; it consisted of alternating layers of wood and metal, and was called the Orgone Accumulator. This invention was the cause of his downfall, for the Food and Drug Administration objected to the sale of the accumulator on the grounds that there was no scientific evidence that it worked. When Reich declined to obey a court order that forbade him to send accumulators across state lines, he was sentenced to two years in prison, where he died more or less insane.

The thing I found most irritating about Reich was that he seemed incapable of believing in the honesty of anyone who didn't agree with him. He took it for granted that people who questioned his ideas must be motivated by envy or hatred. He even coined a term to describe what was wrong with these unbelievers: they were suffering from "emotional plague," a disease that was supposed to be akin to hysteria. Mary Baker Eddy, founder of Christian Science, had invented an equally convenient explanation of the opposition she aroused: "malicious animal magnetism." (It became such a catch phrase in her movement that it was eventually abbreviated to MAM.) I have always found something peculiarly obnoxious about people who need to fall back on this kind of argument: a blanket dismissal of anyone who refuses to accept them at their own valuation. It is basically an insult to the concept of human intelligence.

At the same time, I caught a whiff of the same kind of prejudice in Martin Gardner's book. Gardner writes about various kinds of cranks with the conscious superiority of the scientist, and in most cases one can share his sense of the victory of reason. But after half-a-dozen chapters, this nonstop superiority begins to irritate; you begin to wonder about the standards that make him so certain *he* is always right. He asserts that the scientist, unlike the crank, does his best to remain open-minded, so how can he be so *sure* that no sane person has ever seen a flying saucer, or used a dowsing rod to locate water? And that all the people he disagrees with are unbalanced fanatics? A colleague of the positivist philosopher A. J. Ayer once remarked wryly: "I wish I was as certain of anything as he seems to be about everything." Martin Gardner produces the same feeling.

Alerted to the difficulties of keeping an open mind, I turned to *The Cancer Biopathy*. First impressions were as bad as I'd been led to expect. There is an atmosphere of folie de grandeur. Reich seems to believe that his discoveries are not only important, but momentous and awe-inspiring. Nevertheless, he says, the tremendous import of these facts already strikes him as less frightening, and in due course the open-minded reader will also find reason to become less worried. One of the "reasons" is that Reich himself has now learned to deal with human irrationality and to better understand what is going on inside people who fall victim to mysticism or the emotional plague. As one who has always been interested in mysticism, I found myself irritated by this attempt to equate it with emotional plague. As far as I could see, the only frightening thing about Reich's ideas was his conviction that he was right and everyone else wrong. It is easy to see that if he had achieved political power, his "enemies" would probably have landed in concentration camps.

All the same, I still found myself unable to share Martin Gardner's deep conviction that Reich's "discovery" is self-evident nonsense. Reich's basic idea is that cancer can only be understood in terms of an all-pervading cosmic energy which is not subject to the mechanical laws of nature. As I had written a book on Bernard Shaw, this notion was familiar to me; Shaw called it "the life force." Bergson called it "élan vital." The biologist Driesch called it "entelechy." The philosopher Whitehead hinted at the same thing when he spoke of the universe as a single living organism.

Shaw had, in fact, advanced a theory of cancer that is startlingly close to Reich's. He believed that the difference between living matter and dead matter is simply that living matter can *conduct* the life force because of its molecular structure. Animal matter is more alive than vegetable matter because it is a better conductor; it carries a higher voltage of the life force, so to speak. If the structure of matter in a living body is changed, it may suddenly begin to conduct a lower voltage of the force, so it becomes virtually a separate organism in the same body. This is cancer. According to Reich, cancer is caused by a blockage of vitality. The devitalized tissues begin to degenerate, in much the same way as if their blood supply was cut off. Black, elongated bodies called T-bacilli are formed, and it is these that produce cancer.

And at this point, I was suddenly struck by a disturbing thought. *Suppose he was right?* This would put an entirely different complexion on the matter. Gardner's *Fads and Fallacies* first appeared in 1952, at the time when Reich was being hounded by the Food and Drug Administration. A preface to the next edition states: "The first edition of this book prompted many curious letters from irate readers. The most violent letters came from Reichians." But then, if Reich was basically correct about something as important as orgone energy, their annoyance would be understandable, for Gardner's chapter on Reich is really a piece of slick, highhanded, deflationary journalism. If Reich was correct, then his personal defects would be irrelevant. How would Sir Isaac Newton—that suspicious, bad-tempered genius—have reacted if his theories had been treated as a joke and all copies of the *Principia* burned? How, for that matter, would Einstein have reacted to public derision and legal sanctions? Can it be doubted that they would also have become a little paranoid?

I read *The Cancer Biopathy,* and was impressed. There could be no doubt that Reich was something of a fanatic; at the same time, he writes with the clarity and detachment of a true scientist. I found a paperback copy of *The Function of the Orgasm,* and experienced the same reaction. Reich's insistence that the sexual orgasm is the key to psychological health aroused my scepticism—it sounded too much like Freud's brand of "reductionism"—but the lucid, logical style compelled respect.

Although *The Function of the Orgasm* and *The Cancer Biopathy* are intended to be Parts One and Two of the same work (*The Discovery of the Orgone*), more than twenty years elapsed between their publication. And it is clear that Reich found himself being swept against his will into the "mysticism" he detested so much. In *The Function of the Orgasm* he explains why he cannot be regarded as a "vitalist." A vitalist believes that living matter differs from dead matter *in kind* as well as in molecular structure. In other words, there is a metaphysical principle of life that exists *beyond* matter. This, says Reich, is a position he totally rejects. The difference between dead and living matter is simply a difference of energy. Living matter is "inhabited," so to speak, by orgone energy. This energy can, according to Reich, transform a sterile bouillon culture into a living culture.

Now clearly, such a distinction is really an evasion. If the orgone energy is merely energy, then it is not alive, any more than electricity is alive. If it is alive, then it must be more than energy; it must be living energy, and somehow different from ordinary energy.

What was happening struck me as amusing. Reich is determined to represent himself as a tough-minded materialist, yet his own discoveries undermine his materialist standpoint. In fact, as I later discovered from Ilse Reich's biography, Reich finally faced up to the contradictions in his position, admitted that orgone energy must be identified with love, and even agreed that this implied the existence of God. There was nothing of this in *The Discovery of the Orgone,* but long before the end of *The Cancer Biopathy* it is obvious that Reich has severe difficulties.

I became fascinated by this enigma of a scientist turning, against his will, into a metaphysical philosopher. Whether he was right about orgone energy became a secondary issue. What I wanted to know was how this Freudian Marxist had come to abandon the scientific and political materialism of his early days.

I began trying to find out more about Reich's life and personality, but it proved oddly difficult. His books contain fragments of autobiography, but there is a curious underlying feeling of inhibition and reticence. The standard histories of psychotherapy—Gregory Zilboorg's *History of Medical Psychology,* for example—either ignore him or dismiss him in a paragraph. Ernest Jones's three-volume *Life of Freud* hardly mentions him. This seemed odd, since Reich's place in the Freudian movement was at least as important as that of Jung, Adler, or Rank.

Then, in 1969, Ilse Ollendorff Reich's *Wilhelm Reich: A Personal Biography* appeared, and it was a revelation. Reich had met Ilse Ollendorff in New York in 1939; she was twenty-nine at the time, and Reich was forty-two. They married two months later, and remained together until 1954, when Ilse found the strain of living with this wayward and paranoid genius too much, and moved elsewhere. Ilse Ollendorff had met Reich at a crucial point in his life, when hostility to his ideas had driven him from Europe. His sense of persecution was mounting; so was his intolerance. In Scandinavia, Reich's relations with his coworkers had been informal, and they called him Willy; in America, he insisted on being called Dr. Reich. (He told A. S. Neill: "In this work any familiarity with me would destroy it. They would encroach on me emotionally.") A paranoid self-assertion is characteristic of his later years, and it was undoubtedly responsible for his downfall. He consistently overreacted to the "persecution" of the Food and Drug Administration. Instead of appearing in court to answer their charges in a reasonable manner, he wrote the judge a four-page letter, more or less denying that the court had any jurisdiction in matters of science. Understandably, the judge granted the injunction. Reich's reaction was to compare himself to Galileo, Jesus, and Giordano Bruno, and to threaten to use his orgone machine to cause storms that would flood the eastern United States. Ilse Reich's biography makes it clear that Reich's imprisonment was entirely his own fault. With a minimum of common sense, he would have had no difficulty staying out of jail.

All this fascinated me. It had not been long since I came across A. E. Van Vogt's "Right Man" theory, and it struck me as one of the most significant developments in psychology since Freud. I will try to summarize it here briefly: in reading reports of divorce cases, Van Vogt became aware of how often they involved a personality-type that he labeled the Right Man or the Violent Man. Such men have an obsession with being *in the right;* under no circumstances could they acknowledge the possibility that they might be wrong, and if someone is tactless enough to try to force them to recognize it, they explode into violence. In the home they behave like tyrants, demanding total submission and obedience from wife and children. The least suspicion of infidelity or disloyalty, no matter how ill-founded, is enough to drive them into a frenzy. Yet they themselves are perfectly capable of sexual lapses—sexual conquest is important to their self-esteem—and expect the partner to treat these with tolerance.

In short, the Right Man is a man whose entire life revolves

around his sense of his own importance; the least challenge to this strikes him as unforgivable. Since our social lives have to be governed by rules of politeness, his colleagues and acquaintances may not even notice that he is a Right Man. But those who live in close proximity to him become accustomed to having to live according to *his* rules, or encounter the full force of his resentment.

There is, of course, a degree of Right-Mannishness in most of us; nobody enjoys having his self-esteem wounded. And a human being without self-esteem is either a saint or a useless weakling. It follows that people who are slightly above average in talent, intelligence, or dominance are more likely to develop into Right Men than the rest of us. One of the most common types is the man whose dominance is slightly higher than his intelligence or imagination, so that he feels that his merits are not being recognized, but lacks the insight to see that this is his own fault.

Right Men with political power—like Hitler or Stalin—are terrifying. And Right Men who regard themselves as "intellectuals" can be almost as dangerous; they are inclined to see themselves as messiahs. On a certain level, their ideas may be brilliant and perceptive—like those of Karl Marx or Mao Tse-tung. But at a certain point, the factor of resentment creeps in, and the ideas are distorted by obsessions and vendettas.

Right Men are made, not born. "Rightness" involves a degree of self-deception: it can happen little by little, over many years; the fabrication of excuses for convincing oneself that certain painful misjudgments never happened, that it was the fault of other people . . . Dogmatism is substituted for open-mindedness, bullying for persuasion. Although Ilse Ollendorff met Reich only after he came to America, it is clear from her biography that Reich was an altogether more reasonable, open-minded character in his European days. This could be because some of his associates—like Ola Raknes, Nic Waal, and A. S. Neill—were also talented and strong-minded, and stimulated a certain self-appraisal. His threefold rejection—by the Psychoanalytic Association, by the Communist Party, and by his adopted country Norway—seems to have produced a crisis of misery, which Reich solved by becoming more aloof, more suspicious, and more resentful. His second wife (or rather consort, they were never officially married) Elsa Lindenberg, decided not to accompany him to America because his outbursts of temper were becoming too much of a strain. Ilse Ollendorff was to write: "I know what Elsa must have gone through in those days, because fifteen years later I went through the same experience. No matter how much love, devotion and understanding one might bring to the situation, there was a point when it became a question of life or death, a matter of retaining one's own integrity and individuality or submitting completely to Reich."

When Elsa Lindenberg, living penniless in Sweden, later wrote to ask Reich for help, he sent her only twenty-five dollars. By that time, she was another who had "betrayed" him.

Ilse Ollendorff Reich's biography makes it very clear that Reich became a highly developed example of the Right Man type. (She mentions, for example, his pathological jealousy: ". . . he would accuse [me] of infidelity with any man who came to his mind as a possible rival, whether colleague, friend, local shopkeeper, or casual acquaintance." It seemed to support Martin Gardner's theory of Reich as a crank messiah. Yet at the time I came across Ilse Ollendorff Reich's book, I was working on a book called *The Occult,* and was intrigued to realize that Reich's discovery of orgone energy had several times been anticipated in the past century and a half. Franz Anton Mesmer believed that the universe is permeated with a kind of life-fluid, and his views gained wide acceptance in the decade before the French Revolution; in the 1840s, Baron Karl von Reichenbach renamed Mesmer's fluid "odic force," and was convinced that it is the principle of health in human beings. Half a century later, Dr. Walter J. Kilner of St. Thomas's Hospital, London, rediscovered the "fluid," which he called "the human aura"; Kilner even invented a transparent screen, stained with special dye, which he claimed could enable anyone to see this aura. These men failed to convince their fellow scientists; but this was not the case with Dr. Harold Burr, of Harvard, whose experiments with trees in the 1930s established beyond all doubt that there *is* a weak electrical field associated with life, and that this field can be registered by a delicate voltmeter. In animals and human beings, this field is affected by illness, which can also be detected on the voltmeter. In recent years, the "human aura" has again become the subject of widespread scientific research as a result of the experiments of Professor Semyon Kirlian, who believes that he has established a method for photographing the "life field" of living creatures with the use of highly charged photographic plates.

In the light of this impressive, if controversial, body of evidence, Reich's orgone theory began to sound altogether less like the idée fixe of a Right Man.

It was at this point that our family doctor, Andrew Crawshaw, mentioned that his sister and brother-in-law worked in association with England's leading Reichian therapist, Robert Ollendorff, whose sister had become Reich's second "official" wife. He also pointed out that Ollendorff had been in poor health recently, and suggested that if I wanted to meet him, I shouldn't delay too long. Accordingly, I went to stay for a few days with Raymond and Jennifer Pietroni in Camberwell, and was introduced to Ollendorff and his wife Kirstie.

My first reactions to Robert Ollendorff were ambivalent. I think I had expected to meet someone a little like Reich—Germanic, impressive, rather authoritarian. Ollendorff was none of these things. He was witty, loquacious, and mischievous, and I soon realized that he was determined to be liked rather than respected. He was profoundly antiauthoritarian, a born anarchist, and I think his professional associates sometimes found his puckish unpredictability a strain. He had a mannner of dropping bombshells into the middle of abstract conversations; when we were discussing Reich's disagreements with Freud he suddenly remarked: "Mind, even Reich was afraid to admit that a doctor sometimes has to sleep with his patients to get to know them." I have no reason to suppose he ever did anything of the sort—he gave the impression of having a singularly happy and untroubled home life. But it wasn't entirely a perverse desire to shock. He was raising an important and basic implication of Reichian therapy out of a sheer Viennese passion for ideas. (He was not, in fact, a Viennese—he was born in Breslau—yet he always seemed to me such a typical example of the Jewish-Viennese intellectual that I found this hard to remember.)

That first evening at the Ollendorffs', I tried out the orgone box which was in the corner of his office. It was a large box, about half the size of a telephone booth. The walls were roughly six inches thick, made of alternating layers of metal and asbestos (or other organic material). There was a large hole in the door, about a foot square, through which I could look when I was seated on the chair inside the box. Ollendorff took my temperature before I went inside; it was normal. The box itself felt oddly warm, and I wondered whether it might be standing close to a radiator. I reached out and touched the metal walls; they were cold to the touch.

It seemed an odd arrangement. I asked Ollendorff what made Reich think that alternate layers of metal and asbestos would somehow trap the energy? If it can get in, what is to stop it getting out again? Ollendorff explained that the original idea had been simply to trap the energy from "bion cultures"—cultures that radiate orgone energy—by reflecting it back from metal walls. The culture was placed inside a large metal box, and the experimenter studied it by looking through the hole in the door. In the original box, a layer of wood was added on the outside to stop the energy escaping into the laboratory—organic material is believed to absorb orgone energy. To Reich's surprise, the box not only trapped the energy from bion cultures, but absorbed energy from outside; even when the box was empty, they noticed the characteristic blue color of orgone energy. The more layers they added, the better it worked.

At this point I emerged from the box, and Ollendorff took my temperature; it had risen by 2.5 degrees Fahrenheit.

I was impressed, and I was surprised when Ollendorff told me that he was not convinced on the subject of orgone energy. "I am not a physicist." He added with a touch of malice: "And neither was Reich." But then, he pointed out, it made no difference whether you believed in the orgone or not, provided you accepted Reich's original hypothesis that *some* form of vital energy is discharged in the sexual orgasm. Even the most sceptical would find that hard to deny. Whether it is ordinary physical energy, "bio-energy," or a universal life-energy is beside the point. Reichian therapy simply depends on the notion that some form of energy gets blocked, and that the blockage causes neurosis, another name for energy-stagnation.

What sort of a person *was* Reich? I wanted to know, and was surprised when Ollendorff said he had never met him. When Hitler came to power in 1933, the twenty-one-year-old Ollendorff was arrested as a known Communist sympathizer, and spent nine months in a concentration camp. His sister Ilse had already left

Germany to go to England; when he was released, Robert went to Tanganyika. It was there that he came across the books of Reich, and was fascinated by them. Sometime around the New Year of 1940, he heard, to his astonishment, that he had just become the brother-in-law of his hero. By this time, Ollendorff had made a belated decision to become a doctor, and began his medical studies in England. When it came to studying Reich's therapeutic methods, Ollendorff studied with Reich's pupil and friend Ola Raknes in England. After the war, it would have been easy enough to step on a plane and visit the Reichs at the Institute in Rangeley, Maine. In fact, it would surely have been the obvious thing to do, since he was now practicing Reichian therapy, but by this time Ollendorff had learned more about Reich's personality— from Raknes, among others—and I suspect that he realized that closer acquaintance might be a mistake. Reich was beginning to develop the authoritarianism of the stereotypical German professor, and Ollendorff was too deeply antiauthoritarian to be anybody's disciple; he and Reich would probably have quarrelled violently within twenty-four hours. Ollendorff half-admitted as much to me one morning as we sat in the local pub. "It is probably as well that we never met."

So far I had met no one who had actually known Reich, and I found it difficult to get a picture of him as a human being. Then my old friend Rudi Nassauer—novelist and wine merchant—mentioned that he knew an expatient of Reich who lived in London. Her name was Constance Rooth-Tracey. I lost no time in writing to ask if I could go and see her, and a couple of weeks later I called at her flat in a quiet road to the north of Regent's Park. She proved to be a lady of independent means, now in her sixties, who had gone to Reich in 1936 to be treated for depression. The treatment lasted for three years, and although it was unfinished when he left for America, she had no doubts about its success.

It was obvious that she still regarded him with a respect verging on worship. When I asked her if it was not true that Reich had been an explosive character, she shook her head. He *could* be, with people he distrusted; but for those he liked, he had nothing but warmth and kindness. And although she told me a great deal about Reich's personality and his methods of treatment, she neglected to mention that when she went to see Reich in Maine in

1948, they had a blazing quarrel and parted on hostile terms. (I learned this a few years later from her daughter, Mrs. Suzanne Burford.) I am inclined, in retrospect, to believe that she preferred to remember the earlier benefits and kindness she had received from Reich, and to forget that, by 1948, he had become an altogether more prickly and difficult character.

I asked her about Reich's therapy, and she surprised me by saying that the most important thing he taught her was how to breathe. She explained that Reich had noticed that people under tension inhibit their intake of oxygen. Conversely, the first thing we do when we feel relieved or happy is to take a deep breath and relax. According to Reich, people with psychological problems breathe shallowly in order to create less vital energy, which in turn makes their impulses easier to master; it could be compared to deliberately playing a scratched record at low volume so as not to be upset by the scratch. This shallow breathing eventually becomes an entrenched habit. So Reich insisted that the first step toward overcoming nervous tensions is to learn to breathe deeply, using the stomach and solar plexus as well as the chest.

At this point she told me to lie flat on the carpet, and to breathe "normally." Apparently my breathing demonstrated that I was experiencing nervous tensions (which was true; I felt silly lying there). What I had to learn was to breathe *out,* because it is out-breathing—the sigh of relief—that relieves nervous tensions. Reich, she said, repeated over and over again the phrase: "Out-down-through." "Out" referred to the lungs, "down" to the stomach, and "through" to the genitals. Correct breathing should go all the way to the genitals, producing deep relaxation . . . I did my best, but I have never felt at home in situations like this; I think she regarded me as a poor student. When I left that afternoon, I had no doubt that Reich had been a man who could command enormous loyalty, and who felt at home in the role of a father-figure to his female patients, but I still had no idea of what Reich had been like as a person.

Some weeks later, Robert Ollendorff wrote to say that his sister Ilse was coming to stay that month, August 1972; if I wanted to meet her, I could go and stay overnight. I immediately bought her book on Reich—so far I had made do with the London Library's copy—and reread it. Again, I was struck by the lack of actual per-

sonal description of Reich. She tells of her first meeting with him
in October 1939: "He was a striking figure with his grey hair,
ruddy complexion and white coat." That is all. Most women, writing of a famous man they had been married to, would try to con-
vey some basic impression: "His eyes, that looked as if they were
laughing at some secret joke," or "He had an odd way of
chuckling suddenly from the depths of his chest," but not Ilse
Ollendorff. I wondered if she ended by disliking him so much that
she couldn't bring herself to give any personal details. The photograph of her on the book jacket made her look rather formidable,
like a strong-minded school principal.

When I met her, I realized how misleading a photograph can
be. Ilse Reich was a slim, attractive woman whose hair was still
black, although she was in her sixties. She was one of those lucky
women who are not much affected by age—in whom a teenage girl
seems to lurk just below the surface. I could see why Reich lost no
time in grabbing her. She was gentle, intelligent, and rather shy.
(Before she came into the room Ollendorff told me: "I have always been in love with my sister.") Such women seem to be made
to be carried off by dominant males. What puzzled me was why
Reich had not stayed married to her.

She responded with frankness to most of my questions. The
marriage had been successful for many years; it began to go wrong
after the Oranur experiment, when a tiny quantity of radium
placed in an orgone accumulator made everyone sick. Reich
believed that it was not ordinary radiation sickness; the emana-
tions of the radium somehow combined with orgone energy to
produce a deadly negative energy. Ilse became seriously ill; Reich
had a heart attack after the experiment. Under increasing pressure
from the FDA, Reich was becoming pathologically suspicious, and
began accusing Ilse of infidelity with all and sundry.

I accepted this explanation with my own reservations, recalling
A. S. Neill's comment that Reich had become distinctly more aggressive and thin-skinned when he visited him in 1947. It was also
while talking to Ilse that it suddenly struck me that Reich was a
typical example of Van Vogt's Right Man. What she said about
his fits of jealousy—always totally unfounded—confirmed this. I
was unable to bring myself to ask her whether Reich himself was
unfaithful. But on my way back to Cornwall on the train, I found

the answer in her book. When she came back from a vacation in England in 1947: "Reich put me through a third degree questioning . . . He asked especially if I had been faithful to him during those two months. I almost had to take an oath of fidelity before he would be satisfied . . . I was not allowed to question his faithfulness to me during that period, but I was quite certain that he did not apply to himself the same standards that he expected of me. In fact I knew that he had had an affair . . ." She adds that by 1952 Reich's persecution mania had increased to an extent where he made her write periodic "confessions" of her dislike of him and antagonism to his work—a technique, she remarks, reminiscent of Stalin.

The jealousy was confirmed by A. S. Neill, whom I met at about the same time on a trip to East Anglia. Apart from Raknes, Neill remained Reich's closest friend, one of the few with whom he never quarreled. Yet in spite of his trust in Neill, Reich could not prevent himself from asking his second "wife," Elsa Lindenberg, if she had ever slept with Neill.

Neill also had strong feelings of loyalty towards Reich; he even described him to me as "lovable." He made me begin to wonder whether I was not being hasty in concluding that Reich was an out-and-out Right Man. Obviously, Reich could inspire great affection and devotion, and such men must radiate human warmth as well as dominance. Neill spoke of Reich's relationship with his son Peter, the obvious love and trust between them. But then, Reich could take his son's total loyalty for granted because he did not suspect sexual infidelity.

I could also see exactly why Reich was so fond of Neill, and why the two had never quarreled. If I said that Neill was a born flatterer I would be putting it too strongly, and perhaps implying a weakness of character that was certainly not present in him. At the same time, he had a charming tendency to belittle his remarkable achievements (which included some skillful novels), and to imply that other people were in every way more brilliant and perceptive. (In this respect, he reminded me strongly of Henry Miller, whose charm was also based on a combination of modesty and a capacity to radiate admiration.) After all, Neill had no need to be charming to me. I was there as a kind of journalist, researching a book on Reich, intruding into the private life of an old man in poor health. If he knew anything about me at all, it was probably based on newspaper publicity from the days when I was inappropriately labeled an "Angry Young Man." Yet he somehow managed to imply that it was entirely his good fortune to be questioned by such an important and brilliant writer on the subject of his important and brilliant old friend. Understandably, I found him delightful. Who could resist a man who could write in a letter: "[Your book] shows me so clearly the gulf between the man of talent (me) and the man of universal insight (you)."

Still, it struck me later that this sentence from Neill also pinpoints why his opinion of Reich is not entirely to be trusted. It occurs in a letter about Reich's *Murder of Christ,* which Neill goes on to describe as "the most important book I have ever read." Now, like *Listen, Little Man!, The Murder of Christ* is one of Reich's later attempts at self-justification. His thesis is that mankind is so rotten with "emotional plague" that the healers and preachers of universal love are automatically murdered. Neill told me a story of how Reich, at a party, overheard a woman say that Krishnamurti was the most Christ-like man she had ever met. "Then why hasn't he been murdered?" asked Reich.

What Reich was trying to do, of course, was to explain why he himself encountered so much hostility and misunderstanding. His answer: Christ encountered the same kind of thing. Like Christ, he (Reich) is attacking the antilife armoring of modern man, and hatred is the natural reaction of the sick to those who want to bring them health.

The trouble with this explanation is that it is at base untrue. It is untrue in the case of Jesus, and particularly untrue in the case of Reich. Jesus was disliked by the Romans because he represented a political threat, and by his own people because nations with strong religious traditions detest upstarts who want to alter things. For the Romans, he was a religious nut; for the Jews, an irreligious rebel. Reich aroused hostility because he seemed to be what he *was:* a paranoid egoist. The only thing Reich and Jesus have in common is that they were both widely regarded in their lifetimes as cranks and charlatans. It is simply not true that mankind murders its saints as a matter of course; a glance at any volume of *Lives of the Saints* will show that the majority of them died surrounded by weeping disciples.

Because of his deep loyalty—his feeling of being one of Reich's few friends in a hostile world—Neill overlooks this element of self-deception in Reich. This is probably what friends are for, but I am less happy about Neill's tendency to deceive himself. In *Wilhelm Reich—The Evolution of His Work* David Boadella quotes Neill: "In 1947, and again in 1948, when we walked through the Maine woods together, he would suddenly stop and fire a question at me: 'Do you think I'm crazy, Neill?' My reply was always the same: 'Crazy as a coot!' I can still see his warm face at times like these and the visual memory brings me utter sorrow. I cannot think that Reich became crazy. He may have showed himself to be capable of illusion. We all have more or less paranoid fantasies . . ." But Reich was not, as Neill here implies, a nice, reasonable man with a touch of persecution mania. *The Murder of Christ* and *Listen, Little Man!* reveal massive self-deception and full-blown paranoia. Again, Neill's answer "Crazy as a coot" implies: "Just as I am myself." But this is an evasion. Reich did not mean "Am I a revolutionary eccentric?" He meant "Am I mentally unbalanced?" Neill is not to be blamed for trying to reassure his old friend; but that is no reason why his readers should allow themselves to be taken in.

When I tried to write up my notes on my meetings with Ollendorff, Constance Rooth-Tracey, Ilse Reich, and A. S. Neill, it struck me that I was still as far as ever from the "truth about Reich." Was he, as Ollendorff and Neill believed, a typical "Outsider," a man driven by a peculiar kind of honesty, an inner vision of truth, which he had to pursue even at the cost of health and sanity? Or was he merely an egoist tormented by a desire for "recognition," by the hunger for self-esteem?

I had to admit that what intrigued me about Reich was that there was no simple answer to the problem. Reich *was* a misunderstood man of genius; he was also a touchy egoist who became his own worst enemy. He was a man of profound and important insights who was also capable of embarrassing intellectual naïveté (such as his notion that human aggressiveness could be blamed on the desire for private property). He was a complex human being who craved simple answers to the mysteries of the human mind. There is something almost Shakespearian about the tragedy of his life—the flawed strength that became self-destructive, the powerful spirit undermined by rage and suspicion.

In short, what kept drawing me back again and again to Reich was the fascination of the strange no-man's-land between genius and insanity, greatness and paranoia, self-belief and self-deception. For the same reason, I have always been fascinated by that other paranoid man of genius, August Strindberg—and, to a lesser extent, by the brilliant and vitriolic Frederick Rolfe who, with typical self-aggrandizement, preferred to be known as Baron Corvo.

While I brooded on this, and tried to get it down on paper, it struck me suddenly that I had stumbled on an important basic insight, one that applies to all human beings, not just the dominant few. It is this: every one of us is a mixture of two elements, which could be labeled "personality" and "impersonality"; but in each one, *the proportions are different*. We are all interested in ourselves, in achieving our ambitions. But we all have other interests that attract us for nonpersonal reasons: ideas, music, poetry, books, nature, science. We say they take us "out of ourselves," meaning out of the *personal* self. Even the least intelligent human being has certain nonpersonal interests—if only a newspaper crossword puzzle, or the fortunes of a football team. But in men and women of talent, the dichotomy is particularly obvious because talent involves self-expression—that is, expression of the two aspects. We could picture them as the dark and light side on one of those Chinese symbols of yin and yang. The dark side is yin, the impersonal, the receptive; the light side is yang, the personal, the ambitious, the self-assertive.

If we think of various men of genius, we can see that the two sides can be found in different proportions. The greatest self-expression springs out of impersonality—what Keats called "negative capability." We can see this in Dante, Leonardo, Shakespeare, Mozart, Goethe, and Einstein. The very fact that we know so little about Shakespeare is a proof of his self-effacement. His friend Ben Jonson, an altogether more dominant man, made sure posterity would be familiar with his own biographical details.

In Beethoven, we can see the personal element becoming dangerously enlarged; his bitter quarrels sprang out of touchy pride, not from any sense of lack of recognition. Nevertheless, he maintained his creative balance, and produced works of impersonal genius. It is when we descend to men of lesser genius that ego begins to tilt the balance on the side of the personal. The result is usually disaster.

There is an anecdote about Poe that perfectly illustrates the two elements; it can be found in Hervey Allen's *Israfel*. A female admirer, Mrs. Gove Nichols, describes how Poe confided in her one day: "I write from mental necessity—to satisfy my taste and my love of art. Fame forms no motive power for me . . ." He insisted that he had absolutely no interest in "the plaudits of the mob." On her next visit, as they walked along a hilltop, Poe said suddenly: "I can't look on all this loveliness till I have made a confession to you. I said to you, when you were here last, that I despised fame. It is false. I love fame—I dote on it—I idolize it—I would drink to the very dregs the glorious intoxication. I would have incense ascend in my honor from every hill and hamlet . . . Fame! Glory!— they are life-giving breath, and living blood. No man lives until he is famous! How bitterly I belied my aspirations when I said I did not desire fame . . ."

In saying "I write from mental necessity," Poe recognizes that great literature springs out of the impersonal. But "No man lives until he is famous" is his admission that he has not achieved that level of impersonality. This can be seen in his work in a constant straining for effect. His most ambitious attempt at an "impersonal" book, *Eureka*—a kind of philosophy of the universe—is almost unreadable, simply because we sense that it is a fraud, a piece of overblown, sham profundity, a frantic bid for fame. It was this unsatisfied craving for fame that turned Poe to the alcohol that eventually destroyed him; the alcoholism was a response to the feeling: "I deserve some compensation . . ."

In general, then, craving for "recognition," for ego-satisfaction, is a hindrance to genuine creativity. And there are many men of talent, even of genius, who arouse in us an instinctive distaste because we sense that their "impersonality" is a pretense, that their "desire for truth" is really a desire for fame. When grape-seeds are crushed inside the grape, the wine has a bitter flavor; too much "personality" has the same effect on a work of art.

All of which, I believe, explains why Reich arouses such ambivalent feelings. No one who reads his books can regard him as a downright fake; the mind behind them is too powerful and analytical—he is too obviously "on to something." But he is always stepping beyond the justified self-belief of the scientist who knows the importance of his own work into the shrill self-assertion of a recognition-starved ego. Even Neill noted the ambivalence in him. "I think he deceived himself when he reiterated his desire to be free from recommendation" (i.e., from the acclaim of fellow writers). If Reich was really so unconcerned, why, Neill wondered, did he send him two dozen copies of the English translation of *The Function of the Orgasm*? What use could Neill possibly have for them except to send them to people who might use their influence? Ilse Reich also noticed her husband's dualism about recognition. "Although he chided Neill about the importance of world recognition, he was very pleased—and wrote to his friends about it—when in 1944 his name appeared both in the *World Almanac* and in *American Men of Science*. I have often wondered about his clinging to these straws of official recognition despite his denial of their having any real value." She was also amused to observe that when Reich gave an appointment to a stranger, "he always went through the same routine . . . playing the great scientist . . . He would be in his study, deeply engrossed in writing, wearing a freshly laundered laboratory coat. He would give the visitor the impression that he did him a great favor by interrupting such important work to see him." Einstein, on the other hand, struck people with his complete naturalness, the total lack of desire to impress; he once remarked to Leopold Infeld: "I appear to myself as a swindler because of the great publicity about me without any real reason."

It is true, of course, that Einstein achieved a secure celebrity at an early age. But the real difference between them lies in that inner balance between personality and impersonality. In Reich, personality, hunger for recognition, outweighed the impersonality of the scientist; therefore he was vulnerable to snubs and disappointments that would have glanced off Einstein with no effect.

In short, it boils down to a question of self-discipline, that is to say, to a factor that is almost totally ignored in the psychology of Freud and Reich: human freedom. Chuang Tzu remarked: "Those who follow the part of themselves that is great become great men; those who follow the part of themselves that is small become small men." The more we study the downfall of Reich, the more we realize that *this* is the problem: that tendency, in moments of crisis or emotion, to give way to the "small" part of himself.

Reich's tragedy was avoidable, and this is the source of his fascination. He was not a stupid and pig-headed monomaniac whose self-destruction was inevitable. He was a highly intelligent and perceptive man who might, with different tactics, have ended by achieving world renown. The fascination lies in that odd tendency to make the wrong choice and ruin his own chances.

Yet was Reich entirely to blame for ruining his chances? The more I studied the development of his ideas, the more I became convinced that most of the blame should be placed on the sexual theory and its originator. Freud insisted that all mental illness is sexual in origin. Any follower who showed any tendency to question—or broaden—this view was promptly expelled from the movement. Reich was in no such danger; he embraced the sexual theory with a total commitment that must have been gratifying to Freud. Even when Freud himself began to dilute the theory—first with the concept of the death-urge, then with a more specifically social theory of neurosis—Reich remained inflexible, convinced that Freud was becoming senile.

But suppose the sexual theory was fundamentally wrong? I had never been particularly happy with Freud's type of "reductionism" —the tendency to explain the genius of a Leonardo or Dostoevsky in terms of sexual repressions—but had never doubted that Freud was one of the great scientific emancipators. However, when I began to read Freud systematically, and the major books about him, my misgivings became insistent. What bothered me was not simply that Freud was a neurotic bully, an intellectual dictator with certain affinities with Stalin, but rather the recognition that the sexual theory was Freud's attempt to explain certain observations that he made while working with Breuer in Vienna, and studying with Charcot in Paris. And when I came to look closely at this evidence, it struck me, quite simply, that Freud was totally mistaken. On the basis of this evidence, the sexual theory was nonsense. A study of some of Freud's best-known cases—Little Hans and the Wolf Man—deepened this conviction. The reasons are set out at some length in the second chapter of this book.

But if Freud's fundamental concept is unsound, what justification can there be for writing a book about Reich, except, perhaps, to dismiss him as a man who based his life-work on an erroneous theory? Why, for that matter, did I continue to find Reich as fascinating as ever? The answer struck me as I attempted to apply some of the results of "split-brain research" to the Freudian theory of the unconscious mind. If Roger Sperry and Robert Ornstein are correct in asserting that we have *two* people living inside our heads, then the sexual theory becomes doubly unnecessary. But here it proved that Reich's instinct—so closely related to that of D. H. Lawrence—had been absolutely sound. Where he differed from Freud about the role of sex, I felt that Reich was correct. I have to admit that the sudden intellectual vistas that opened up when I reached this conclusion struck me as a revelation. It all required another lengthy chapter of exposition. But there was no help for it; either it had to be said, or I had to abandon the book. I can only advise readers who want to stick to biographical details to skip Chapters Two and Four, and return to them when they have time. An alternative plan would be to read them first; I feel they are the core of the book.

It should hardly be necessary to add that this work is not intended primarily as a biography of Reich. As soon as I began to study the available material, I formed the impression that Reich had no intention of allowing anyone to write a frank and fully documented biography. Possibly this view is unfair, but my overall impression is that Reich was determined to be in charge of his own "public image." He certainly felt that his ideas were more important than his personal history. But the real reason, I believe, is that he was obsessed by the idea of achievement—staking his claim to be a great discoverer—and had no wish for the world to know about his failures, his compromises, his moments of self-doubt. He spent his life trying to impose his view of himself on his contemporaries.

Inevitably, he failed. I am not now speaking of his failure to establish the importance of his discoveries; history may yet prove him right. But it is impossible for a man who has written a dozen or so books, and made a wide impact on his contemporaries, *not* to leave behind all the necessary clues for an assessment of his personality.

In fact, before I had written more than a few dozen pages, I had ceased to regret the gaps in the biographical information. The book became a quest for the real Wilhelm Reich, and I became fascinated by the game of hide-and-seek.

I doubt whether Reich would have been pleased with the result. But it demonstrates, I think, that he was right about one thing. His ideas *were* more important than his personal history.

CHAPTER ONE

For seven hundred years, the great Austrian empire, under its rulers the Hapsburgs, dominated the politics of Europe. In April 1897, a month after Wilhelm Reich was born, that empire slid into the first stages of its final disintegration. The events of that month doomed Europe to the First World War, and, coincidentally, they doomed the unborn child inside Frau Cecile Reich to a lifetime of frustration and failure.

Since Reich's own career is so closely bound up with that anarchic new world that emerged from the war, let us examine how the great collapse came about.

By the end of the nineteenth century, the Austro-Hungarian empire had spread itself too far afield. It had too many ill-assorted subjects—Austrians, Italians, Poles, Czechs, Germans, Hungarians, as well as half-a-dozen other minor nationalities—and great social changes were ripping apart the old fabric. The revolutions of 1848 had shaken everybody. The young Emperor Franz Joseph came to the throne determined to show Europe that all this revolutionary nonsense was just a passing fad. Instead, he watched the empire undermined by military defeat, then by the revolutionary mutterings of his own subjects. And as things went from bad to worse, the aging emperor made a mistake: he decided that the answer lay in finding a strong man and making him Prime Minister. He chose Count Casimir Badeni, a Polish nobleman who was also the governor of Galicia. Confronted with so many squabbling nationalities, Badeni tried to improve the situation with a few concessions all around. On April 5, 1897, he brought into effect the Badeni Language Ordinances, which declared that from then on, German would no longer enjoy an unfair advantage as the bureaucratic language of any given area; minority languages—like Czech and Hungarian—would also be permitted in the Civil Service. It sounded—as everyone will admit—like a harmless and sensible measure.

A few weeks later there occurred another event that made the future look even more promising. For a long time Russia had been making threatening noises about the Balkans, and the Austrians had been making allies wherever they could find them. And now, quite suddenly, the Russians experienced a change of heart, and offered peace. They had their eyes on the Far East, and wanted to avoid problems at home. Austria could hardly believe its good fortune, and lost no time in signing an entente cordiale, agreeing to ignore the Balkan problem until a later date.

These two events, both of which occurred just before Reich was born, should have ensured a long period of peace and prosperity. In fact, they turned Austria into a powder keg. Without the Russian threat to hold them together, Austria's dissatisfied nationalities began to squabble in earnest, and the German-speaking Austrians were angrier than the rest. It was all very well to give rights to the Czechs and Poles and Hungarians, but that meant eroding the rights of the Germans. The Austrian bureaucracy was run almost entirely by middle-class Germans, and it was their jobs that were threatened by this irritating liberalism. They rose up as one and protested loudly; the Members of Parliament even threw inkwells at the Speaker of the House. Of course, nobody really expected the government to take any notice. In imperial Austria, the ruling classes made the decisions, and the middle classes did as they were told. And then, to everyone's bewilderment, the emperor gave way, and dismissed Badeni. The middle classes, rather

startled and dismayed by their own power, relapsed into as-
tonished silence.

These events, which took place during the first months of
Reich's life, were really the beginning of the end. The German
middle classes wanted the old imperial Austria back again, but it
was dead and waiting to be buried. The Czechs and all the smaller
nationalities wanted a new democratic Austria, with equal chances
for all. The Germans pulled one way, and the Czechs pulled the
other, until eventually the empire tore apart down the seams. The
small Balkan states, which had always been so much trouble, also
began protesting about their rights; when Serbian patriots assassi-
nated Archduke Franz Ferdinand at Sarajevo in June 1914, the
powder keg finally exploded, and the seven-hundred-year-old empire crumbled like a demolished building.

Wilhelm Reich was born on March 24, 1897, in Dobrzcynica,
in the province of Galicia. Count Badeni, the exgovernor of Galicia, was still Prime Minister, and no one yet realized the extent of
the troubles that were about to descend on him.

The Reich family was Jewish, and its various branches were
well established in Austro-Hungary; some were even members of
Parliament. A mere half-century before, that would have been
unthinkable—Austria, like Germany and Russia, had a powerful
tradition of anti-Semitism. But the revolutions of 1848 had
changed all that, and in Germany and Hungary, as well as Austria,
Jews had their civic rights like anyone else.

The Jews themselves had also been accommodating. The Reich
family, for example, which numbered a famous rabbi among its
ancestors, was now thoroughly assimilated into the Austrian state.
Reich's father, Leon Reich, was a wealthy farmer who supplied
beef to the German government. He had abandoned his Judaism,
and his two sons were given a secular education.

The few comments Reich made about his father make it clear
that he was an extremely dominant and bad-tempered individual,
who ruled his farm despotically, and expected total obedience.
There is nothing very surprising about this; anyone who has read
Austrian novels about the period—for example, Joseph Roth's
Radetsky March—will know that the Austrian landowner was still
regarded as a feudal baron. But Reich's comments also suggest
that his father was a fairly typical "Right Man"; Ilse Reich speaks

of him as "rather brutal," with a feudal attitude towards his family
and employees, and intensely jealous of his wife, Cecile. She, on
the other hand, seems to have been a placid, sweet-natured
woman who took her husband's dominance—and violent temper—
for granted. Ilse says of her: "She is reported as having been rather
unintellectual and not very clever, a good housewife, and her own
mother, Grandmother Roniger, is known to have talked about her
as *das Schlaf* (the lamb) which in German very definitely has the
connotation of 'the dumb one.'" Cecile Reich bore her husband
only two children: Wilhelm, and a younger brother, Robert, born
in 1900. Wilhelm seems to have inherited his father's disposition;
Robert was more like his mother.

There was still plenty of anti-Semitism in Austria in the late
nineteenth century, but Wilhelm and Robert would not have noticed it. Leon Reich had bought a large farm at Jujinetz, in Bukovina, where the chief language was Little Russian (or Ukrainian).
There were Jewish children in Jujinetz, but they spoke Yiddish. In
any case, Willy and Robert were not allowed to play with them.
The Reich family was "rather stuck-up, and put a very pronounced stress on German culture."

So the Reich boys had a Ukrainian nursemaid, then private tu-
tors. Presumably the farmhands regarded them as "the young masters." Like any children of a rich landowner, both went in for
hunting, shooting, and fishing. Neill told me Reich was an excellent horseman and a crack shot. The descriptions of his early life
quoted by Ilse make it sound idyllic, like something out of Turgenev's *Sportsman's Sketches*.

Then, when Reich was thirteen, a curious event occurred, about
which, unfortunately, we have practically no information. Neill
told me that Reich had "caught his mother in bed with his tutor,"
but that may only have been a manner of speaking. What seems
quite clear is that Reich somehow discovered that his mother was
having an affair with his tutor, and betrayed her to his father. As a
result, his mother committed suicide.

This event is enough to make us realize why Reich was so silent
about his early years. Yet although we know so little about it, it is
important to try to understand it more fully. Again, the concept of
the Right Man provides some vital clues. The faithful wife is an
important part of his psychological foundations. It enables him to

see himself as he wishes to—as the patriarchal figure who deserves universal respect. He is capable of beating her black and blue if she even smiles at another man. To actually *know* that she has permitted another man to possess her is enough to dislocate his sanity. If she deserves thrashing for smiling at another man, what does she deserve for . . . for . . . the idea is unthinkable, enough to threaten madness.

It is necessary to try to envisage what happened during the next days or weeks. She would probably be locked in her bedroom, and the servants given orders not to go near. And Reich's father, trying to soothe the hurt by talking about it—still hoping, in some irrational corner of his mind, that he will wake up and find it was all a nightmare—shouts at her for hours at a time, asking how a respectable woman could do anything so wicked, so unutterably evil. Some morbid element in him wants to know exactly how it all came about. When did the tutor first indicate that he was attracted by her? When did he first kiss her? Terrified of provoking him further, she sobs and protests that she cannot remember. But he *has* to know. He even speaks softly and reasonably, giving her the hope that if she only tells him everything frankly, they might attempt a reconciliation. And as she finally begins to tell him in detail, he listens silently and intently; for a few minutes, they are almost close again. When she comes to the admission of infidelity, of how the man helped her unbutton the dress and pull it over her head, he feels himself engulfed in a kind of blackness; again, it has passed beyond the bounds of his response. He is sorry now that he only threw the man out; he has visions of torture, of flaying alive, of disemboweling. At the same time, there is an obscure pleasure buried in the torment; he could almost wish that he had been in the next room, spying on it all through a hole in the wall . . .

Finally, after days, perhaps weeks of this third degree, he has made his point; she is utterly convinced that she is evil, that she is a nobody, a nonentity, who ought to wither away under this burning glare of her husband. She is amazed that he has taken it so badly, that she has hurt him so deeply; she never realized that she was taking such an irrevocable step. If she was a woman of more spirit, she would leave him and try to start her life over again. But she is crushed, and the realization that this place can no longer be her home, that things can never be the same again, fills her with a

sense of total defeat. All she can do is to weep, and hope that it
will melt him as it has in the past. And even now, her helplessness
produces an automatic response of tenderness, the desire to take
her in his arms and tell her that everything is all right. But it
would not be true. What she has done is as unforgivable as
murder. She has literally divorced herself from him. He feels an
utterly implacable sense of hatred and rejection.

And so finally, incapable of further response, she makes the ultimate act of contrition, and takes her own life. Oddly enough, the
effect on her husband is not to produce remorse or self-condemna-
tion. He still feels that she committed an unforgivable crime. But
she has now compounded the offense by finally deserting him.
While he could see her weeping, he could feel that there was some
normality in the situation. But now she has gone, it has become a
confused dream. She has committed the ultimate infidelity . . .
Perhaps Van Vogt's most interesting observation about the Right
Man is that although he is capable of deserting his wife and leaving her penniless, he can be totally shattered and undermined if
she leaves him. A Right Man in this situation may experience nervous breakdown, or commit suicide. In the case of Reich's father,
the breakdown took the form of a loss of the will to live. A sense
of duty towards his sons kept him from committing suicide. But a
few years later he did the next best thing, and deliberately contracted pneumonia by standing in a freezing pond for hours in
cold weather, holding a fishing rod. The aim of the stratagem was
to ensure that his sons would be able to collect his insurance, but
it failed in its purpose; for some reason, the company refused to
pay up.

From our point of view, the main question is what effect all this
had on Reich. Ilse Reich speaks of it as "the most severe trauma of
his early years" and leaves it at that. But it is necessary to realize
that Reich had much in common with his father, and that consequently, his own reactions to his mother's infidelity and suicide
would be very similar to those of his father. Why *did* he feel im-
pelled to tell his father that she was having an affair? Ilse Reich
tells us on his own authority that he admired his mother and felt
little love for his father; so why betray her? The answer is surely
that Reich was as deeply shocked by her infidelity as his father
was. He *also* felt betrayed. He felt that in this matter he was on his

father's side. She deserved the most severe punishment. But then, Reich was only thirteen; his capacity for vindictiveness was not as developed as his father's. The suicide would be a greater shock to him because by that time he must already have regretted the misery he had caused her. And undoubtedly, he would never cease to regret the incomprehensible rage that had made him tell his father what he had discovered. Six years later, when he met Freud, he would suddenly understand the precise nature of that rage.

Before we leave this subject of Cecile Reich's suicide, it is worth raising one interesting question. Why *should* a man like Leon Reich experience such hard, unforgiving rage at his wife's infidelity? Of course, all men would prefer their wives to be faithful, as a matter of emotional security, but the majority of men, like the majority of women, can forgive a lapse. So why should a "Right Man" treat it as a crime?

This is not the place to explore the problem, but it is worth bearing in mind that Reich's later psychology was partly an attempt to explain the origin of what we would now call "male chauvinism."

The death of Leon Reich—from tuberculosis, which developed from the pneumonia—took place four years after his wife's suicide, in 1914. By that time, Willy was attending a school in Czernowitz (Chernovtsy), the capital of Bukovina, returning to the farm at weekends to help his father. After Leon's death, he continued to run the farm while working for his exams, which he passed with honors in 1915. In 1916, Reich joined the army while his brother went to live in Vienna with relatives. The farm, apparently, was lost, although none of the fragmentary accounts of Reich's early life explain how this came about. What *is* clear is that the Reich brothers had now lost the financial security which they had taken for granted from childhood.

Reich apparently enjoyed army life. He became a lieutenant, and fought in the Italian campaign. Admirers of Reich may find it difficult to understand how such a passionate critic of human aggression could enjoy the army; but Ilse Reich clearly has no such problems. She writes: "He was not a pacifist by nature, and the responsibility for a group of people was much to his liking." What she is saying, clearly, is that Reich was a highly dominant and aggressive young man, who thoroughly enjoyed being in command

and giving orders. He probably thought and behaved very much like those young officers portrayed by Tolstoy in *Anna Karenina,* or like Robert Musil's Ulrich, "the man without qualities," who felt that civilians are spineless and undisciplined, and that army officers are the world's natural élite. She mentions that he always wore spurs, although he was in the infantry, and that when he was on leave in Vienna he went riding at its exclusive Reitschüle. It seems that Reich's values were those of any other dominant, upper-class young officer in imperial Vienna.

But Reich was not upper class, he was middle class. Moreover, he was Jewish, and, worse still, he was penniless. So although he may have been tempted by the idea of an army career, he must have realized it was out of the question.

The alternative was some sensible, middle-class occupation. Reich decided on law—or perhaps had it decided for him by the relatives who had been looking after Robert. Exams were never a problem for him; he matriculated at the Faculty of Law—in the University of Vienna—in 1918. But legal studies bored him; he may also have reflected that even after taking his degree, he might spend years waiting for his first big case. In mid-year he switched to the Faculty of Medicine. War veterans were permitted to reduce a six-year course to four, presumably to compensate for the two years wasted in the army; Reich's natural brilliance ensured that he had no difficulties in compressing six years' work into four. He and Robert shared a small apartment with another student; the rent, apparently, was paid by Robert, who had a job. Their agreement was that when Willy had graduated, he would support Robert during his studies. They were half-starved much of the time, and this may have contributed to Robert's early death at twenty-six. Photographs of Reich at this period show a thin young man of unprepossessing appearance, whose set face displays nervous tension. Ilse says that he was "an outstanding student, a leader in student discussions, liked by many, but disliked by others because of his brilliance." But people are never disliked for their brilliance; only for the bumptiousness and conceit that so often go with it. So we have to envisage Reich as an intense, impatient young man, distinctly humorless—as he remained all his life—who struck many people as self-obsessed. People who liked him were impressed by the quickness of his mind. People who disliked him probably re-

ferred to him as a "clever Jew-boy." He was half-starved, had no
parents, and we are probably justified in assuming that the relatives who had looked after Robert had now lost all interest in the
Reich brothers; or perhaps, like so many Viennese after the war,
they themselves were starving. In any case, it was now "Reich
against the world."

At this point, the outward events of Reich's life become less important than the ideas that began to possess him. Historically
speaking, he was lucky; he was a naturally brilliant young man
who found himself suddenly in the center of a whirlpool of new
ideas. For psychologists, Vienna meant Freud, Jung, and Adler.
For musicians it meant Schönberg and his school. For painters,
Klimt, Egon Schiele, Richard Gerst, and Oskar Kokoschka. For
architects it meant Adolf Loos and the building without ornament.
For philosophers, it came to mean "the Vienna school"—when
Reich came to Vienna, Wittgenstein was training there while
working as a schoolteacher.

In *The Function of the Orgasm* Reich tells how, one day in
January 1919, a note was passed surreptitiously around the
class. Someone felt that it was time that sex was openly discussed
at the medical school, and suggested a seminar on the subject. A
group of students argued that sex was being neglected at the university, and that there ought to be a course in "sexology." Thirty
or so students supported the idea, and the course ran throughout
1919. By the fall, all but eight of them had lost interest and
dropped out, and Reich had become the leader of the group. He
had also discovered the subject that was to absorb him—in fact,
obsess him—for the rest of his life.

Modern readers will assume that a course in sex meant a course
in the ideas of Freud. This is untrue. Freud came fairly late to a
field that had already been exhaustively explored by writers like
Krafft-Ebing, Hirschfeld, Forel, Bloch, and Ellis. In fact, one of
the earliest systematic works on the human sexual impulse—and its
deviations—was written when Freud was only eight years old. *The
Psychology of Human Drives* by Jacob Santlus (1864) argued
that human drives can be divided into the psychological and the
spiritual, and that it is the interaction of the two that produces
sexual deviations. Twenty-two years later the first great classic
in the field, Richard von Krafft-Ebing's *Psychopathia Sexualis*,

in which the terms sadism and masochism were coined, appeared. (The book became an immediate best-seller, with the result that the British Medico-Psychological Association debated whether to cancel his honorary membership.) In 1899, Dr. Magnus Hirschfeld, himself a homosexual, launched his *Yearbook of Sexual Deviations,* and later founded the Institute of Sexual Science in Berlin, specifically for studying sexual illness. In England, Havelock Ellis' *Studies in the Psychology of Sex* caused widespread scandal in the late 1890s; the English, unlike their continental neighbors, believed that sex should be discussed only by doctors behind locked doors. The classic history of English sexual mores had to be written by a German, Ivan Bloch.

Most of these writers were inclined to approach the subject in a pragmatic, almost mechanistic manner. Masturbation and *coitus interruptus* were supposed to cause nervous illness; a great deal of time was spent arguing whether sexual perversions were inborn or acquired. Krafft-Ebing is always falling back on phrases like "hereditary mental disease," "congenital psychopathic disposition," and "defective moral sense." The matter was further complicated by a vague general assumption that sex was something that made its appearance at puberty, in the form of a drive called "the libido," a scientific euphemism for lust. Since sex was basically the procreative impulse, the task of the sexologist was to explain how it became perverted into homosexuality, sadism, fetishism, and so on. At times it sounds almost as if they suspect that sexual deviations are caused by different types of germs.

Such were the topics discussed at early meetings, and Reich's reaction was one of positive and instantaneous distaste. In *The Function of the Orgasm* he wrote that Krafft-Ebing and the rest "made sexuality seem bizarre and strange." He goes on irritably: "A natural sexuality did not seem to exist. The unconscious was full of nothing but perverse impulses." Reich was basically an idealist and—oddly enough—something of a puritan. To understand what disturbed him so much, one has only to open Krafft-Ebing or Hirschfeld at almost any page. This, for example, from Krafft-Ebing.[1]

"Case 39. X, merchant . . . He would accost some prostitute and ask her to go to a shoe shop with him, where he would buy her the handsomest pair of shoes made of patent leather . . .

When this had taken place, she had to go about in the street, walking in manure and mud as much as possible, in order to soil the shoes. Then X would lead the person to a hotel, and, almost before they reached the room, he would cast himself at her feet, feeling an extraordinary pleasure in licking them with his lips. When he had cleaned the shoes in this manner he paid her and went his way."

As one turns the pages of *Psychopathia Sexualis* one glimpses typical phrases: "Without any teaching he began to masturbate and always during the act there were mental pictures of bleeding women"; "Later the mere idea of old, ugly women's heads in night-caps was sufficient to induce an erection"; "From the age of twelve, there was masturbation with the employment of furs, or by means of taking a furry dog to bed"; "By means of large sums of money he would induce prostitutes to lie on their backs and allow him to urinate and defecate in their mouths"; ". . . visited prostitutes, had them purchase a living fowl or rabbit, and made them torture the animal"; "She likes best to perform anilinctus on old men . . ." As the grisly procession of freaks winds on over hundreds of pages, it begins to seem that half the human race is sexually twisted, and that even "normal sex" is rather disgusting. Understandably, the twenty-two-year-old Reich, himself highly susceptible to the attractions of the opposite sex, felt that all this had little to do with the mystical force that binds Tristan to Isolde or Faust to Marguerite.

It was not all that much better when they invited a Freudian to come and talk to them. Reich "instinctively" disliked the approach the speaker took, and felt the lectures were too coldly clinical, like a discourse on poetry by someone who is interested only in its grammatical structure.

But Freud differed from Krafft-Ebing and the rest in one fundamental respect. At least no one could accuse him of not seeing the wood for the trees. Freud went behind the rather pathetic manifestations and spoke about the hidden power that produced them. For this he borrowed the ready-made term "libido"; but it meant something completely different from the sex-drive of the early sexologists. Freud's libido was an immense force, perhaps the greatest of all natural forces. When frustrated, said Freud, it turned into anxiety and neurosis.

Now Reich was also less interested in human sexual peculiarities than in the force that lay behind them, and Freud's concept of the libido produced in him an effect of revelation. What excited him so much was his feeling that this libido was nothing less than the force of life itself. If so, this concept could unify all the "vital sciences"—biology, psychology, zoology—as Newton's concept of gravity unified the physical sciences. It would be nothing less than the key to the mystery of life. In a lecture to the seminar in the summer of 1919, Reich compared the libido to electricity, which can never be observed directly, but only through its manifestations—light, heat, and so on. One day, Reich said, it should be possible to measure the libido as directly as we can measure electric current with a voltmeter. His fellow students were so impressed that they voted him leader of the seminar for the following fall.

The irony is that Reich's conversion to Freudianism was based on misunderstanding. By the time Reich came to Vienna, Freud had long ago abandoned the idea of the libido as a hidden force that could explain neurosis. He had never really been happy with this explanation, and tended to use it as a convenient label for various unknown psychic factors, rather as old map makers labeled certain regions "terra incognita." Freud's approach was basically far more pragmatic than Reich's. It is true that in a very early paper, written a quarter of a century before, Freud had attempted to construct a kind of working model of the mind as a piece of "neurological machinery," driven by a kind of nervous energy (called "quantity of excitation"), but he abandoned the paper almost as soon as it was finished, and the "Project for a Scientific Psychology" remained in manuscript until after his death. Freud's biographer Ernest Jones said he was ashamed of it.[2] In fact, Freud was never much interested in theories and working models; he liked to observe neurosis firsthand with his patients and then, very cautiously, try to draw conclusions. In 1926 he entirely abandoned the libido theory.

Reich's approach was as far from this cautious pragmatism as it could be: he was interested in the idea of a meaning and purpose in nature. He read August Forel's book *The Sexual Question* because it was one of the key works on sexology, but he was more interested in Forel's early work on ants, in which Forel pointed out the highly *purposive* nature of ant organization. It is almost as if the ant colony is a single organism, directed by some purpose that is greater than any individual. From Forel, Reich turned to the work of the vitalist philosopher Hans Driesch, who had abandoned biology when he became disillusioned with the "machine theory of life" that was current in the 1890s. Driesch had become convinced that life is basically purposive. For example, if he destroyed half a sea urchin's egg with a hot needle, the remaining half developed into a perfect but half-sized embryo—not, as one might expect, into a half-embryo. So a living organism could be constructed out of one of its parts. On the other hand, no one would expect to construct a machine out of a single screw.

But while Reich found Driesch's disproof of the "machine theory" convincing, he was unable to accept the next stage of the argument: that the "purpose" of living organisms exists beyond nature, outside space and time. Driesch called this purpose "entelechy," but Reich was intelligent enough to see that he was really letting in God by the back door; he felt that the larger problem was avoided by the use of a single word.

He found the ideas of Henri Bergson more satisfying than those of Driesch, largely because Bergson plays his cards more cautiously. He rejects mechanistic materialism without taking flight into metaphysics or religion. Yet Bergson's élan vital is basically the same thing as Driesch's entelechy. Bergson may be more "scientific" than Driesch, but his arguments lead to the same conclusion, which is plainly inevitable; life must either be a product of matter—as fire is of coal—or it must have an independent existence *beyond* matter. The first view leads to materialism, the second to vitalism—or religion. And although Reich claimed to reject Driesch's vitalism—he dismissed him with the sneer: "He later found refuge among the spiritists"—he himself remained fundamentally a vitalist. He even admits, in *The Function of the Orgasm,* to being impressed by the principles of Buddhism, and by Rudolph Steiner's anthroposophy. Nevertheless, he looked for scientific justification for his vitalism, and found it to some extent in the work of Paul Kammerer, a biologist who believed that the will plays a fundamental part in evolution. There was a point when it looked as if Kammerer had proved his case through his experiments on midwife toads. Reich was also excited by the work of Eugen Steinach, who showed that animals, and people, can be rejuvenated by means of sex hormones. Old rats on which he performed an operation to increase their output of sex hormone became as virile and aggressive as young rats—for a short time. It seemed to demonstrate a direct connection between the sex drives and the force of life.

Reich took the opportunity to visit Kammerer, Steinach, Adler, Freud, and Stekel (one of Freud's leading disciples). He found all but Freud disappointing. Kammerer was a charming, upper-class Viennese, something of a Don Juan, who struck Reich as "not particularly interesting." This kindly and elegant man may have found the young Reich a little too intense. Steinach was exhausted, and complained about the persecution to which he was being subjected by his academic colleagues. Reich's own persecution mania was not yet sufficiently developed to enable him to sympathize. Stekel impressed Reich unfavorably because he seemed anxious to please. This seems to fit with the little we know of Stekel's character; he was one of the more lightweight of Freud's followers, and one historian of psychoanalysis has remarked that "his interest in sexuality remained quasi-pornographic."[3] As for Adler, he had already broken with Freud, and spent most of his time railing against him.

Freud himself was a different matter. As Reich wrote in *The Function of the Orgasm,* he found Freud simple, direct, and honest. While each of the others seemed to be playing some part—the Professor, the *Menschenkenner* (judge of human nature), the distinguished scientist, Freud seemed to be devoid of pretensions, and Reich was greatly struck by his "piercingly intelligent eyes."

What emerges clearly from Reich's description is that he believed that he had encountered in Freud a completely balanced and healthy man. The comment about the others "playing roles" is significant, for Reich later developed the notion of "character armor," which the weak develop to cover their insecurity. Freud alone seemed above this need. And, oddly enough, this still seemed true to Reich thirty years later, when he tape-recorded a series of interviews that have been published as *Reich Speaks of Freud.* Reich told the interviewer, Dr. Kurt Eissler, that he felt that most psychoanalysts were "genitally disturbed," and that this was why they hated his orgasm theory of sexuality. Eissler asked him: "You think that extends to Freud too?" and Reich flatly denied it, saying that he was impressed by Freud's vitality and strength of will. But this remark was made before the publication of the first volume of Jones's life of Freud in 1954. When Reich read this, it apparently struck him as a revelation, and he wrote a letter to Eissler admitting that he now realized that Freud was not a "genitally healthy man." The biography, he wrote, revealed that Freud had suffered from a form of impotence during his five years' engagement to a girl who was completely dominated by her neurotic mother. As a result, Freud was inhibited from honestly investigating the subject of genitality. This, says Reich, is why Freud found it impossible to accept his own orgasm theory.

Reich was not entirely incorrect in supposing that Freud had his sexual problems. Ernest Jones writes that "the more passionate side of married life subsided with him earlier than it does with many men." The evidence suggests that he became impotent, or simply lost interest in sex, before he reached his mid-forties.[4] On the other hand, Reich's explanation of Freud's hostility has an air of rationalization. The truth is that the two men were so totally unlike that it would have been impossible for them to remain on friendly terms for any length of time. Freud required disciples rather than followers; and when the disciples showed the slightest tendency to think for themselves, he felt betrayed and rejected them violently. In his book on Freud's relations with his disciple Tausk, Paul Roazen points out that Freud only felt comfortable in the role of father-figure; yet his theory of the Oedipus complex implies that there is a deep, unconscious hostility between father and son. He expected to be stabbed in the back, and reacted to any sign of supposed hostility with ruthless and total rejection. He threw out his disciples like an angry father disinheriting his sons. Such a rejection brought Jung to the brink of mental breakdown in 1913, and actually drove Tausk—a rather self-pitying character—to suicide in 1919. In matters involving loyalty, Freud had more than a touch of paranoia. But then, so had Reich, and with two such powerful characters, the relationship was bound to end in rejection.

CHAPTER TWO

If we are to understand the developments during those crucial years, 1920 to 1927, when Reich clashed with Freud, it is necessary to speak of the history of psychoanalysis.

When Freud was studying medicine in the late 1870s and early 1880s it was still generally accepted that mental illnesses were physical in origin. "Mental diseases are brain diseases," said Wilhelm Griesinger, the dean of nineteenth-century psychiatrists. And in his comprehensive history of psychiatry, *The Discovery of the Unconscious,* Henri Ellenberger remarked: "Occasionally a physician was appointed medical director of a mental hospital, his only qualification being that he was a good student of brain anatomy." This mechanistic theory of mental illness was known as "organicism" and, as we have noted, Freud himself was inclined to accept it in his early days. His teacher in Vienna was Theodor Meynert, one of the leading figures of the organicist school.

In 1869, an American named George M. Beard introduced an interesting change of emphasis when he suggested that mental illnesses were diseases of the nervous system, due to a lack of such chemicals as phosphorus. This lack caused nervous exhaustion, or "neurasthenia." Beard's neurasthenia immediately became a fashionable disease. In that age of masculine men and feminine women, it was regarded as shameful to be nervous or hypersensitive; now Beard had shown that neurosis was no more degrading than catching cold.

Beard was anything but a dogmatic mechanist. He recognized that in America, the problem of neurasthenia was due mainly to the increasing pressures of a competitive society. He was also acute enough to see that freedom itself—religious and political—can raise its own distinct problems and add to the tension of everyday life; for a man with no idea of how to use it, freedom can be destructive. Beard also produced simple comparisons to explain his concept of nervous exhaustion and nervous energy; human beings can be likened to storage batteries, charged with a certain reserve of nervous force; people with low reserves are prone to breakdown. He also liked to compare this nervous force to money; a man of high vitality is a kind of millionaire; a man who overdraws his account goes into nervous bankruptcy.

Little by little, psychology was moving away from pure "mechanism." But the process was painfully slow, since the alternative—what might be called "dynamism"—aroused such intense hostility among men of science. The man who was almost entirely to blame for this was Franz Anton Mesmer, the discoverer of "animal magnetism," whose revolutionary ideas had electrified Europe in the 1770s and 1780s. Mesmer was detested because he was regarded as a kind of mystic or occultist. (We have already noted the remarkable resemblance between his ideas and those of Reich.) And for most of the nineteenth century, the medical profession continued to regard his name as a synonym for charlatanism.

Unfortunately for the progress of psychiatry, the same judgment was applied to the discovery of Mesmer's pupil, the Marquis de Puységur: hypnosis. Puységur and his brother were treating a young peasant named Victor Race for asthma, and one day, as Race was being "magnetized," he fell into a trance. And although "asleep," he was able to obey simple orders and answer questions; he actually seemed more intelligent in this state than when awake. Other hypnotized patients could not only diagnose their own illnesses, but could also describe their future developments. Hypnotism also became a sensation in Europe in the late eighteenth century, but fell into disrepute with the downfall of Mesmer. When the brilliant young doctor E. J. Georget defended mesmerism (already confused with hypnosis) before the French Academy of Sciences in 1826, he was interrupted by cries of "Charlatan!" In England, pioneers of hypnosis like John Elliotson, James Esdaile, and James Braid met with bitter opposition that damaged their careers. No amount of medical evidence could convince doctors that hypnotism was not some disguised form of "occultism." It was widely believed that hypnotized people had second sight—in fact, there is some impressive evidence for the theory[1]—and an erudite English lady named Mary Ann South even tried to prove that it was the basic secret of the alchemists. For hypnotherapy, it was a matter of guilt by association.

For the advocates of hypnosis, the year 1882 was the turning point. This was due to the work of two men, one famous, one unknown. The unknown was a French country doctor named Auguste Liébault. As a medical student in the 1840s, Liébault had come across an old book on "magnetism"; he tried it out and found that it worked. Because his patients—mostly poor peasants—were suspicious of the method, Liébault offered hypnotic treatment free. He even wrote a book about it, but it sold only one copy in ten years. For forty years, Liébault cured all manner of illnesses by soothing the patient into hypnotic sleep, and then suggesting that he would wake up feeling better. In 1882, he tried the method on a patient of the successful neurologist Hyppolite Bernheim, and succeeded in curing a case of sciatica that had failed to yield to Bernheim's methods. Surprisingly, Bernheim did not follow the usual medical precedent and denounce the "magnetist" as a fraud; he went to study Liébault's methods at his country surgery, was impressed by them, and decided to adopt them. He and Liébault became known as the founders of the "Nancy school" of hypnotherapy.

Bernheim's discovery of hypnosis had been anticipated by his colleague—and rival—Jean-Martin Charcot, the most celebrated doctor in France. As a young intern, Charcot had been appointed to the Salpêtrière, a hospital that was basically a poorhouse for old women. There he had been fascinated by cases of hysteria—that is, by patients who might exhibit anything from hysterical convulsions to hysterical pregnancies; some even performed the apparently impossible feat of bending backward until their heads touched their heels. Charcot left the Salpêtrière and slowly gained celebrity as an expert on geriatrics, kidney diseases, and disseminated sclerosis. At thirty-six, he was appointed chief physician at the Salpêtrière, and set out to solve the mystery of hysteria. In 1878, he discovered that some of his most spectacular hysterics were deeply susceptible to hypnosis, and proceeded to study the subject with his usual methodicalness. And in February 1882—the year that Bernheim was convinced by Liébault—he succeeded where so many others had failed, and persuaded the Academy of Sciences to listen with serious attention to a paper on hysteria and hypnosis. It must be stated immediately that he succeeded largely because he had made a fundamental error that took the sting out of his advocacy: He was convinced that hypnosis is itself a pathological condition, a form of hysteria, restricted to the mentally ill. Bernheim flatly opposed this view, pointing out that it is easier to hypnotize a healthy and intelligent person than a mentally disturbed one. Charcot declined to believe it. Like many great discoverers, he was a less than satisfactory human being: dominant, egotistical, dictatorial, and pig-headed. But the Academy of Sciences was charmed by his view that hypnosis is a form of sickness, and dropped their opposition to the subject. It had been precisely ninety-eight years since their colleagues had condemned Mesmer.

Charcot's trouble, quite simply, was that he tended to think in rigid categories, which meant that he saw only what he was looking for. And his personality was so strong that his patients were inclined to exhibit precisely the symptoms he expected from them. In short, Charcot's mental make-up contained a great deal more "personality" than "impersonality." Fortunately for himself, he was highly successful, and had plenty of opportunity to indulge his craving for applause. His lectures were virtually stage performances:

[His patients] were always ready to . . . exhibit his famous three stages of hypnotism: lethargy, catalepsy, somnambulism, all invented by the Master, and hardly ever observed outside the Salpêtrière. Some of them smelt with delight a bottle of ammonia when told it was rose water, others would eat a piece of charcoal when presented to them as chocolate. Another would crawl on all fours, barking furiously when told she was a dog, flap her arms as if trying to fly when turned into a pigeon, lift her skirts with a shriek of terror when a glove was thrown at her feet with a suggestion of being a snake . . .[2]

But Charcot's great achievement was to make the medical profession aware of the basic similarity between hypnosis and hysteria. Many patients suffered from hysterical paralysis of the limbs or speech muscles. Charcot hypnotized a man in front of the audience, then told him that when he was slapped on the back, his arm would become paralyzed. Charcot woke him up and slapped him on the back; instantly, the man's arm became paralyzed.

Unfortunately, the tendency to think in rigid categories made Charcot miss the true significance of his demonstrations: that hysteria and hypnosis were both *forms of suggestion*. According to Charcot, hypnosis *is* hysteria, a pathological condition. As to how hysterical patients became "hypnotized" in the first place, Charcot had an ingenious answer: the original trauma produced a condition of shock which was, in fact, a "hypnoid state"; and in this state, any suggestion of paralysis could lead to the real thing.

Bernheim was less inclined to allow his preconceptions to distort his observation. Yet absurdly enough, he went on to make the opposite error. He saw clearly that both hypnosis and hysteria were due to suggestion, which led him to wonder whether suggestion would not be equally effective when the patient was wide awake. He found that it was. So Bernheim came to place increasing emphasis on the waking state, which in turn led him further and further from those strange mysteries of hysteria, and the unconscious mind, that had so intrigued Charcot. Bernheim, like Charcot, failed to make the tremendous discovery that was staring him in the face.

The man who made it was, of course, Sigmund Freud, who spent some time studying with Charcot while the latter was still conducting his experiments in hysteria and hypnosis. What struck Freud, with the force of revelation, was that if the "unconscious mind" can produce the phenomena of hysteria and hypnosis, *then it must be far more powerful than the conscious mind*. Freud was the first to grasp the full significance of that word "unconscious."

Freud's mind had already been prepared for the discovery by a
case with which he had been concerned in 1881, four years before
his visit to the Salpêtrière. His friend and colleague Josef Breuer
had been treating a young woman named Bertha Pappenheim,
who was suffering from periodic hypnoid states, and paralysis of
her right arm. Bertha's everyday self alternated with a semicon-
scious self who spoke only English, and suffered from various hallucinations. Perhaps the most curious thing about this trance-state
was that it caused Bertha to relive events that had occurred precisely one year earlier—even to the exact day and hour. She also
spoke sentences that seemed confused and meaningless, sometimes
in a mixture of four or five languages. She periodically exhibited
other hysterical symptoms: deafness, dumbness, a squint, and an
inability to swallow food or drink.

One day as the girl lay in her "absent" state, muttering occasional words, someone in the same room repeated one of her
phrases. The girl took up the phrase and began to tell an imaginary story. The longer she talked, the more fluent she became. Finally, she woke up, feeling calm and relieved. The inference
seemed to be that talking had helped her to get something "out of
her system."

Breuer now tried questioning the "absent" girl about her hysterical symptoms; she would describe what had originally caused
them, and wake up feeling better. For example, she explained her
inability to drink by telling how she saw a dog drinking from a
glass of water. Having said this, she demanded a drink, swallowed
it down, and woke up cured of this particular symptom. She eventually described how the original trauma had been caused as she
sat by the bedside of her dying father. She had fallen asleep with
her arm over the back of the chair, and her arm went to sleep. In
this state she had a waking dream, or a nightmare, in which she
saw a black snake writhing towards her father; she tried to drive it
off, but the arm was paralyzed. She tried to pray, but could only
remember some verses in English. A train whistle woke her up.
The next day the sight of a bent branch in the garden reminded
her of a snake, and her arm became paralyzed; she also found she
could only speak in English. The same thing would occur at inter-
vals whenever some snakelike object triggered the hallucination.

After telling Breuer about this dream of the snake, she woke up cured.

What Charcot had to say seemed to throw a great deal of light on the case of Bertha Pappenheim (or "Anna O," as she became known in the annals of medicine). The original trauma occurred in a nightmare—a "hypnoid" state; the sight of the branch the next day was the posthypnotic suggestion that caused the paralysis, just as Charcot had caused it by a slap on the back. The case also seemed to bear out another theory of Charcot's: that certain people seem to be in a state of *permanent* "somnambulism," and in such people, paralysis (or other hysterical symptoms) can be induced even without hypnotic suggestion. Clearly, this applied particularly to people whose vitality had been reduced by illness, or a series of shocks and defeats.

Now before Charcot, the most widely held theory about hysterics was that they were "putting it on," exaggerating their symptoms to gain attention. Charcot exploded this conveniently simplistic notion. What he showed, in effect, is that *hysteria is a physical symptom caused by the subconscious mind.* Everyone experiences its simpler forms every day. We know that talking about itching can make us itch. Every child has felt his handwriting "freeze up" when the teacher peers over his shoulder. We can be put off our food if someone talks of something disgusting.

Symptoms like this hardly suggest the enormous power of the unconscious mind. But it is a different matter when a woman's stomach swells up with a "phantom pregnancy," or when a hypnotist causes a wart to vanish by hypnotic suggestion, or a blister to appear by telling the subject that he has touched him with a red-hot iron. These effects are far beyond the power of the conscious will, and it was Freud whose intuition went to the heart of the matter. The unconscious must be somehow far *weightier and heavier* than ordinary consciousness. It could be compared to the ballast in a ship; no one can see it, and it has no obvious effect. Yet without it, the ship would bob around like a cork and overturn in the first high wind. Moreover, if the ballast moves in a storm, the ship may well capsize.

This idea of the unconscious had been around for more than a century—ever since Leibniz first used it in his *Monadology*—but no one had ever grasped its full significance. Leibniz was only talking about unconscious perceptions, which he called "little perceptions," meaning that they are too lightweight to make themselves felt by consciousness; he obviously saw the unconscious as a narrow, penumbral area of consciousness. In *The Philosophy of the Unconscious*, published in 1869, Eduard von Hartmann expanded Schopenhauer's idea that *nature* is driven by an unconscious will, but he failed to apply the idea to man. As far as common usage went, to do something "unconsciously" meant to do it absentmindedly.

Freud was the first to see that the unconscious was something far more mysterious than absent-mindedness. Breuer and Charcot taught him that the basic mechanism of neurosis is *suggestibility,* that is to say, that Charcot's "grand hysterics" with their strange ailments were simply amplified versions of the simple mechanism that makes us itch when someone talks about itching. The mechanism can be seen clearly in the case of Bertha Pappenheim. In *Studies in Hysteria* Breuer writes that she was an inveterate daydreamer, and that "her states of feeling always tended to slight exaggeration." That is to say, she was highly imaginative and highly suggestible. Her father's illness plunged her into depression, and from then on, the course of the illness could be likened to a game of tennis between her conscious and unconscious mind. Depressed by the illness, the conscious mind plunges into pessimism about the future. The highly suggestible unconscious mind responds with its own sense of foreboding and misery, which in turn intensifies the depression of the conscious mind, which in turn influences the unconscious, which in turn . . . And so the game of tennis continues, the depression deepening as it shuttles back and forth between the conscious and the unconscious. When the unconscious is healthy, we experience a sense of inner support, of vitality bubbling up from the depths; when it is sick, we have a sense of inner collapse, lack of energy, a feeling like that of walking on thin ice. In Bertha's case, the steady leakage of vitality gradually eroded the usual difference between sleeping and waking, until dreams invaded the conscious mind, producing hallucinations.

This brings us to the oddest part of the story. In recognizing the immense power of suggestibility, Freud had, in effect, discovered the basic mechanism of hysteria and neurosis. Yet he failed to recognize the central role of the "tennis-playing mechanism." What blinded him to its importance was his increasing conviction that the conscious mind was little more than a puppet of the unconscious. It may have been a disadvantage that he made his "discovery of the unconscious" through the case of Bertha Pappenheim, for Bertha was an extreme case of its disruptive powers. She might break off a conversation with Breuer to climb a tree; a moment later, brought back to her previous train of thought, she would continue where she left off, with no memory of climbing the tree. This looked remarkably like what was once called "demoniacal possession," in which the mind becomes a *slave* to "demonic" forces. From cases like Anna O and the hysterics of the Salpêtrière, it was easy for Freud to jump to the conclusion that the conscious mind is a slave to the demonic forces of the unconscious, that free will is an illusion.

With the wisdom of hindsight, we can see that Freud was simply rushing from one extreme to another. The nineteenth century was inclined to overestimate the power of reasoning and conscious decision; Freud declared that they were practically nonexistent. We can grasp the flaw in his logic if we turn to the analogy of the ship. It is true that a shift in the ballast can cause the ship to tilt or capsize, but it cannot make it turn around and go in the opposite direction; only the captain can do that. He is in charge, not the ballast.

The conclusion of Bertha Pappenheim's illness makes the same point. "The patient had formed a strong determination that the whole treatment should be finished by the anniversary of the day on which she moved [from Vienna] into the country," says Breuer. In other words, at a certain point she made a decision that it was her *conscious will* that mattered, not her unconscious terrors. In fact, she described the original trauma—the snake dream—on the exact anniversary, and woke up cured.

But Freud, dazzled and excited by his "discovery of the unconscious," overlooked the significance of this kind of evidence. Instead, he pursued a rather dangerous line of argument. If the unconscious is so powerful, then surely there is reason to suspect that *it* makes all the decisions that appear to emanate from consciousness? The "id" pulls the strings, and consciousness dances. This was to become one of the most fundamental assumptions of psychoanalysis.

But it raises another question. If our motivations are not what we think they are, then what are they? In other words, what motivates the unconscious?

When we look at it more closely, we can see that the question is really based on a linguistic misunderstanding. To say that the unconscious mind is more powerful than the conscious mind is not the same thing as saying that it is the puppet master. An elephant is stronger than a man; but it can still be controlled by him. The correct wording of the question is not *"What* motivates the unconscious?" but *"How* is the unconscious motivated?" We can then see the answer quite clearly: by the suggestions of the conscious mind. If I anticipate excitement, the unconscious provides me with energy; if I anticipate boredom, it withdraws energy, and I feel oddly dull and empty.

Because he failed to grasp the "tennis mechanism," Freud had to find another powerful factor that could explain how the unconscious produced neurosis—a kind of hidden irritant, like the pearl in the oyster. His eventual conclusion was that this factor is sex, and in creating the sexual theory, Freud once again pushed the unconscious mind into second place. He was repeating, in a different form, the error of Charcot and Bernheim.

This point is so crucial to the understanding of Reich that it is important to grasp its full implications before we continue.

The "tennis mechanism" described above would nowadays be called a "feedback mechanism." Feedback occurs when part of the product of a system reenters the system itself, as when a businessman plows some of his profits back into his business. In the same way, when you drive your car, the alternator produces electricity which recharges the battery, which in turn is essential to starting the car. This image, in fact, describes one of the fundamental operations of the unconscious.

It might help this discussion if we try to demystify this term "unconscious." For all practical purposes, it is simply the *mechanical* part of a person's being. As Leibniz pointed out, I "know" many things of which I am not conscious. For example, if someone asked me to make a sketch of the keyboard of a typewriter, I would have no idea where to put the various letters. But I could soon work it out by drumming my fingers on the desk. *They* know where the keys are, even if my "conscious mind" doesn't.

This kind of knowledge, learned knowledge, is stored fairly near the surface of my unconscious. Deeper down is the knowledge my ancestors have acquired in the past two million years of evolution; deeper still, the knowledge of our prehuman ancestors. Man has no less than three brains—what might be called the human brain, the mammal brain, and the reptile brain. The whole complex, including the nervous system, could be compared to a sophisticated computer. This computer is basically what Freud meant by the unconscious.

The "conscious me" is in charge of this computer. This statement has to be qualified immediately. I cannot make my feet warm merely by wanting to. Yet I can make my heart beat faster by thinking about something that alarms or excites me. I can release sex hormones by thinking about something that is sexually exciting. With a little training in techniques of meditation, I can even make my heart beat slower. Personal evolution, "growing up," is largely a matter of achieving greater control over the computer. A young girl cannot stop herself blushing when someone pays her a compliment, while a mature woman doesn't blush. On the whole, it would be true to say that the "conscious me" is intended to be the master of the computer.

But then, one of the main functions of the unconscious is to preserve our health; not merely on the level of destroying germs, but also on the psychological level of keeping us optimistic and full of energy. The unconscious is our basic life-support system.

Here again we approach the heart of the matter—the unconscious does this according to instructions, or hints, from the conscious mind. And the conscious mind takes its hints from the surrounding world, which it "scans" like a radar signal. When I wake up in the morning I "scan" the day ahead, asking myself how much energy I shall require to get through it. If it is the first morning of a vacation, I demand, and get, a large supply. If it is a wet December morning, with a prospect of tiresome problems, my "heart sinks," and it costs me an effort to get out of bed. This explains why, after six months at work without a vacation, human beings begin to feel "run down." They are not genuinely *tired;* it is simply that the unconscious mind responds to negative signals by rationing the energy supply. The "car battery" fails to recharge, and we find it hard to get started. During a vacation, the unconscious responds to positive signals by releasing a flood of vitality.

In short, the chief role of the unconscious is that of a servant; it could be compared to the nurse who hands the surgeon his instruments: energy, concentration, sharpened perception, and so on. Neurosis develops when the surgeon gets at cross-purposes with the nurse, and the nurse becomes increasingly sullen and resentful. This was the aspect of the unconscious that impressed Freud: its power to cause headaches, paralysis, suicidal impulses. But he totally overlooked its positive powers. Every child has noticed that Christmas can be completely unlike other holidays, that it can have an air of "magic." This is the feedback mechanism working positively; a continuous barrage of pleasant anticipation has persuaded the subconscious to release enormous quantities of vitality. A saint who is confident of the love of God may float into mystical ecstasy; he attributes this to God, but it would be more accurate to give the credit to the "computer." The saint who goes into the wilderness to pray is deliberately providing himself with the conditions in which he can achieve mystical ecstasy, or plunge into a "dark night of the soul." Since human beings are inclined to be pessimistic, most people whose lives are uneventful are more likely to slip into neurosis than ecstasy.

Which brings us to the major point: that the "feedback mechanism" *is* within the control of the conscious mind. It is not necessary to provide the mind with a series of pleasant stimuli: *merely to think*. Wordsworth's *Ode on Intimations of Immortality* provides a case in point. It begins with the famous lines about childhood—how meadow, grove, and stream seemed "apparelled in celestial light," and how, now he is an adult, "there hath past away a glory from the earth." Yet a few lines later he explains that the fit of depression has already passed: "A timely utterance gave that thought relief/ And I again am strong." This could be called "the Wordsworth effect." Instead of contemplating its problems with passive misery, the mind takes an active attitude towards them, and quickly regains a feeling of control over its own destiny.

For this is, of course, the central issue. Has the mind a degree of control over its own destiny? Or are we the playthings of forces far greater than ourselves? Freud took the latter view; consequently his psychology is basically pessimistic. On the other hand, the post-Freudian psychologist Abraham Maslow created a basically optimistic psychology on the recognition that most healthy people experience "positive feedback"—which he called the peak experience—every day of their lives. The importance of his observation is that healthy people have learned the trick of regulating their vital economy to produce peak experiences. It would be missing the point to say that they have peak experiences because they are lucky enough to be healthy. They have learned the trick of causing the unconscious mind to respond to positive suggestion, which elicits a response of vital energy, but also of *meaning*. The meaning inspires the conscious mind with a sense of purpose, and there is no more certain way of ensuring a subsidy of energy from the unconscious than to possess a sense of purpose. This, in turn, guarantees physical health. The Viennese psychiatrist Viktor Frankl made a similar discovery when he was in a concentration camp during World War II: the prisoners with a sense of purpose lived longest, while those who surrendered to despair and monotony were most susceptible to illness. For the demoralized prisoners, the unconscious had abandoned its work of "support."

Frankl has an equally significant observation that makes the opposite point. When prisoners from Auschwitz were moved to Dachau, the journey took three days, during which time they were overcrowded and half-starved. At Dachau they were kept standing in the freezing rain all night because someone had fallen asleep and missed the roll call. Yet, Frankl said, they were all relaxed and happy, laughing and telling jokes—*because Dachau had no incinerator chimney*.

What is significant here is the recognition that the conscious mind can *choose* to which elements in its situation it will decide to give prominence. The prisoners had *almost* every reason for pessimism, and the lack of a chimney can hardly be called a positive element in normal circumstances. Yet when consciousness selects this one element for notice above all others, the unconscious promptly responds with a surge of sheer exhilaration. Again, we observe the vital importance of this element of freedom, the mind's freedom to choose its attitudes.

The "computer" is not simply our vital support system; it is also an immense reference library. An interesting example is cited by the poet Coleridge in *Biographia Literaria*: an illiterate young woman fell into a "nervous fever" and began to speak in Latin, Greek, and Hebrew. It looked like some odd form of "demoniacal possession" until a doctor discovered that the girl had been brought up by a pastor who spoke all three languages, and was in the habit of wandering around the house intoning his favorite passages from the classics. The girl's unconscious mind had "recorded" the words, and she repeated them in her delirium.

In a more recent case, a subject under the influence of a psychedelic drug told the doctor, Jean Houston, that he was in ancient Athens listening to Socrates. Asked what Socrates was saying, the patient said "I don't know—he's speaking in Greek." The doctor had taken a degree in classical Greek, and asked him to repeat what Socrates was saying: whereupon the man repeated the words in classical Greek.[3] In this case there was no revelation of a childhood spent in the house of a Greek scholar, but Dr. Houston found nothing unusual in the episode; she had studied other cases in which people gave details of life in ancient Egypt or medieval Europe, and was convinced that it was a matter of unconscious learning from television or magazines. The mind literally tape records everything it sees and hears, but the memories can only be played back if a certain part of the brain is activated.

The implications are startling. In the 1880s, the Dutch psychologist and poet Frederik van Eeden performed an interesting experiment with a ten-year-old girl; he taught her French under hypnosis. When awakened, the girl had no knowledge of the language. Then one day, Van Eeden told her that when she woke up, she would remember everything she had learned; to the girl's utter amazement, she was suddenly able to speak French. But Dr. Houston's observations suggest that there is no need for a patient to be taught a foreign language; if a hypnotist could gain access to the out-of-the-way corners of the subject's computer library, he would probably find that she has already picked it up unconsciously.

Freud's disciple Jung became aware of an even stranger aspect of the unconscious, and thereby earned the Master's enmity and suspicion. In *Memories, Dreams, Reflections,* he tells how he asked Freud's opinion of parapsychology, and how Freud rejected it "in terms of so shallow a positivism" that Jung became angry. At this moment Jung had a curious sensation "as if my diaphragm were made of iron and were becoming red hot." There was suddenly a loud report from the bookcase, and as Freud leapt up in alarm, Jung said: "That is an example of a so-called catalytic exteriorization phenomenon." Freud replied "Bosh," whereupon Jung asserted that there would be another report in a moment; a second loud detonation immediately sounded from the bookcase.

By "exteriorization phenomenon," Jung meant what would be more generally called a "poltergeist effect." In the late nineteenth century, investigators of "paranormal phenomena" became aware that these strange goings-on—loud bangs and raps, objects flying through the air—are not necessarily the work of disembodied spirits, but are usually due to the presence of a disturbed child or adolescent *who is totally unaware of being the cause.* Now while it is credible that the unconscious mind can produce remarkable effects on one's own body—even to religiously induced stigmata—it is altogether more difficult to see how it could possibly exert a direct influence on physical objects. If "psychokinesis" is a genuine phenomenon, then the powers of the unconscious mind are far greater and far stranger than Freud had even begun to imagine.

What it amounts to, then, is that Freud's failure to recognize the feedback mechanism of neurosis left him free to construct a theory that was a rationalization of his own pessimism and sense of insecurity. Man is essentially a creature—an animal—at the mercy of instinct. Inhibited by civilization, his sexual drive festers in the unconscious mind, producing all kinds of mental illness. Later, when Freud began to recognize the inadequacy of the libido theory, he discovered another "instinct" to which he could attribute all man's problems: the death-instinct, a built-in urge towards death, which man attempts to redirect by turning it outward toward other human beings. The "thanatos" theory is the ultimate expression of Freud's pessimism, his conviction that human beings are the slaves of forces greater than themselves. Freud was already in the process of formulating the theory when he met Reich in 1919.

All this should make us aware of the fundamental objection to psychoanalysis. Neurosis is caused by "negative feedback," which produces an increasing sense of suffocation, of *loss of freedom.* Its cure entails positive feedback, which produces an increasing sense of freedom. This is closely bound up with a sense of meaning, of

the value of conscious effort. Clearly, a psychotherapy based on
the conviction that freedom is an illusion is handicapped from the
beginning. The tracking-down of sexual traumas and repressed
guilt-feelings may raise the patient's hopes, and so improve his
general outlook, but the Freudian "philosophy of helplessness" en-
sures that his attitude remains passive, so the basic problem remains. The only true cure of neurosis is for consciousness to
throw off its passivity, to become aware of its freedom. (For example, the philosopher William James began to emerge from a
nervous breakdown when he decided to accept Renouvier's definition of free will: "The sustaining of a thought because *I choose to*
when I might have other thoughts.") Freud's basic outlook actually sustains the essence of the neurosis while attempting to cure
it. This could be compared to the way that doctors, in the days before Semmelweis, used to attend women in childbirth immediately
after lancing a boil or performing a postmortem, then wonder why
their patients died of puerperal fever.

Wilhelm Reich was fundamentally optimistic, and, as we shall
see, he instinctively recognized this self-contradictory element in
Freudian psychotherapy. His later developments may be seen as
an attempt to break away from this basically negative outlook and
to develop a more dynamic and creative theory of sexuality.

It is interesting to observe the way that Freud used the insights he
derived from Breuer and Charcot to build up the sexual theory,
and then turned this into "an impregnable bulwark of dogma"
(his own expression).

Curiously enough, the first hints for the sexual theory came
from Breuer himself. In describing the case of Bertha Pappenheim
in *Studies in Hysteria* (which he coauthored with Freud), Breuer
tactfully omitted to mention one of its more embarrassing compli-
cations: the fact that he and his patient became strongly involved
emotionally. Freud later told this part of the story to his biographer Ernest Jones. Bertha was an attractive and intelligent girl,
and Breuer devoted far more time to the case than most doctors
would have considered appropriate. His wife became so jealous
that Breuer was finally forced to tell his attractive patient that he
was withdrawing from the case. By this time, Bertha had improved
so much that he felt he could do this with a clear conscience. That

evening he was summoned to see her, and found her suffering a particularly violent attack of her "secondary personality." She lay with her legs open, apparently in the throes of childbirth (or sexual intercourse). Breuer was deeply shocked; the girl came of a puritanical family which never spoke about sex. The "childbirth" was, of course, hysterical, and even Breuer could see that he had been cast in the role of father or lover. He gave way to panic, and left for Venice with his wife the next day.

After his return from the Salpêtrière, Freud himself became increasingly aware of the erotic relation that could develop between doctor and patient. Jones relates how one day a female patient flung her arms around Freud's neck; fortunately (he adds), they were interrupted by the entrance of a servant. The episode apparently came as a revelation to Freud, who suddenly recognized that a successful cure might even depend on the patient falling in love with the doctor. Freud called the phenomenon "transference"; twenty years later, he made the significant remark that it proved to him that the origin of all neurosis is sexual. This seems to be a curious piece of reasoning. After all, "transference" can happen to anyone in the field of medicine, or even education. If a tubercular woman falls in love with her doctor, or an economics student with her professor, does this also prove that tuberculosis and economics are sexual in origin? The plain fact is that love springs out of admiration, and that therefore *any* relationship between mentor and pupil, or healer and patient, provides the basic situation.

After the episode of the enamored patient, Freud began questioning other patients about their sex lives—to the detriment of his practice—and became increasingly convinced that all neuroses could be traced back to an early sexual trauma. Many female patients obligingly furnished details of how they had been seduced by their fathers at an early age, and for a while Freud actually held the view that the majority of neuroses were caused by such seductions. His willingness to entertain such an untenable view indicates his determination to create a "sexual theory." By 1897, two years after the publication of *Studies in Hysteria,* he had come to recognize that the majority of these accounts were fantasies. Far from persuading him that he had been pursuing the wrong line of reasoning, it only confirmed his belief in its correctness. Why should they lie about being seduced by their fathers, unless they harbored a secret wish to be seduced? Freud quickly generalized this notion into the Oedipus complex: that the daughter has a secret desire to replace her mother; the son, his father. It also followed that the son must harbor an unconscious enmity towards his father, a desire to kill him, and a fear of being killed by him (or, at the very least, castrated).

Breuer sensibly felt that all this was going a little too far; he probably suspected that Freud was becoming a crank. He could accept that sex might be the origin of some neuroses, but surely not *all?* Freud, by now totally committed to his sexual theory, accused Breuer of betraying him, and broke off the relationship. Even Jones has to admit: "The scientific differences alone cannot account for the bitterness with which Freud wrote about Breuer in the unpublished Fliess correspondence in the nineties. When one recollects what Breuer had meant to him in the eighties, his generosity to Freud, his understanding sympathy, and the combination of cheerfulness and intellectual stimulation that radiated from him, the change later is indeed startling." And he excuses Freud by suggesting that Breuer had a certain small-mindedness that was "very alien to Freud's open-hearted and generous nature." To anyone who has read his account of the relation between Freud and Breuer, this conclusion will seem an inversion of the truth.

In retrospect, we can see that "the sexual theory" was a logical outcome of Freud's failure to grasp the feedback mechanism of neurosis. By totally disregarding the role of the conscious mind, Freud threw all the emphasis on the unconscious. He saw the unconscious as a kind of oven that incubated the neurosis. But in that case, what does it incubate? Freud's answer: repressions. "Obsessional ideas are invariably self-reproaches which have reemerged from repression in a transmuted form and which always relate to some sexual act that was performed with pleasure in childhood." The idea of repression also enabled him to explain Charcot's grand hysterics; they were simply diverting the energy of repression into physical channels, as a kind of safety valve.

This reasoning led Freud to the next stage in the theory. If the unconscious is a kind of oven that incubates the repressions and causes them to fester, then it is essentially passive. And the job of the psychotherapist is to try to dig into it to remove the festering splinter. How can he do this? At first, Freud believed that the answer lay in hypnosis. This dissatisfied him because a large number of patients failed to respond to hypnosis. But again, Breuer had provided him with the vital hint: the "talking cure" that had worked so impressively with Bertha. By 1895, Freud had developed the famous free-association technique: asking the patient to lie down on a couch and tell the psychiatrist everything that came into his or her head. In effect, Freud had now taken the same step as Bernheim: that of shifting the emphasis back from the unconscious to the conscious mind. But in so doing, he was also shifting his attention from the phenomena that had so impressed him at the Salpêtrière, as well as losing sight of the significance of suggestibility.

For more than half a century, the "sexual theory" remained one of the unquestioned dogmas of psychoanalysis; anyone who questioned it was likely to find himself vigorously ejected from the movement. Freud's leading followers—Jones, Melanie Klein, Karen Horney, Helene Deutsch, A. A. Brill, H. W. Frink—shared his conviction that the early rejection of the sexual theory was due to some survival of Victorian prudery, and to unconscious dishonesty on the part of its opponents. The cautious reservations of Breuer, Jung, Adler, and the rest were somehow mythologized into underhand attempts at counter-revolution, a kind of psychological Trotskyism.

Yet now that all the initial major figures in psychoanalysis are dead, it is possible to look back on its early history with a certain objectivity. It seems clear that most of Freud's major cases can be interpreted without the sexual theory. Since a conviction as important as this demands justification, I will devote a certain amount of space to it. We may begin by considering the case of "Little Hans"—regarded by Freudians as one of the most striking applications of the theory of childhood sexuality.

At the age of four, not long after the birth of a baby sister, Little Hans developed a phobia about going outdoors; he said he was afraid of being bitten by a horse. This detail struck Freud as highly significant, since he regarded the horse as a symbol of male sexuality. From Little Hans's father—an enthusiastic disciple who had attended Freud's lectures—he elicited the following facts about

the child's sexual development. At the age of three, Hans had
shown an unusual interest in his "widdler"; when his mother
caught him holding it one day, she threatened to cut it off. Hans
replied that he would widdle with his bottom. When his mother
undressed, Hans looked at her intently, and asked if she had a
widdler, commenting: "I thought you were so big you'd have a
widdler like a horse." On vacation with his parents, Hans slept
with them—which, Freud assured them, aroused sexual feelings in
the child. At four-and-a-half, when his mother was bathing him, he
asked her why she was so careful not to touch his widdler; she
said it would be "piggish." "But great fun," said Little Hans.

He seems to have been an affectionate child, initially jealous of
his baby sister, but soon becoming fond of her. (Freud himself
had, as a child, wished his baby brother Julius dead; when the
baby died, Freud experienced strong guilt feelings. He was now
convinced that all children harbor these homicidal feelings.) Little
Hans also put his arms around a boy cousin and developed a crush
on a seven-year-old playmate.

When Hans began to exhibit reluctance about going into the
street, explaining that he was afraid of being bitten by a horse,
Hans's father decided that the horse symbolized a large penis,
which had frightened the child at some stage. Freud instructed the
father to tell Little Hans that he really wanted to sleep in his
mother's bed, and that he was afraid of horses because he took so
much interest in their widdlers; predictably, Hans got worse.

The child explained that his fear of horses was due to an episode at Gmunden, when a friend's father had told her: "Don't put
your finger near that horse; it could bite." The father rejected this
straightforward explanation, and told Hans that he thought it was
a widdler he was afraid to put his hand to. "But widdlers don't
bite," said the puzzled child. "Perhaps they do," said his father
cryptically.

The following day, Hans admitted that he still put his hand on
his widdler every night. Later he told his father that he no longer
held his widdler, but agreed that he still wanted to. His father
suggested he should sleep in a sack with his hands outside.

On a visit to the zoo, Hans showed fear of the elephant and
the giraffe; his father told him that this was because large animals
had big widdlers. Hans denied this. When Hans subsequently

dreamed of two giraffes, Freud explained that it was "a matrimo-
nial scene transposed into giraffe life." Hans really wanted to
sleep with his mother and satisfy his curiosity about her genitals.
He also came to the conclusion that Hans really hated his father
and wanted to kill him; horses, he said, symbolized the father.

In the event, Little Hans's phobia vanished of its own accord.
The case is nevertheless regarded as one of Freud's major tri-
umphs; one psychoanalyst speaks of it as "a remarkable achievement . . . one of the most valued records in the psychoanalytical
archives." But unless one is already totally convinced by the sexual theory, it is difficult to endorse this assessment. In fact, it
seems to be an almost grotesque example of Freud's tendency to
impose his sexual obsessions on any problem that came to his notice. Anyone who has children knows that they take an interest in
their sexual organs, and in any others that present themselves for
inspection. Unwise parents may threaten to cut off their male children's penises, but it seldom causes any deep disturbance; children
know that adults are always making threats they don't mean to
carry out. On the other hand, the idea of unknown danger causes
deeper worry: the thought that if they touch a certain wire they
may be electrocuted, that if they reach out to stroke a dog or a
horse, it might bite off a finger. In nervous children, such fears
easily turn into phobias. All the evidence suggests that it was not
his father Hans was afraid of, but real horses. Freud's explanation
that Hans's fear of "black things" on horses' eyes and noses were
based on his father's glasses and mustache proved to be another
bad guess; it turned out that Hans meant ordinary blinkers and
harnesses. Looking over Freud's account of the Little Hans case,
it seems clear that he only complicated the problem by assuming
that the child's fear of real horses was somehow connected with
his interest in his penis. Fortunately, Hans seems to have been
healthy enough to throw off the effects of his father's attempts at
psychoanalysis.

One further example will serve to illustrate the Freudian
method. The case of the Wolf Man is regarded as one of the most
significant in the history of psychoanalysis, and various documents
relating to it have been collected into a full-length book.

The Wolf Man was a young Russian, probably called Sergei Petrov, who came to Freud about 1910 in a state of deep depression.

His vital powers had reached such a low ebb that he was unable to
dress and feed himself; he suffered from permanent constipation
so that he needed enemas twice a week. These symptoms immediately indicate a typical case of "life failure." Because the unconscious mind has withdrawn all inner support, life seems permanently gray and meaningless; the eyes can see that something is
beautiful, but there are no feelings to respond. The state has
been portrayed by many Russian novelists—Russians seem particularly prone to it—and Dostoevsky's Stavrogin (in *The Possessed*)
is a revealing example of the condition.

What emerged in Freud's analysis was that Petrov was jealous
of his elder sister, who took pleasure in teasing him, particularly
showing him pictures of a wolf in a story book, which terrified him
into screams. At the age of six, Petrov had a nightmare of six mo-
tionless white wolves sitting in a tree outside the bedroom window; hence the patient's nickname.

Where sex was concerned, the story sounded fairly promising.
The Wolf Man had a sister who was two years his senior, and who
had a thoroughly sensual nature. She played sexual games with
him when he was about three and handled his penis. The preco-
cious child waved the organ at his nurse, who told him that children who did that kind of thing were likely to have it cut off. Such
threats are, according to Freud, a fundamental cause of neurosis.
Petrov's adult sex life was also rather odd; he was sexually
obsessed by servant girls who were on all fours scrubbing the
floor; he liked to have intercourse with them in this position.

After some years of analysis, Freud explains, he came to an interesting conclusion: that the basic trouble lay in a "primal scene"
witnessed by the Wolf Man at the age of eighteen months. He had
wakened up in his cot, says Freud, to see his parents, both in white
nightshirts, making love "in the animal position." This, Freud
believed, led to a homosexual fixation on the father and a desire
to be beaten by him. Hence the wolf nightmare, and the obsession
about servant girls on all fours. The wolf dream had somehow
reversed the "primal scene"; instead of waking suddenly and seeing
his father engaged in coitus, he wakened and saw white wolves
looking in passively through the window.

After many years of treatment, the Wolf Man was much improved, though by no means cured—he continued to have nervous

troubles, and to be a thoroughly inadequate human being to the end of his life. Nevertheless, Freudians have always regarded the case as a convincing proof of the theory that the cause of neurosis lies in childhood traumas.

Freud himself wrote an impressive paper about the case shortly after it was concluded in 1914; it was called "From the History of an Infantile Neurosis," and it has become a classic of psychoanalytic literature. But there is one point that is less than satisfactory; Freud never actually tells us how he found out about the scene witnessed by the eighteen-month-old baby. He simply states it as a fact. "I have now reached the point at which I must abandon the support I have hitherto had from the course of the analysis. I am afraid it will also be the point at which the reader's belief will abandon me. What sprang into activity that night out of the chaos of the dreamer's unconscious memory-traces was the picture of copulation between his parents, copulation in circumstances that were not entirely usual . . ." But from this point on, he refers to the "primal scene" as an established fact. A page later he admits that he is inclined to be critical "towards the acceptance of this observation of the child's." And in the next paragraph, he explains that the wolf picture that used to terrify Petrov so much showed it standing upright with its hands stretched out, and that his patient "thought that the posture of the wolf in this picture reminded him of that of his father during the constructed primal scene." Here the use of the word "constructed" seems odd.

When the Wolf Man was eighty-three, he wrote an autobiographical memoir, which was published, together with Freud's original paper, in a book called *The Wolf Man and Sigmund Freud*.[4] It also contains essays by other leading Freudians who had dealings with the Wolf Man. Oddly enough, the vital question of whether the child actually saw the primal scene, and later described it to Freud, is left in misty ambiguity.

The problem is solved by consulting the second volume of Jones's *Life of Freud*; it contains the throwaway admission: "The patient could not recollect the incident . . . but the mass of converging evidence was so convincing that in Freud's judgment the reconstruction reached the same degree of certainty as an actual memory." Which leads one to wonder why, in that case, Freud failed to tell the reader about this "mass of converging evidence."

It is the memoirs of the Wolf Man that make clear just how far
Freud has, once again, imposed his own preconceptions on the
case, and how, in doing so, he has completely overlooked the obvious explanations of the Wolf Man's mental troubles. The Wolf
Man explains that there was a long history of mental illness in his
family—a detail that Freud has unaccountably forgotten to mention. His paternal grandmother committed suicide; his grandfather
became highly eccentric; his paternal uncle suffered from severe
obsessional neurosis; his own father was a manic depressive; his
sister committed suicide; his mother was permanently ill. The
Wolf Man himself emerges as an intelligent but extremely weak
and self-pitying character; when he lost his fortune in the Russian
Revolution, he expected Freud to support him and, in fact, Freud
collected sums of money for him for many years. In 1938, after
the suicide of his wife, he told a Freudian analyst with characteristic self-pity: "I have always had bad luck. I am always subject
to the greatest misfortunes." The rest of the book makes it clear
that it was his own weak and rather unpleasant character that was
largely to blame.

The most interesting fact to emerge from the book is one that
Freud completely suppressed: that the origin of the illness lay in
his sister's suicide. Freud not only plays down the suicide: he insists that the Wolf Man was rather pleased and relieved by it.
"When the news of his sister's death arrived, so the patient told
me, he felt hardly a trace of grief. He had to force himself to show
signs of sorrow, and was able quite coolly to rejoice at having now
become sole heir to the property." What the Wolf Man himself
says could hardly be more different. "After the death of Anna,
with whom I had had a very deep, personal, inner relationship,
and whom I had always considered as my only comrade, I fell into
a state of deepest depression. The mental agony I now suffered
would often increase to the intensity of physical pain. In this condition I could not interest myself in anything. Everything repelled
me and thoughts of suicide went round in my mind . . . I had
fallen into such a state of melancholy after Anna's death that
there seemed to be no more sense or purpose in living, and nothing in the world seemed worth striving for. In such a state of mind
one can hardly interest oneself in anything." He was, in any case,
of a romantic and pessimistic disposition; he identified himself

closely with the romantic poet Lermontov, who died in a duel. Now, with the complete collapse of all sense of purpose, his inherited melancholia caught up with him. "My thoughts and feelings seemed to be paralyzed. Everything that went on before my eyes was unreal to me; it all seemed a bad dream." Again and again he makes it clear that he was suffering from dissociation from reality that comes with complete collapse of the will. "I experienced everything as unreal and dreamlike." And the fact that he was wealthy, and could travel around Europe with a valet and personal physician, gave him no incentive for effort. He could indulge his misery and self-pity.

In the course of the long analysis, Petrov must have told Freud these things. Why, then, does Freud fail to mention them? Because he is intent on imposing his own purely arbitrary notion of the "primal scene," and establishing this as the cause of the Wolf Man's chronic depression. To mention Petrov's own account of his early life and his sister's suicide would render his own sexual explanations superfluous.

Understandably, then, Freud regarded the sexual theory with jealous concern, and became deeply resentful and suspicious of anyone who questioned it. In a footnote to the Wolf Man paper, he comments that at the time of writing "I was still freshly under the twisted reinterpretations which C. G. Jung and Alfred Adler were endeavouring to give to the findings of psychoanalysis." The bitterness of the comment seems out of place, since Jung and Adler were not denying the sexual theory: only attempting to broaden the scope of psychoanalysis. And as late as 1937, the comment Freud made on the death of Adler revealed that the almost paranoid bitterness was still there: "For a Jew-boy out of a Viennese suburb a death in Aberdeen is an unheard-of career in itself, and a proof of how far he had got on. The world rewarded him richly for his service of contradicting psychoanalysis." Something of the attitude behind these comments is revealed in a passage in Jung's autobiography: "I can still vividly recall how Freud said to me, 'My dear Jung, promise me never to abandon the sexual theory. That is the most essential thing of all. You see, we must make a dogma of it, an unshakeable bulwark.' He said that to me with great emotion, in the tone of a father saying, 'And promise me this one thing, my dear son: that you will go to church every Sunday.' In some astonishment I asked him, 'A bulwark—against what?' To which he replied, 'Against the black tide of mud'—and here he hesitated for a moment, then added—'of occultism.' " To understand this remark we must bear in mind that Freud's psychology had its roots in Mesmer, and that because of the association with Mesmer, hypnosis had been discredited for almost a century. Freud was determined that none of this "occultist" mud should stick to psychoanalysis. Yet Jung is strictly fair when he adds: "To me the sexual theory was just as occult, that is to say, just as unproven an hypothesis, as many other speculative views."

The standard histories of psychoanalysis have created the legend that it had to overcome the frenzied resistance of puritans. There was, of course, a great deal of resistance; Professor Raimann, of the Psychiatric Clinic in Vienna, was expressing a widely held view when he declared: "Any man who concentrates his attention so exclusively on sex must be some sort of pervert . . ." But it was not because Freud spoke openly about sexual matters that he was so passionately condemned; we have seen that sexual psychology was widely and openly discussed in Europe long before Freud. What aroused the hostility was the widespread feeling that Freud was propounding a theory of neurosis that was *fundamentally untrue:* the notion that it was *always* due to sexual repressions. Much of the opposition came from sensible people, like Breuer and Jung, who felt that the sexual theory was arbitrary and unbalanced. Bernard Shaw put his finger on the problem in the preface to his novel *Immaturity*: "As I write, there is a craze for what is called psychoanalysis, or the cure of diseases by explaining to the patient what is the matter with him: an excellent plan if you happen to know what is the matter with him." Freud's notion of what was the matter with his patients seemed to be based on purely arbitrary interpretations of their dreams or admissions to the psychoanalyst. The kind of inferences that Freud drew in cases like the Wolf Man and Little Hans give the impression that psychoanalysis is more akin to palmistry or astrology than to the science of psychology.

All this has considerable relevance to the relationship between Freud and Reich. What becomes clear, from a study of Freud's relations with his leading followers, is the intensity of the conviction that "he who is not with me is against me." When anyone showed the least sympathy for his ideas, Freud was immediately willing to treat them as friends and allies. If this friendly attitude had the desired effect of turning the sympathizer into a whole-hearted partisan, Freud was satisfied. During the probationary period the admirer was allowed to raise questions and doubts, and even to think for himself. But this was only so that the ultimate triumph of the psychoanalytic doctrine would be the more complete. If it finally became clear to Freud that there was still a basic difference of outlook, and that the admirer was not willing to be received into the church of psychoanalysis with all the sacraments, patience gave way to hostility; clearly, the disciple was perverse and unworthy, flying in the face of his own salvation—not to mention that he was a potential danger to the salvation of others. In effect, if not in fact, there was a ritual of excommunication, not unlike that applied by the Jewish faith to its heretics. The unbeliever was solemnly anathematized and placed on a list of "prohibited persons." The intention was to break his spirit, to make him feel cast into the outer darkness.

For those less totally involved in psychoanalysis, or whose support was too valuable to throw away, less than total submission was demanded. Freud remained a lifelong friend of the novelist Thomas Mann, and one result of this strange alliance was Mann's essay "Freud and the Future," a speech made in Vienna on Freud's eightieth birthday, in which Mann skillfully avoids the real issues by treating Freud as a descendant of Schopenhauer and Nietzsche and generalizing about his courage in the face of "persecution." But the story of Freud's relationship with the great satirist Karl Kraus is rather more characteristic. Kraus was the editor of the leading satirical magazine *Die Fackel* (*The Torch*), and in 1904, Freud made the first friendly overture in a letter, congratulating him on his "perceptiveness and courage." For a while they remained on cautiously friendly terms, regarding one another as two revolutionaries. But as Kraus became more aware of the implications of psychoanalysis, he found it basically detestable. He wrote perceptively: "Psychoanalysis is the disease for which it claims to be the cure," recognizing that the whole Freudian attitude encourages dependency, self-pity, and sickness. He also reacted strongly against Freud's attempts to explain the genius of men like Leonardo and Dostoevsky in terms of penis envy and Oedipus complexes.

The Vienna Psychoanalytic Society finally decided to retaliate, and in January 1910, a disciple named Fritz Wittels read a paper called "The Fackel Neurosis." Its main point was that Kraus's longstanding enmity to the conservative newspaper *Neue Freie Presse* (*The New Free Press*) was due to the fact that Kraus identified the *Presse* with the father's large penis, which corrupts (or pollutes) the world, while Kraus's own *Fackel* was a small penis, which was nevertheless capable of destroying the father's large penis. Wittels explained Kraus's hatred of cheap journalism as another form of his Oedipus complex. The comments of the rest of the group—as recorded by Otto Rank—make it clear that they regard this tissue of humorless absurdities as a serious defense of psychoanalysis. Freud expressed himself as being in agreement with Wittels' paper, and thanked its presenter for his "many sacrifices." He appears to mean that Wittels has stuck out his neck and exposed himself to attack in *Die Fackel,* a position that he, Freud, would be unwilling to take.[5]

The only member of the group who had anything to say in favor of Kraus was Viktor Tausk, who was himself noted for his biting wit and the sharpness of his tongue; Tausk commented that the conservative press *was* vulgar, and that Kraus was right to do battle against it. Tausk was one of Freud's most brilliant and trusted disciples; but his comment suggests—to anyone who knows Freud's character—that this was not a position he would be able to hold for long. In fact, the story of Freud's subsequent relations with Tausk—which finally came to light half a century after Tausk's death—is a striking example of Freud's pitiless hostility towards anyone he felt to be drifting away from total allegiance. In this case, the problem was not that Tausk came to have doubts about the sexual theory, but that his brilliance became a threat to Freud. Lou Andreas-Salomé, the woman who had once rejected Nietzsche, and who later became Tausk's mistress, wrote in her *Freud Journal* that the tragedy of Tausk's relation with Freud was that "he will always tackle the same problems, and the same attempts at solution, that Freud is engaged in." And according to Paul Roazen's account of the relationship,[6] Freud was always afraid that Tausk would anticipate some of his own discoveries. In

the early days of their relationship, Tausk was emotionally dependent on Freud towards whom he felt immense gratitude for direct-
ing him into psychoanalysis. As Tausk's self-confidence, and prominence in the movement, increased, Freud began to experience
his usual misgivings. During World War I, Tausk was away from
Vienna, and his independence increased; yet his personal attachment to Freud remained as strong as ever. Like so many of
Freud's male disciples, Tausk found it hard to realize that the act
of thinking for himself—even along strictly Freudian lines—was
enough to arouse Freud's desire to get rid of him. Roazen comments: "Freud's male pupils wanted his love, but he gave it only if
they came close to castrating themselves as creative individuals."

Tausk, for all his intellectual vitality, had one basic flaw: he
was a pessimistic romantic, with a strong vein of self-pity. With
ruthless calculation, Freud used this weakness to undermine and
destroy him. When Tausk returned to Vienna after the war he had
financial and emotional problems, including troubles with women.
He asked Freud for psychoanalysis—at that time the group held
the theory that all psychoanalysts should be psychoanalyzed—and
Freud coldly and decisively refused him. Nevertheless, he recom-
mended him to be analyzed by one of his female students, Helene
Deutsch, who was herself being analyzed by Freud. The gesture
was clearly intended as an attack on Tausk's self-esteem—the implication being that not only was he Freud's inferior, but even the
inferior of one of Freud's female students. The arrangement also
had the cunning advantage of allowing Freud access to Tausk's innermost thoughts via Helene Deutsch, who had no hesitation in
repeating them. Tausk pleaded that surely Freud's reasons for refusing him did not apply to a son? The comment was naïve; Freud
told others that Tausk was a "dog on a leash," implying that he
might bite; besides, Freud's theory of the Oedipus complex meant
that his objections applied *especially* to a "son." Freud had the
upper hand, and he had no intention of showing mercy. Roazen
remarks: "Freud was through with Tausk, no matter how difficult
it might prove for Tausk to accept the rejection."

On 3 July, 1919, Tausk wrote two letters, one to Freud and one
to his mistress, while he sipped slivovitz; then he tied a curtain
cord around his neck and shot himself through the temple. He blew
off part of his head, and strangled as he collapsed. When Tausk's

son went to see Freud two days later, he found him "formal" and "standoffish." There is no other record of Freud's reaction to the suicide. He probably felt that Tausk's downfall was entirely Tausk's own fault, and that he had got what he deserved.

Tausk's suicide in 1919 left an obvious gap in the ranks of the disciples, most of whom were now past middle age. That gap was to be filled by Wilhelm Reich. Unfortunately for Freud, and also, it turned out, for his new disciple, Reich also lacked the temperament to become a voluntary eunuch.

CHAPTER THREE

More than three decades after that first meeting with Freud, Reich told Dr. Kurt Eissler: "When I first met Freud, there was immediate contact—immediate contact of two organisms, an aliveness, interest, and going to the point. I had the same experience with Einstein when I met him in 1940. There are certain people who click, just click in their emotional contact . . . I knew Freud liked me. I felt it. I could see it. I could talk to him straight. He understood what I meant in an immediate way."

There is no need to doubt Reich's claim that Freud took an instant liking to him. He even put his finger on the reason, with characteristic lack of modesty: "You see me now? I am quite alive, am I not? I am sparkling, yes? He had the same quality. He had an aliveness which the usual human being didn't have . . ." That is to say, Freud, like Reich, was a man of genius, and men of genius usually have a discernibly higher voltage than mediocrities. Roazen has commented that Freud preferred people with less formality and more sparkle; Reich certainly fit into this category.

In view of Freud's unfortunate experience with disciples like Adler, Jung, and Tausk, it may seem surprising that he accepted

Reich so easily. But Reich himself offers an important clue when he says: "In 1919, there was a very small circle. There were only about eight men. At the Psychiatric Clinic, they were laughed at. In the medical school, they were laughed at. Freud was laughed at." Even in his mid-sixties, Freud had still not gained general acceptance. As a consequence, he and his disciples had developed a kind of siege mentality: the faithful band against a hostile world. Reich came to him as a brilliant young medical student and ex-army officer. Freud could not afford to reject such potentially valuable support. Neither was there any reason why he should; he had not yet achieved the world fame that was to arrive in the last decade of his life. According to Reich, Freud was a lonely man who had little social intercourse with his followers.

The followers were, inevitably, a rather uninspiring group; inevitably because Freud, as we have seen, always managed to break with his more interesting admirers. Ernest Jones writes uncharitably: "The reader may perhaps gather that I was not highly impressed with the assembly. It seemed an unworthy accompaniment to Freud's genius, but in the Vienna of those days, so full of prejudice against him, it was hard to secure a pupil with a reputation to lose, so he had to take what he could get."[1] And "what he could get" included, in those early days, Jung, Adler, and Stekel. By 1919, even Stekel was classified with Jung and Adler as a traitor. Oddly enough, the break had occurred on account of Tausk. Stekel and Adler were editors of the psychoanalytic journal *Zentralblatt,* and in 1911 Freud tried to induce them to accept Tausk as a supervisor of book reviews—in effect, a third coeditor. Stekel dug in his heels, and Freud tried to persuade the publisher to sack him. When this move failed, Freud set out systematically to persuade every other member of the staff to resign, then helped to found another journal, *Internationale Zeitschrift.* It was typical of Freud that, when his authority was defied, he would move heaven and earth to punish the offender.

At the time Reich joined Freud's circle, the "senior disciple" was Paul Federn, a talented and compassionate analyst whose qualities were personal rather than intellectual; he was romantic, idealistic, and notoriously absent-minded. Next to Federn in order of seniority came his friend Eduard Hitschmann, whom Federn had introduced to the group as long ago as 1905; he was a worthy but dull character who admired Freud to the point of worship; Freud found his plodding intellect mildly irritating. These were the "elder statesmen" after the departure of Jung and Adler. Younger followers included Karl Abraham, Otto Rank, Theodor Reik, Herbert Silberer, Hermann Nunberg, Hanns Sachs, and Sandor Ferenczi. The Welshman, Ernest Jones, a disciple and founder of the British analytical movement, also spent much time with Freud in Vienna. Ferenczi, based in Budapest, was one of the most charming and talented members of the Freud circle, and Freud had a deep personal liking for him. Hanns Sachs was a plump, lively bachelor who loved attractive women and good wine; he went to Berlin in 1920, leaving the group considerably duller. Karl Abraham was a dedicated psychoanalyst with a precise and formal manner; his scientific abilities were highly regarded, and he was not above exploiting petty jealousies within the group. Hermann Nunberg, a man of sour disposition, was another systematic intellect who tirelessly arranged and rearranged Freud's ideas. Theodor Reik, later well known as a popularizer of psychoanalysis, is described by Roazen as "a heel-clicking admirer of every word Freud wrote," a description that applies to most of the group. Ernest Jones later became Freud's biographer; Paul Roazen, whose *Freud and His Followers* is based on interviews with people who knew Freud, devoted many pages to correcting Jones' distortions of psychoanalytic history. He describes Jones as "spiteful, jealous and querulous"—qualities that frequently emerge in Jones' treatment of rivals in the Freud biography.

Of all the group, only three could be described as having ideas of their own: Paul Federn, Otto Rank, and Herbert Silberer. Federn was a socialist who believed that psychoanalysis would one day free man from his mental chains. His writing style lacks Freud's clarity; Roazen speculates that this was because his ideas differed from Freud's, but as he was anxious not to bring this into the open, he wrote obscurely to hide the differences. Otto Rank was an unattractive, withdrawn little man, who had remained a loyal Freudian throughout the period of the defection of Jung and Adler. In the early 1920s, he was, next to Ferenczi, Freud's favorite disciple, a position that aroused the envy of Abraham and Jones. His break with Freud was to be slow and painful; but in 1919 he was still a "heel-clicking admirer."

Apart from Rank, the most potentially brilliant and original of
Freud's followers was Herbert Silberer; he was a man of independent means and the only member of the Vienna group who
was not Jewish. At the time Reich met Freud, Silberer was already
under a cloud, and scarcely ever came to meetings. Roazen offers
the suggestion that this was because the other members were suspicious of gentiles. But a far more important reason can be found
in Silberer's book *Problems of Mysticism and Its Symbols,* published in 1917.[2] It deals with the interpretation of dreams and
myths from a Freudian standpoint, but this is a deeply Jungian
work—in fact, more "Jungian" than anything Jung himself had
written up to that date. (In his autobiography, Jung mentions that
it was Silberer's book that sparked his interest in alchemy.) Silberer frequently quotes Jung with approval, and this in itself would
have been enough to explain Freud's increasing hostility, but there
was an even deeper cause for offense. Silberer had no doubt that
the various myths of alchemy and mysticism could be interpreted
according to the sexual theory; but he also insists that they can be
interpreted "anagogically"—that is, allegorically or mystically—as
evidence of man's striving for spiritual fulfillment. In short, Silberer takes the view that man's higher needs—for example, the
need for God—are as fundamental and instinctive as the need for
sex and dominance. Silberer must have recognized that in these
matters he was in fundamental opposition to Freud's pessimistic
reductionism. But he made the curious mistake of thinking that
their grounds for disagreement were unimportant when balanced
against his wholehearted admiration and devotion, and his support
for the sexual theory. He was genuinely hurt and mystified by
Freud's increasing rejection of him. In April 1917 he proposed
calling on Freud, and received the following note:

Dear Sir,
    I request that you do not make the intended visit with me. As
the result of the observations and impressions of recent years I no
longer desire personal contact with you.

                                        Very truly yours,
                                        Freud.

Silberer, like Jung and Tausk before him, had been "excommunicated," and the rejection had on him an effect similar to that on Jung and Tausk—Freud undoubtedly had some curious power of arousing a sense of guilt and unworthiness in those he rejected. Silberer sank into a state of depression verging on mental breakdown. At the age of forty—in January 1923—he hanged himself from the window bars in his home, leaving a light propped in such a way that his wife would see his face when she came in.

Reich's own account of the immediate rapport between himself and Freud needs to be supplemented with the information that Roazen gleaned from people who knew them both. As Roazen wrote in *Freud and His Followers*: "Even as a relative newcomer to psychoanalysis in the early 1920s, Reich seemed excessively self-assured; at any rate, Freud would not countenance his arrogance. At one of the private meetings at Freud's home he said to Reich: 'You are the youngest here, would you close the door?' Freud kept his distance from Reich . . ."

Whether or not Freud had his reservations about Reich, the older disciples certainly had. Reich's temperament would now be described as "pushy"; it seems that he enjoyed emphasizing that he was one of the few members of the group with a training in biology and science. Reich obviously found it hard to dissemble his impatience, telling Eissler that he found the circle intensely dull, and comparing himself complacently to a shark in a pond full of carp. But there could be no doubt about his brilliance, and the insight he showed in diagnosis. He was proud of the fact that he was a clinician and that he declined to speculate. Freud was delighted by this pragmatic approach, and it was the foundation of the warm regard he originally felt towards Reich. Freud told a friend of his daughter Anna that Reich was "the best head in the Association." According to his own account, Reich's rise in the Freud circle was astonishingly swift. He called on Freud for the first time around February 1919, soon after the commencement of the first sexology seminars. (This was also the period when he called on Adler, Stekel, Kammerer, and Steinach, a circumstance that suggests that he was anxious to make as many distinguished contacts as possible.) By March, he told Eissler, Freud was already sending him patients. This speaks well for his persuasiveness and charm—he was, after all, a medical student who had received only a few months' training, with four years of study still ahead of him. In the following year he became a fully fledged member of the Vienna Psychoanalytic Society.

It is a pity that there are so few personal accounts of Reich in those early days. In later years, the break with Freud, and his own highly unorthodox views, raised a cloud of hostility that colors nearly all references to him by his contemporaries of that period, and even these references are so infrequent that they point to a conspiracy of silence—or at least, a reluctance to increase Reich's importance by discussing him. But there is a chapter in *The Function of the Orgasm* that can help to fill the gap by making it possible to understand why he made such an impact on the Society. It is based on the first paper he ever wrote under the influence of psychoanalysis, "Ibsen's Peer Gynt, Libido Conflicts and Hallucinations,"[3] and it has a vigorous directness that suggests the work of a young convert. It begins:

> The subject of psychoanalysis was great and moving. To the thought of the average man, it came like a slap in the face. You imagine that you can determine your actions by your own free will? Indeed not! Your conscious actions are only a drop on the surface of an ocean of unconscious processes of which you can know nothing, and besides, you would be afraid of knowing them. You pride yourself on the "individuality of your personality" and the "breadth of your mind"? Naïve! Really, you are only the plaything of your instincts, which do with you what *they* want. Of course, this offends your vanity, but—you were just as offended when you had to learn that you had evolved from the monkeys, and that the earth on which you crawled was not the center of the universe, as you once believed. You still believe that the earth is the only star among billions of stars which is inhabited. In brief, you are conditioned by processes which you do not control or even know, and which you fear and misinterpret. There is a psychic reality that reaches far beyond your consciousness. Your unconscious is like Kant's *Ding an sich* [thing in itself]: it cannot itself be apprehended, it can only be recognized in its manifestations . . .

These last two sentences help to explain the tone of sheer joyous delight in which Reich explains that human beings have no free will and are really the playthings of their instincts. When he speaks of a psychic reality beyond consciousness, he sounds like a Roman Catholic speaking of the Vicarious Atonement, or a Spiritualist referring to the realm of the supernatural. Freud has produced upon Reich the same effect that Charcot earlier produced on Freud. He has discovered the unconscious, and glimpsed its tremendous implications. He sees it as a realm of mystery, the source of all life, the great Unknown. (In German, *unbewust* means both unconscious and unknown.) This is why he can feel so cheerful about informing human beings that they are mere insects on a second-rate star. Like a religious convert, he feels that the unimportance of man is a small price to pay for the reality of God.

Yet this same chapter on Peer Gynt also points to the basic flaw in Reich's make-up, the weakness that would destroy him. There is ominous significance in his remark that when he met Freud and understood his ideas he felt himself to be an outsider, like Peer Gynt.[4] "His fate seemed to me the most likely outcome of an attempt to step out of line with official science and traditional thinking."

Reich is already casting himself in the role of misunderstood martyr, and in this same chapter he also reveals a slightly paranoid tendency to see the world in terms of the lost and the saved. He explains that schizophrenics—patients who have lost touch with reality—have no sense of the boundary between the ego and the universe, the inner and outer worlds, but they at least are better off than the "Babbitts"—the self-centered bourgeoisie—who "have no idea of this harmony, feeling their beloved egos, sharply circumscribed, to be the center of the universe. The profundity of some mental patients makes them more valuable, from a human point of view, than the Babbits [sic] with their nationalistic ideals." One senses danger in this identification with mental patients and hatred of the Babbitts (after all, Sinclair Lewis' character, whose name has become a synonym for bourgeois mediocrity, is basically a naïve and warm-hearted person, for whom the novelist clearly feels affection). Reich's further comments on Peer Gynt suggest that he has become entangled in some singularly muddled thinking. Ibsen's play is about the misery of unconventional human beings who will not compromise or capitulate to the boredom and shallowness of everyday life. Ibsen's drama, says Reich, will not become outdated until the Peer Gynts are proved to be right. But anyone who has ever read *Peer Gynt* knows that it is the story of an overimaginative but basically worthless individual, a dreamer who can never come to terms with reality, and whose life is a failure. It seems curious that Reich should choose to identify with this particular "outsider," and it is even more dangerous to assume that the Peer Gynts are surrounded by impotent midgets who feel an instinctive hostility to all dreamers and idealists. Reich seems to be deliberately setting the stage for his own tragedy.

The original Peer Gynt paper was instrumental in gaining Reich the status of guest member of the Vienna Psychoanalytic Society —a remarkable achievement for a twenty-three-year-old medical student. With a paper on hysterical conversion symptoms, read before the Society on October 13, 1920, Reich was received into full membership.

Current psychoanalytic practice dictated that Reich himself should be psychoanalyzed, but three attempts were unsuccessful, all broken off by Reich himself while still unfinished. In her biography of her husband, Ilse Reich clearly feels that there is something of a mystery here, or, at least, an interesting revelation of Reich's inner conflicts. "The reason for the failure of all Reich's attempts at personal analysis will have to be discovered at some future date, if at all, by a person trained in the field of depth psychology." But closer analysis can suggest more straightforward motives. The first person to make the attempt was Isidore Sadger, an undistinguished member of the circle whom Jones describes as "a morose, pathetic figure, very like a specially uncouth bear." Sadger's lack of tact and social polish were overwhelming. At one social gathering, he opened a conversation with a distinguished literary lady by asking abruptly: "Have you ever occupied yourself with masturbation?" Reich himself may have been arrogant and tactless, but his family background and his training in the officer corps had given him a certain polish and finesse. It is easy to see that he would have found it difficult to open his soul to a man like Sadger. The next analysis was undertaken by the generous and good-natured Paul Federn, who even brushed aside the question of fee. As the senior disciple, Federn could probably afford to regard Reich's youthful aggressiveness with a tolerant eye. But this tolerance seems to have eroded fairly quickly, and even as early as 1923 (according to Reich), Federn had come to share the general view of him as a troublemaker. No details are known, but a letter written by Reich to Federn in 1926[5] offers certain clues. Reich is protesting at having been overlooked for the office of secretary of the Society, and seems anxious to convince Federn that his complaint is not prompted by "petty personal feeling." He says that when he was previously rejected for the post, he—the "aggressive, paranoid and ambitious" type—shrugged his shoulders and harbored no grudge. This makes it fairly clear that it was Federn who had used the words "aggressive, paranoid and ambitious," and who had accused Reich of frustrated ambition. This seems to suggest that Federn had a very clear insight into Reich's short-comings, as well as into his basic motivations.

The third analysis was undertaken by the brilliant Hungarian, Sandor Rado, a friend of Ferenczi. This was in later years, after Reich's final meeting with Freud, by which time Reich's own views were highly developed. Reich's only comment is that "Rado was very jealous, awfully jealous." Again, there is no need to look for deeper motivations. Most of the Freud circle detested Reich, and he returned the feeling. It was not in his nature to lie down on a couch and pour out his inmost thoughts. The only man to whom he would have been willing to open up his soul was Freud, and Freud was not interested.

The patient whom Freud sent to Reich in March 1919 was a youth suffering from obsessive symptoms, the chief of which was a compulsive need to hurry. Reich proceeded according to the Freudian rule book; the patient lay on a couch, and the analyst sat by his head (so he could not see the analyst's face); the patient was then asked to talk, to say anything that came into his head. Reich soon uncovered the cause of the neurosis: as a child, the patient had committed a theft from a big store, and ran away in panic, afraid of being followed. The memory had been repressed, according to Reich, and now made its reappearance in this inability to walk at the normal pace.

The diagnosis seemed to verify Freud's theory about the repression of deep anxiety. But what about the sexual element? Freud had stated dogmatically: "Obsessional ideas are invariably self-reproaches which have emerged from repression in a transmuted form, *and which relate to some sexual act that was performed with pleasure in childhood.*" Reich had no difficulty in getting around this problem, explaining (in *The Function of the Orgasm*) that the youth's anxiety was due to an "infantile fear of being caught masturbating."

In short, Reich, like Freud, accepted the sexual theory as an "unshakeable dogma." The solution of the problem of mental illness consisted quite simply in probing around until the repressed sexual trauma was located. If there was no sign of a specifically sexual trauma, this was only a proof of how deeply it had been repressed. Reich was absolutely confident that neurotic symptoms came from repressed desires and that if the analyst did his work correctly the unconscious sexual wish would be discovered. He explained that a hysterical girl's fear of being attacked by a man with a knife is a desire for sex that has been repressed by social morality, and has vanished into the depths of the unconscious. The neurotic symptom is due to her desire to masturbate or lose her virginity.

The explanation is important, not simply as an expression of Reich's orthodox Freudianism, but because it reveals something fundamental about Reich's whole approach: his extreme *literal-mindedness*. It is a characteristic that remained with him throughout his life, and which throws an important light on his development. He craved the kind of down-to-earth certainty that a mathematician would find in a table of logarithms or an engineer in his calculator. He wanted one explanation, and one only. This can be seen in the case cited above. The story about the patient stealing and hurrying away provides an adequate explanation of the neurosis. The masturbation theory is superfluous and unlikely; fear of being caught masturbating would hardly cause someone to walk faster, even if he made a habit of masturbating while walking. But if the theft story provided an adequate explanation, then the Freudian theory became unnecessary, and such a possibility had to be avoided at all costs. But then, the theft story would also give rise to some awkward questions. Why should he have *repressed* the memory? It is surely more likely that he would have brooded on it and become the victim of a guilt neurosis? But neurotic symptoms seldom appear out of the blue, without some background of guilt and depression. This can be seen in the case of Anna O. Her inability to swallow was caused by seeing a dog drink out of a glass; but this was only the *secondary* cause. The primary cause was the depression, *the stagnation of vital energy,* that resulted from watching her father die slowly. And if Reich's patient suffered from guilt feelings—either about masturbation or theft—there must also have been a more immediate cause of vital-stagnation, domestic tensions, adolescent sexuality, educational problems. By choosing to accept the Freudian view, Reich had solved the problem by slide rule. The method ignored all inconvenient complexities.

Yet for a man of Reich's temperament, the Freudian method also had frustrating drawbacks. To begin with, there was the old problem of how to gain access to the patient's unconscious mind. In the "talking cure," the patient disgorged vast heaps of disconnected fragments, through which the analyst had to search for months or even years. It was a slow, frustrating business, unsuited to Reich's impulsive temperament. But there was an even more embarrassing problem. Freud's original theory declared that once the repressed symptom had been located, the cure was virtually complete. Once the problem had become conscious, it would vanish. But what if this failed to happen? Shortly after Reich became a full member of the Society, Freud sent him a patient who was suffering from general neurasthenia—headaches, back pains, lack of concentration—and compulsive masturbation. Oddly enough, the masturbation failed to provide much relief. Reich's analysis uncovered an incest fantasy—he does not state whether the person concerned was the patient's mother or sister—and, for the first time, the patient masturbated with satisfaction. According to Freudian theory, this should have solved the problem. The patient was now admitting his incestuous desires and using them as masturbation fantasies. And in fact, the symptoms vanished—for a week. Finally, says Reich, he corrected the patient's feelings of guilt about his masturbation and enabled him to obtain complete gratification. This caused immediate improvement, so that after nine months it was possible to discharge him. Yet although Reich had taught the patient to improve his masturbation techniques, there was still no complete cure. What had gone wrong? Why did the admission of the incest fantasy to consciousness fail to cure the neurosis? Was it, perhaps, not the true cause of the problem? We might raise the equally interesting question: what had gone right? Why did Reich's lessons in masturbation improve the patient's condition? No subtle Freudian theory is needed here. One of the original symptoms was lack of concentration. The patient was masturbating, as he was living and feeling, half-heartedly. Reich taught him to put his mind to it, to *focus* the imaginary source of his gratification, and there was an improvement. This seems to suggest that the lack of concentration was a *cause* as well as a symptom. And this view is in accordance with the "feedback theory" of neurosis outlined in the last chapter. Practical problems produce a sense of impotence, the futility of effort. The unconscious mind responds to this sense of futility by constricting the energy supply, which increases the feeling of impotence. "He who desires but acts not, breeds pestilence," said William Blake, putting his finger on the root cause of all neurosis. If the conscious mind can be persuaded to focus, then the vicious circle of impotence and lack of concentration can be broken. The unconscious responds by supplying more energy. And the stagnating marshes of neurosis are irrigated by a sense of purpose.

If Reich glimpsed this explanation, he instantly rejected it. It would have contradicted his premise that man has no free will, that he is the "plaything of his instincts," "a little worm in the stream of his own feelings." But there *was* another explanation that was altogether more consistent with Freud's sexual theory: that the patient had improved because he had achieved *a satisfactory orgasm*. There was, admittedly, nothing in Freudian theory about satisfactory orgasms, but at least Reich's idea was in the basic Freudian spirit.

Another case seemed to point to the same conclusion: that of a young waiter who had never, in all his life, experienced an erection. His penis remained permanently flaccid. The treatment continued, without success, for three years. By the end of that time, all Reich had discovered was that at the age of two, the waiter had glimpsed his mother giving birth, and received the impression of a large bloody hole between her legs. Apart from his impotence, the waiter showed no sign of serious disturbance; he was good-tempered, well-balanced, able to cope with everyday problems. Here again, if Freud was correct, the discovery of the "primal scene" should have brought about a cure. In fact, it made no difference whatever. There was clearly a *blockage* of some kind, a failure of vital energy to achieve its proper discharge. Yet this insight was of no use to the patient; he had to be discharged uncured. The chief lesson that Reich drew from this case was that the patient was *too* well adjusted.

Freud himself had already reached the conclusion that certain neuroses had their cause in blockage of sex-energy. He called these "actual neuroses"—those that were caused by some everyday sexual problem, such as *coitus interruptus* or excessive masturbation. (This was supposed to produce headaches, back pains, etc.) Unlike "psychoneuroses," actual neuroses were not caused by childhood guilts or traumas; in fact, they were semiphysical in origin. One of Freud's earliest insights into the sexual theory came in Paris, when he overheard Charcot telling a colleague about a young woman whose hysteria was due to her husband's impotence. "In these cases," said Charcot, "it is always the genital thing." Those words—*"la chose génitale"*—struck Freud as a revelation. A year later, another colleague confirmed the insight when he told Freud that a female patient suffering from anxiety neurosis needed "repeated doses of a normal penis." Freud concluded that in these cases, the patient's system becomes poisoned with stagnant sexual energies—perhaps some actual chemical substance that needs to be metabolized by normal sexual outlet, as food needs to be digested. By labeling such problems "actual neuroses," he was able to keep them in a separate compartment, and turn his clinical acumen to the more interesting riddle of the psychoneurosis.

Some of Freud's colleagues—Stekel, for example—were inclined to reject this notion of "actual neurosis." After all, it was almost non-Freudian to believe that there are neuroses that were not due to repressions and buried traumas. Reich, as usual, went to the opposite extreme. It seemed to him far more likely that *all* neuroses were due to "the genital thing." In *The Function of the Orgasm,* Reich claims that among the hundreds of cases that he treated, there was *not a single woman* who was not suffering from total absence of vaginal orgasm. Between sixty and seventy percent of the men had severe genital problems, either in the form of failure to obtain an erection or premature ejaculation. He concluded that some form of genital sickness was always present in female patients as well as in most males. When an elderly lady came to Reich with a tic of the diaphragm, Reich taught her to masturbate, and the tic vanished. This, he felt, proved his point. He later formulated his basic conviction in the following uncompromising words: "My contention is that every individual who has managed to preserve a bit of naturalness knows that there is only one thing wrong with neurotic patients: *the lack of full and repeated sexual satisfaction.*"

During these first few years in the psychoanalytic movement, Reich seems to have had no suspicion that he was moving swiftly towards heresy. He even seems to have been unaware of the amount of hostility he aroused. He told Eissler that as soon as he came in, there was an immediate stir; he seemed to feel that everybody enjoyed this. In *The Function of the Orgasm* he compares himself to the baby elephant in Kipling's *Elephant's Child,* always rushing around full of "satiable curtiosity," getting spanked by the grown-ups, and almost ending up as a crocodile's dinner. The "grown-ups" of Freud's circle had much the same attitude to Reich in those early years—tolerance mixed with irritation. And between 1919 and 1922—when he obtained his degree—the time during which he could make a nuisance of himself was limited. Life was exceptionally full. In 1921, while working in the Vienna University Hospital, he married a fellow student, Annie Pink, described by Ilse Ollendorff as "one of the most attractive, brilliant and sought after of the girls at the university." Now that Reich had a considerable psychoanalytic practice, his finances had begun to improve, and his wife's father eased the burden by contributing to her support. But life was not all work and study; Reich was musical and played the cello and piano. In music, as in science, he was attracted by Vienna's revolutionaries, and joined the Schönberg Society. Some of Schönberg's early works—like the "monodrama" *Erwartung*—are positively Freudian in content, and could explain Reich's attraction.

After graduation, Reich took a two-year postgraduate course in psychiatry—the study of serious mental illness—at the Neurological and Psychiatric Clinic of the university. His chief, Wagner-Jauregg, was Austria's most eminent neurologist, a remarkable clinician who had made the discovery that cretinism is due to iodine deficiency, thus ending the incidence of the disease almost at a stroke. At the time Reich became his student, Wagner-Jauregg was working on a cure for paresis with malaria therapy, a discovery for which he would receive the Nobel Prize in 1927, the first psychiatrist to do so. Wagner-Jauregg and Freud had been students together, and addressed one another with the familiar *du;* but while Wagner-Jauregg liked and respected Freud, he regarded the sexual theory as nonsense, and, according to Reich, lost no opportunity to poke fun at Freud's obsession with sexual symbols.

It was here that Reich had the opportunity to study psychotic patients, that is, patients who were insane rather than merely neurotic. No attempt was made to cure them, except by chemicals, such as bromides. Reich was touched by the predicament of these patients. It was obvious that they were confused and in urgent need of help. The foundations of their lives had crumbled, and, in order to cling to something, they had created a world of imagination and delusion. Yet the psychiatrist could only ask preposterous questions: "How much is two and two?" and "What is the difference between a midget and a child?" Reich was embarrassed by this kind of insensitivity and even wrote a play about the misery and bewilderment of such patients. Here we glimpse the essential Reich, the psychologist and artist who has the power to see the world through the eyes of a psychotic patient. This insight into the *existential* world of the psychotic not only distinguishes Reich from clinicians like Wagner-Jauregg, but also from psychologists like Freud. Yet again, the remarks carry with them a sense of foreboding—a feeling that Reich understood the psychotic mentality a little too well for his own good.

Working under Wagner-Jauregg and Paul Schilder, Reich once more became convinced of the correctness of the sexual theory. It struck him that the neurotic disguises the cause of his illness, while the psychotic expresses openly and without shame such obsessions as incest with his parents, and fantasies about smearing himself with ordure. According to Reich, the psychotic has admitted his repressed sexuality into consciousness, while at the same time preserving his defenses against it. So he must place the "blame" on the outer world. He is sane, it is the world that is mad.

Here again, we feel that Reich's insights into the processes of madness are profound; but he is determined to fit them into a rigid

Freudian framework. It is not necessary to be a psychiatrist to know that all madness is *not* sexual in origin. Insanity is the mind's response to a sense of overwhelming discouragement, inability to deal with the problems of existence. This discouragement was expressed by Van Gogh when he wrote: "Misery will never end" just before he committed suicide. We can detect the same sense of futility and despair in many other men of genius who became insane: John Clare, Swift, Hölderlin, Kleist, Schumann, Semmelweis. Reich himself, like Semmelweis, finally became insane because he felt the odds against him were too great. In such cases, insanity is the mind's surrender to despair and exhaustion. But Reich preferred to accept the sexual theory because it provided him with ammunition in his own private war against society. One senses a certain confusion between Reich's clinical observations and his personal convictions. He states that psychotics see through the sexual hypocrisy that surrounds them; far from being trapped in fantasy, they recognize reality for what it is. People *are* "polymorphously perverse," says Reich, and so is society as a whole. We have attempted to repress natural sexuality with the result that all humans are slaves of public opinion. We could be compared to the subjects of an insane tyrant who are forced to guard their speech and actions, who never express themselves spontaneously. Men become so accustomed to this repressed, artificial existence that they come to accept it as natural, as the essential human condition. Here Reich is anticipating the doctrine of the later Freud—of *Civilization and Its Discontents,* with its message that man and civilization are hopelessly at odds. But while Freud accepts this situation with grim stoicism, Reich obviously feels that it can be altered. Like Rousseau, he feels that man is born free but is everywhere in chains; the answer is to get rid of the chains. And, as far as Reich was concerned, this was fairly simple. The trouble lay in man's attitude towards sex, his feeling that it is "dirty" and forbidden. Reich had been strongly impressed by the way that most of his sexually sick male patients seemed to regard sex as an act of aggression, and the male sexual organ as a weapon of violence or a means of proving one's potency. In some, only fantasies of rape could induce orgasm. If only, therefore, man could learn to regard sex as a wholly natural act of tenderness, the problem would vanish.

The "elephant's child" could be stimulating and amusing, but his sheer uncontrolled vitality could be exhausting. Roazen begins his brief account of Reich with the comment that he was "too undisciplined (and original) to stay permanently within the psychoanalytic orbit." One has the feeling that the adjectives have been carefully chosen.

Even as early as 1922, it must have become apparent to many members of the Society that there was a basic divergence of opinion between Reich and Freud. In *Beyond the Pleasure Principle* (1920) Freud had postulated the concept of the "death-instinct" to explain human self-destructiveness. In 1922, Reich attended the International Psychoanalytic Congress in Berlin, where Freud spoke on the ego and the id, which introduced a new and bewildering complication into psychoanalysis. Freud had explained neurosis as the ego's defense against the dangerous forces of the id, that is, against repressions. But, what happens, for example, if a man becomes impotent because he harbors unconscious incest wishes? Clearly, there is no *conscious* wish to become impotent, but neither can the id be responsible, since it lacks all moral feeling. So what *is* responsible? Freud solved the problem by inventing another part of the mind: the superego. This, said Freud, is an unconscious part of consciousness, and it plays the role of policeman and guardian of public morals. In old-fashioned terminology, it was known as conscience. Like all moralists, it can be cruel and ruthless. The superego also explained why some patients only got worse under treatment. They didn't *want* to get better; the superego was determined to inflict punishment.

This ingenious idea had an immediate appeal to psychoanalysts —even to those who had been dubious about Freud's earlier idea of the death-instinct. The superego seemed an altogether better explanation of human self-destructiveness than the death-instinct. The idea was accepted more or less unanimously. But Reich was not entirely happy. These new theoretical formulations were very interesting but the real work continued to be done in the laboratory. In fact, the movement was too prone to lose itself in theory. What was needed was a revival of interest in the practical side of psychoanalysis. Reich was already assistant director of the Psychoanalytic Polyclinic, in which free treatment was offered to working-class Viennese. In the train on the way home from Berlin,

Reich suggested to some younger colleagues that what was needed was a "technical seminar" to supplement the work of the Polyclinic—regular meetings of psychoanalysts to thrash out better techniques. The idea was applauded. Back in Vienna, Reich tried it on his older colleagues, and was delighted when they also seemed to find it exciting. Roazen remarks cynically, evidently quoting some of these older colleagues: "A continuous case seminar at the Institute in Vienna was partly invented as a way of keeping Reich within bounds; he was asked to show, as the clinical material came up, where the standard technique was misguided." If this is true, the "elephant's child" had no suspicion that their enthusiasm was basically a desire to keep him out of mischief. Eduard Hitschmann, the director of the Polyclinic, was appointed head of the seminar. Reich was regarded as too inexperienced for such a post, but he became the most enthusiastic contributor to the seminars. In 1923, Nunberg replaced Hitschmann; then, in 1924, Reich finally reaped the reward for his eagerness, and became seminar leader, a position he held until 1930. The group met once a week, to discuss actual cases and the methods they were using to deal with them.

Life was treating Reich well. In 1924 his first child, Eva, was born; she would always remain his favorite. He had acquired the reputation of being the most brilliant of the younger psychoanalysts, and his practice, and income, increased accordingly. At this point, it would probably have been easy to settle for respectability and comfort. But Reich's driving energy and unsatisfied ambition kept him from being contented with this kind of success. The spectacle of his brother Robert's failure may have provided another incentive. The hardships they had endured as students led Robert to develop tuberculosis. He had spent some time in Romania, where he married; by 1925 he was back in Vienna with his wife and child. Reich helped provide for them until 1926, when Robert died; but after this, he declined all help to the widow. Ilse Reich explains that this was probably due to his loathing for "bourgeois parasitism." Reich was, apparently, a completely unpredictable mixture of generosity and meanness.

But the success was not unmixed. It seems to have been during the first year of the technical seminar—1923—that the older members began to feel strong misgivings about Reich, which were

probably a reflection of Freud's own changing attitude. In January
of that year, he delivered a lecture about the elderly lady whom he
had taught to masturbate, and it seems to have been well-received.
So was another paper he gave in October about a woman with
delusions of persecution; Reich emphasized the role of her genital
problems. But in November, when he delivered a paper on the
theme of genitality, he was surprised by the coolness he encountered. The old guard was deeply, if politely, resistant to Reich's
new idea that mental illness was due to lack of adequate orgasms.
Two of them told Reich that they knew of any number of female
patients with normal sex lives. And Reich himself had to admit
that he knew of many male patients who were neurotic *and* capable of orgasm, sometimes several times in one night. But the more
he thought about it, the more convinced Reich became that the orgasm lay at the root of the problem. After all, a satisfactory orgasm was more than a mere physical discharge of sperm; it should
also be a discharge of emotional tension, resulting in total relaxation. And the same should apply to women; neurotic patients
might be able to achieve clitoral orgasm, but not what at the time
was believed to be the more deeply satisfying vaginal orgasm.

In his enthusiastic innocence, Reich seems to have been unaware of how far these views would grate on his colleagues—and
particularly on Freud. At the beginning of his career, Freud had
embraced the simplistic view that most disturbed patients had
been sexually assaulted by parents in early childhood; he soon
recognized the absurdity of this opinion, but it remained a source
of reproach, and derision, on the part of his enemies for many
years. His belief in unconscious repression was a great deal more
convincing, and easier to defend. The years had seen a gradual
refinement of the Freudian position, with the emphasis slowly
shifting from sex and the unconscious to the ego and the death-
wish. Now only the most hostile of Freud's opponents would accuse him of being a sexual pervert, and intellectuals such as
Thomas Mann classified him with Nietzsche and Schopenhauer as
an explorer of the unconscious. Just as Freud was receiving the
recognition, and respectability, that were his due, here was this
tactless iconoclast reducing the whole thing to crudely simplistic
terms and threatening to bring the whole sexual theory into disrepute. How could state counsellors and university chancellors take

psychoanalysis seriously when it proclaimed that mental health depended on achieving satisfactory orgasms? How could the general public come to terms with a theory that taught elderly ladies to masturbate?

What was happening, of course, was that Freud's circle was reacting to Reich's orgasm theory in much the same way that the psychiatrists of the older school had reacted to Freud's early theories. They were inclined to look for purely personal motivations, that is, to Reich's own psychological problems and peculiarities. As a young man, he was bound to exaggerate the importance of sexual potency. (Freud called the orgasm theory "Reich's hobby horse.") And then there was Reich's aggressiveness and ambition; he was determined to attract attention at all costs, and what better way to do so than by proclaiming half-truths in a loud and confident voice? Reich later told Eissler that in 1923 Paul Federn began to speak against him to Freud. The precise date can probably be pinpointed as that day in November when Reich read his paper on genitality to the Society.

Reich's development of his ideas during the next two years tended to confirm his colleagues' low opinion. He was becoming increasingly preoccupied with the problem of "sexual stasis"—exhibited in patients like the waiter who experienced a deadness in the genitals. Reich was convinced that the cooperativeness and politeness of such patients was a defense mechanism, an unconscious resistance to the psychotherapist. But how could it be broken? He was impressed by a case he observed at the clinic, when a catatonic patient suddenly exploded into excitement and rage, then became "normal" for a time. Catatonia is a kind of stupor, and the rage had dissipated the stupor. The patient told him that the explosion had given him pleasure. It had somehow "unfrozen" his vital energies. There was an obvious parallel between a case like this and that of the impotent waiter. The waiter was also sunk in a kind of stupor, and his politeness was really a form of resistance. If he could have been provoked into an attack of rage, might that not have been the beginning of a cure?

This again struck the circle as highly unorthodox. Nunberg felt that the analyst's job was to win the patient's trust and cooperation. Reich's attitude seemed to be the opposite: that it would be better for the analyst to uncover the patient's latent hostility and bring it into the open. It was easy to feel that this was just another symptom of Reich's own aggressiveness.

Freud himself was far from happy, either with the orgasm theory, or with Reich's preoccupation with latent hostility. When Reich brought him the bulky manuscript of *The Function of the Orgasm* in 1926, Freud winced at the title, then commented pointedly: "That thick?" Since the book was dedicated to Freud, Reich understandably felt this to indicate a lack of enthusiasm. This was confirmed by the length of time Freud took to read it—two months or so (he was usually a quick reader); and his final comments were only politely encouraging. Reich sensed a distinct coolness. Then, in December 1926, Reich gave a talk to the circle on the problem of "resistance." He raised the question of which should be tackled first: the neurotic symptoms, or the "latent negative attitude" towards the analyst. Freud asked irritably whether it would not be better to "interpret the material in the order in which it appears." He was, in effect, telling Reich not to split hairs. Reich felt the members of the seminar were pitying him, but, he said, "I remained calm."

The real cause of Freud's increasing hostility was simple, although Reich was too absorbed in his own ideas to recognize it. Reich was developing the libido theory just as Freud was abandoning it. At a fairly early stage, Freud had, in effect, replaced the libido with the "pleasure principle"—the desire of the id to have its own way. Now he had gone "beyond the pleasure principle"; the libido had almost vanished from his theories. For Reich, the optimistic romantic, the libido remained the core of psychoanalysis, a kind of Niagara of vital energy that had to find its outlet if it was not to become completely destructive. If Reich was correct about the libido, then Freud must be wrong about the death-wish and the superego; there was hardly room for both. It was really a basic clash of temperaments: romantic optimist versus realistic pessimist, and the pessimist was reacting to the optimist with increasing antipathy. Without being fully aware what was happening, Reich was drifting into the same position Tausk had occupied a decade earlier.

The odd thing is that Reich never *did* recognize it, either then or later. Where Freud was concerned, some curious compulsive blind-spot came into operation, which refused to allow him even to consider the possibility that Freud could dislike him. Reich's first wife, a practicing psychoanalyst, was convinced that Freud was a father-substitute; this would certainly explain Reich's life-long loyalty to the man who finally rejected him as decisively as he had rejected Tausk and Silberer. The Right Man theory suggests a further explanation. Freud was the pivot of Reich's self-esteem. He had, in effect, made him, treated him as a favored son, raised him to a position of eminence in the world of psychoanalysis. There was no way in which Reich could reject Freud without disowning a part of himself. In the case of Jung and Adler it had been different; both had already formulated certain basic concepts before they met Freud, and both were able later to reject the sexual theory and return to their own original insights. Reich owed *all* his basic concepts to Freud, and the sexual theory remained at the core of his thinking for the rest of his life. Thus it was necessary for Reich to rationalize Freud's increasing coolness, to believe that it was due to envious colleagues like Federn, who poisoned Freud's mind against him. In the study at Organon there was a large signed photograph of Freud. In the conversations with Eissler dating from 1952, Reich insisted on the continued warmth and understanding between himself and Freud, although this was obviously inconsistent with his expulsion from the psychoanalytic movement. At one point, Eissler speaks of Freud's "meanness," obviously hoping to tempt Reich into denunciation. Reich instantly denies that he had used the word "meanness," so that Eissler is forced to withdraw: "I thought you did . . ." Reich goes on to explain that he was not speaking of meanness, but Freud's "biting irony." All pioneers, he says, need associates and colleagues to help them. And, sooner or later, these colleagues begin to take advantage of the master—inevitably, Reich insists, because pioneers are always ahead of the main body of humanity. And here we can see exactly why Reich would never hear a word against Freud. He has identified himself with Freud. He and Freud were the two great pioneers, misunderstood and reviled by mankind. In a sense, Reich had *become* Freud; the son had replaced the father. He might express pity and sympathy for Freud; but never hostility.

All this enables us to understand the traumatic nature of what occurred soon after the disastrous lecture of December 1926.

Matters seem to have come to a head over the question of Reich's "training analysis." Reich's earlier attempts had been unsuccessful; therefore he still lacked the most crucial part of the psychoanalyst's initiation. Freud felt that it was the only way in which the analyst could personally experience the truth of the theory that he applied to his patients. The training analysis was the equivalent of the Zen Buddhist's *satori,* the Hindu's *samadhi;* it was the "moment of truth." And since Freud was the father-figure of the movement, the master, it was every young analyst's dream to receive his initiation through Freud. Understandably, Freud became more reluctant as the years went by; there were too many young analysts competing for his attention. He even made a rule that he should never be expected to treat members of the Vienna circle. But since he occasionally broke it—we have seen that he treated Helene Deutsch in 1918—disciples continued to hope for this mark of supreme distinction. Reich, like Tausk, believed that he was regarded as a favorite son. Moreover, at some point, Freud seems to have hinted that he would be willing to undertake Reich's training analysis. This would certainly have been a remarkable triumph for Reich; Freud had even refused Federn. To be analyzed by Freud would have been the culmination of his brilliant rise in the movement—almost an indication that Freud regarded him as his successor.

In fact, Freud turned him down. There seem to be no detail of the precise form of the rejection, but Annie Reich told Ilse Ollendorff that Reich found it intolerable, and that it plunged him into deep depression. Shortly thereafter, Reich developed tuberculosis, and had to spend the early months of 1927 at a sanitarium in Davos, Switzerland. It is difficult not to conclude that this was another example of Freud's sinister power to cause self-destructive conflicts in those he rejected.

But Reich, like Jung, was too self-reliant to commit suicide. He spent his months at Davos—until the summer of 1927—revising the manuscript of *The Function of the Orgasm*[6] and writing articles. It was also, clearly, a period of serious mental conflict and self-examination. Ilse Ollendorff reports: "Annie Reich, and with her other Freudian analysts, believe that a 'deteriorating process' began in Reich during his stay at the sanitarium, that he was not the same person after his return, that he must have gained new insights into some of his own problems and been disturbed by them." She expresses her own disagreement, and says she believes this is a rationalization by Annie Reich of her own difficulties in living with Reich "because he was a person with unusual energy." She adds that when *she* lived with Reich she never felt that a deteriorating process was going on until 1951, three years before their separation. But this comment seems irrelevant. No one would have been better able to judge whether Reich had deteriorated than his first wife, and what Reich was like more than a decade later is beside the point. Annie Reich, and other analysts who knew Reich closely, can have meant only one thing: that Reich had lost some of his pliability, his ability to consider other points of view. It was more than a year earlier that Federn had supposedly referred to him as the aggressive, paranoid, and ambitious type, and the element of paranoia was hardening. It is easy to envisage how this came about. What Reich had to face was virtually his own downfall in the movement. Clearly, Freud and his circle wanted no part of the orgasm theory, and their rejection included its originator. On a photograph taken at Davos in February 1927, Reich has scrawled the words "Conflict with Freud." Reich glares at the camera from under lowered eyebrows, his face grim and determined. The first step in his rationalization is clear. Freud has not rejected him on personal grounds—because he is aggressive, paranoid, and ambitious—but purely on theoretical grounds, because he cannot bear to follow Reich to the logical conclusion of his own theories. Therefore Reich is the torchbearer, the true Freudian, *plus royaliste que le Roi.* If he is rejected, it is for complex reasons; partly because of the machinations of the envious Federn, and partly because Freud himself has been blinkered and deceived by self-seeking parasites. Freud is Lear, and Reich is the Earl of Kent, banished because of his honesty and loyalty. This rationalization is clearly expressed to Eissler when Reich declares that Freud was trapped by his loyalty to his followers. Freud's theory of the genitality of infants frightened everyone, and so Freud tried to soften it by inventing the sublimation theory, which was basically an evasion. When his natural development was hampered, Freud went sour and created the theory of the death-instinct. And this, says Reich, is why Freud developed a cancer of the jaw, and why he smoked so quickly and nervously. He wanted badly to say something that he was forced to repress—he was forced to "bite it down." And what Freud was biting down, of course, was the recognition of the consequences of his own genital theory.

It is true that the fully developed form of this rationalization dates from a quarter of a century after the rejection by Freud, but it is also stated, less fully but equally plainly, in *The Function of the Orgasm*. It was the students who were to blame for Freud's surrender to "the world." He felt that Freud's students had sacrificed the libido theory to make psychoanalysis acceptable to the public, and that Freud had tacitly supported this in an effort to avoid divisiveness within the organization. Reich felt that even in 1929, Freud knew Reich was right, but could not support him.

Now all this was, as we know, flatly untrue. By 1926, Freud himself had turned his back on the orgasm theory—this is clear in a book published that year, *Inhibitions, Symptoms, Anxiety,* in which he states in so many words: "Anxiety never arises from repressed libido." If Reich had been honest, he would have faced the truth: that Freud found his orgasm theory simplistic and repellent. With the advantage of historical hindsight, we can see why this was so. Freud was deeply pessimistic. More than a decade earlier, he had told Jung that human culture is a mere farce, "the morbid consequence of repressed sexuality." "That is just the curse of fate against which we are powerless to contend."[7] A man who held this view of the greatest achievements of the human spirit—that is, that culture is a form of neurosis—would hardly be willing to concede that neurosis can be cured by a satisfactory orgasm.

Besides, there was another, and even more crucial, reason for Freud's increasing antipathy to Reich. Reich hints at it several times in his conversations with Eissler, when speaking about Federn's supposed slanders, but seems deeply reluctant to state it outright. He insists several times that he has no idea of the precise nature of Federn's slanders, and when Eissler asks him about Federn, Reich denies having anything to say, but then forces himself to make a statement: that in 1926, he heard rumors that he (Reich) was sleeping with his patients. He says that these were simply slanders invented by Federn, and goes on to speak about the "genital frustration" of psychoanalysts. Many of them insert

fingers into the vaginas of female patients on a pretext of examination, but, he says, when *he* fell in love with patients he made no
attempt to conceal it. He would halt treatment to allow them both
to regain their equilibrium, then they would decide whether or not
to go to bed. Some of his fellow psychoanalysts were less honest
and would masturbate the patients under the pretext of treatment.
Such people felt envious of Reich's much more open attitude.

It is possible, of course, that Reich was speaking of a much
later period; but since he is explaining why the Freud circle became hostile, this hardly seems likely.

Here, then, we have the most basic reason for Freud's change
of attitude towards the one-time favorite disciple. Where "immo-
rality" was concerned, the founder of psychoanalysis was remarkably narrow-minded. Ernest Jones tells how Freud forbade his
wife to stay with an old friend because she had slept with her husband before she was married. He even regarded references to legs
as improper. Such a man would obviously be horrified at the
thought that one of his most brilliant young followers was using
psychoanalysis as an excuse for fornication—and, what was more,
justifying his conduct by an appeal to "the genital theory." Freud
took a strict view of the Hippocratic oath. If Reich was really
sleeping with his patients (and Freud only had Federn's word for
this), then his conduct was not only dangerous to himself, but to
the whole psychoanalytic movement. It could raise a scandal that
would set psychoanalysis back twenty-five years. If this was the
consequence of the orgasm theory, then Freud had practical as
well as theoretical reasons for rejecting it.

It is now possible to understand something of the nature of
Reich's mental conflict during the months in the Davos sanitarium.
He was emotionally dependent on Freud, and Freud had rejected
him. He knew, or strongly suspected, the purely practical reason
for that rejection; he had known since the previous year. What
was now important was to patch up his wounded feelings, to heal
the bruise to his self-esteem, and, above all, to convince himself
that he was right and that his "enemies" were wrong. In order to
erect this structure of self-reassurance, it was necessary to convince himself that Freud was on his side, and that disciples like
Federn were Freud's enemies as well as his own. In the conversations with Eissler, he loses no opportunity to imply that Freud

really disliked Federn. Freud disliked Federn's eyes, says Reich, and once referred to them as "patricidal eyes." (Reich adds thoughtfully that Federn really *had* murderous eyes.) It follows that if Freud disliked Federn, he could not be deeply influenced by Federn's slanders. Ergo, Freud's rejection was not a personal matter; it was a theoretical disagreement about the libido. Moreover, Freud was really on his side; he was simply afraid to say so.

The Right Man has a remarkable capacity for telling himself stories and then believing them. But this kind of emotional self-repair has a basic drawback: it can be wrecked by a single blow of reality. It is no longer safe to be open-minded and flexible, to allow yourself to see the point of view of other people. Those who are very close to you are particularly dangerous, because they continue to treat you on the old footing, and assume the right to contradict or to point out your inconsistencies. They have to be regarded with suspicion and, if necessary, discarded.

If this interpretation is correct, then Reich's months in Davos were a period of mental as well as physical recovery. Physically, Reich was as well as ever; but psychologically, there was a deterioration, an additional layer of paranoid suspicion. This was the deterioration noticed by his wife and close colleagues. Annie Reich was mistaken to believe that he had "gained new insight into some of his own problems and been disturbed by them." Insight into his own problems was the last thing that Reich wanted. It would have undermined the certainties he had taken so long to repair.

CHAPTER FOUR

Thus, at this point—central to Reich's life—we must consider the major issue: *Was Reich's whole life-work based on a fallacy?*

In spite of his "heresies," Reich remained basically a Freudian. He not only accepted the sexual theory; he generalized it to a point where even Freud felt it was a wild caricature of his own position. But we have seen in an earlier chapter that the original sexual theory was partly an outcome of Freud's failure to grasp the immensely *active* power of the unconscious, and the feedback mechanism that plays such a crucial part in the relation between the "ego" and the "id." Does this suggest that Reich's own genital theory was based on the same misunderstanding, and that it was therefore an elaborate mistake?

The first step towards an answer is to try to grasp the essence of Freud's theory of neurosis as it was held in 1926, and to appreciate why everyone, including Reich, regarded it as *self-evidently true*.

Fortunately, Freud himself has saved us a great deal of trouble by providing an admirable summary of his views; it can be found in a short book called *The Question of Lay Analysis,* published in

1926. He begins by explaining the kind of problems that psychoanalysis was devised to try and solve:

> A patient . . . may be suffering from fluctuations in his moods
> which he cannot control, or from a sense of despondency by
> which his energy feels paralysed because he thinks he is incapable
> of doing anything properly . . . He may one day have suffered
> from a distressing attack—unknown in its origin—of feelings of
> anxiety and since then have been unable, without a struggle, to
> walk along the street alone, or to travel by train; he may perhaps
> have to give up both entirely. Or, a very remarkable thing, his
> thoughts may go their own way and refuse to be directed by his
> will. They pursue problems that are quite indifferent to him, but
> from which he cannot get free. Quite ludicrous tasks, too, are im-
> posed on him, such as counting up the windows on the fronts of
> houses . . . But his state becomes intolerable if he suddenly finds
> he is unable to fend off the idea that he has pushed a child under
> the wheels of a car or has thrown a stranger off the bridge into
> the water, or if he has to ask himself if he is not the murderer
> whom the police are looking for . . . It is obvious nonsense, as
> he himself knows; he has never done any harm to anyone; but if
> he were really the murderer being looked for, his feeling—his
> sense of guilt—could not be stronger.
>
> Or again our patient—and this time let us make her a woman
> —may suffer in another way . . . She is a pianist, but her fingers
> are overcome by cramp and refuse to serve her. Or when she
> thinks of going to a party she promptly becomes aware of a call
> of nature the satisfaction of which would be incompatible with a
> social gathering . . . She is overcome by violent headaches or
> other painful sensations when they are most inconvenient . . .
> And finally, it is a lamentable fact that she cannot tolerate any
> agitations which after all are inevitable in life. On such occasions
> she falls in a faint . . .
>
> Other patients, again, suffer from disturbances in a particular
> field in which emotional life converges with demands of a bodily
> sort. If they are men, they find they are incapable of giving physi-
> cal expression to their tenderest feelings towards the opposite sex,
> while towards less-loved objects they may perhaps have every re-
> action at their command. Or their sensual feelings attach them to
> people whom they despise and from whom they would like to get
> free; or those same feelings impose requirements on them whose
> fulfillment they themselves find repulsive . . .

What Freud has described here is basically the obsessive and neurasthenic type of patient. He goes on to explain that the psychoanalyst gets the patient to lie down, and then tries to get him to tell his innermost secrets, for there may be secrets which the patient is not only unwilling to admit to other people, *but even to himself*. The aim of Roman Catholic confession is to get the penitent to tell what he knows; the aim of psychoanalysis is to get the patient to tell *more than he knows*.

After this admirable summary of his aims, Freud goes on to speak of the ego and the id. The ego, says Freud, is a kind of façade of the id, a "frontage"; "the ego lies between reality and the id, which is truly mental."

Now the id, says Freud, is full of cravings and desires—instincts that demand satisfaction. These desires can only be satisfied through the external world. And the ego has the job of acting as intermediary between the id and the external world. The id sees a pretty woman and wants to make love to her. But if the body obeyed its demands, it would land in jail. It is the task of the ego to guard against such mishaps, to act as diplomat, to pay polite compliments to the woman, invite her to dinner, and steer her gently in the direction of the bedroom. Its job is to persuade the id to bridle its passions. In doing so, it replaces the "pleasure principle" with the "reality principle."

In responsible adults, this cooperative principle usually works admirably. But what about in young people, whose ego has not yet developed enough to control the id? When the id makes an instinctual demand which it would like to resist (such as committing incest with the mother), but is too weak to control, it can only *repress* that demand—isolate it, like a telephone operator pulling the plug from a switchboard. But that still leaves an angry person on the other end of the line. Besides, the ego has shirked its proper responsibility in behaving like this, and is "bound to suffer damage in revenge." It has permanently narrowed its sphere of influence, turned a corner of the id into a no-go area. All this led Freud to conclude that "the decisive repressions take place in early childhood," when the ego is weak.

These repressions, he goes on to say, are *always* sexual in nature. "Our opponents have told us that we shall come upon cases in which the factor of sex plays no part. Let us be careful not to introduce it into our analyses, and so spoil our chance of finding such a case. But so far none of us has had that good fortune."

We can thus see clearly how Freud came to formulate the sexual theory. He started by trying to understand why certain patients feel a compulsion to count windows, or experience the delusion of having pushed a child under a bus. He decided that the answer lay in a festering splinter in the unconscious mind, a splinter that owes its origin to a childhood repression, and is invariably sexual in nature.

But in Chapter Two, we have seen that Freud's sexual theory was *not,* as he liked to believe, a rigidly logical deduction from his clinical observations. The germ of the idea was the remark he overheard in Paris, that a certain female patient could be cured by "repeated doses of a normal penis." It seemed to confirm his suspicion that Bertha Pappenheim's problem was basically sexual, as the episode of the violent pelvic movements seemed to suggest. Bertha had lost her father, and now "transferred" her emotional attachment to Breuer. Freud observed the same "transference phenomenon" in his own patients; he later explained that this is what had convinced him that the origin of all neurosis is sexual. Again, when his female patients told him stories of being seduced by their fathers, he concluded that sexual abuse of children was a major cause of neurosis. But even when he decided that such stories were fantasy, this failed to undermine his belief in the sexual theory; on the contrary, it increased it, for why should they fantasize unless they harbored a secret wish to be seduced by their fathers?

Thus Freud came to believe wholeheartedly in the sexual theory of neurosis. But it should also be plain that, on this kind of evidence, he had no right to conclude that the basis of *all* neurosis is sexual. *Any* subject about which we feel strong inhibitions can lead to neurotic symptoms. We can induce a minineurosis instantaneously by solemnly warning someone not to do something. A person who believes that under no circumstances may he clear his throat instantly feels a compulsion to clear his throat. In Catholic Austria, as in Victorian England, sex was a major cause of inhibition; therefore it is not surprising that Bertha Pappenheim made suggestive pelvic movements. If she had been brought up in a nunnery, she might have uttered a stream of blasphemies; and Freud might just as well have concluded that the origin of all neurosis was religious.

How could a man of Freud's scientific training commit such a logical error? The answer seems to be that he was startled by the originality of his insight, shocked by its heterodoxy, bowled over by its simplicity. Besides, its potential for creating scandal was enormous; it might even destroy his career. It was easy to exaggerate the importance of an idea so exciting and so dangerous. We should also bear in mind that Freud had already arrived at one immensely important insight: the existence of the "second mind" in man—the unconscious. It must have been enormously tempting to combine the two insights. This he proceeded to do, allowing the whole theory to be colored by his natural pessimism ("Man is the helpless victim of his appetites and anxieties"). It looked logical; and, as in the case of Darwin, the scandal and controversy it aroused had the effect of establishing it as the major contender in the field.

But sooner or later, it was bound to strike psychologists that this enormous emphasis on sex was purely arbitrary. Neurosis is basically a challenge to our psychic unity, and the most obvious thing about it is its mechanism: the restriction of freedom through self-consciousness. In the late 1930s, the Viennese psychiatrist Viktor Frankl formulated what he called "the law of reverse effort," the recognition that if you become overanxious about anything, you do it badly. Someone who is worried about stammering stammers worse than ever, whereas a stutterer who was *asked* to stutter in a school play found himself unable to do so. It follows that all that is necessary to produce neurosis is *any* kind of obsessive anxiety. Frankl also discovered that he could cure obsessive patients by asking them to reverse the direction of their efforts: by persuading them to do the very thing they were terrified of doing. A bank clerk whose job depended on legible handwriting found that his handwriting was getting worse; and the more he worried, the worse it became. Frankl advised him to practice *trying* to write badly, and the problem quickly vanished.

Here we can see the basic mechanism of neurosis. We can also see that, in this case, the sexual theory is superfluous; the neurosis is triggered by the man's anxiety about his job. And what happens when he tries to write badly? The need to focus his efforts on the task rescues him from his sense of passivity and helplessness. In exercising control, he becomes aware of his freedom. He ceases to "oppose" himself, and the problem vanishes. If the clerk had been anxious about his sexual potency, the same mechanism would have made him impotent, not because sex is the *underlying cause* of his neurosis, but because the "interference mechanism" will operate on *any* cause for anxiety.

This enables us to see why, to a large extent, Freudian analysis works in practice. Neurosis is due to a build-up of anxiety, through a process of "negative feedback." Belief in the analyst reduces the pressure of the anxiety, and the patient's "will to health" does the rest. In fact, any form of "distraction" can produce the same effect. In 1924, Reich treated two women for cardiac neurosis—the sensation that the heart is being "squeezed." When the women were genitally excited, the palpitations and anxiety subsided; inhibition of genital pleasure caused the palpitations to return. Reich concluded that cardiac neurosis is due to the blockage of sexual energy. We can see that this conclusion is less logical then he assumed. *All* anxiety produces a "contraction" of the heart, and focusing upon the feeling of suffocation causes it to increase. (Anyone can make the heart "contract" by thinking about it, just as we can make ourselves itch by thinking about itching.) It was as if Reich's patient was squeezing her own heart, yet was unable to stop, as an embarrassed woman is unable to stop blushing. The harder she tries, the worse it becomes. Stimulation of her genitals would have the effect of distracting her attention from the anxiety to the pleasure she is experiencing, so she relaxes. It would have had much the same effect if she had become absorbed in a good book.

All of which would seem to suggest that the answer to our original question— Was Reich's life-work based on a fallacy?—is quite simply, yes. Reich's work was based on the sexual theory, and the sexual theory is based on a fallacy. But this is to overlook an important distinction between Reich and Freud. Freud's basic outlook was negative; Reich's was positive. For Freud, sex was a mere animal instinct whose frustration led to neurosis. But why is sex so important to us? Because, says Freud, we are nature's slaves, and nature demands procreation. For Reich, as for D. H. Lawrence, sex was the most powerful expression of the force of life itself, man's glimpse of reality. That is to say, where sex is concerned, Freud is a rationalist, Reich a mystic.

But why should this difference in approach make any practical difference, when their actual therapeutic practice starts from the same assumption—that the root of the neurosis is sexual?

The answer to this question is, in fact, of crucial importance to understanding Reich's contribution to psychotherapy, and deserves to be considered at some length.

We have seen that one of Freud's basic misconceptions lays in his notion that the unconscious is the *controller* of consciousness, the "puppet master." So, according to Freud, neurosis can be compared to a volcanic eruption, an explosion that has been prepared in the underground world of the unconscious and which now bursts through the surface into consciousness. In Freud's view, consciousness plays no part in this process, except for being responsible for the original repression. We have seen that this explanation is inconsistent with what most of us know about the mechanism of neurosis: that it is a "feedback" mechanism caused by *self-consciousness*. That is to say, consciousness, *not* the unconscious, is the villain of the piece.

The philosopher Michael Polanyi puts his finger on the central problem when he points out that, when we look *at* something, we cease to see its meaning.[1] A pianist who looked at his hands would paralyze his fingers; in order to play well he must look *beyond* his hands to the music. When you look *at* a thing, you see it but you cease to grasp it. In order to grasp its meaning, you must cease to attend *to* it, and attend *from* it.

Why is it, asks Polanyi, that when I switch my attention back *to* something, I destroy its meaning? He suggests that "to attend *from* a thing to its meaning is to *interiorize* it, and to look instead *at* the thing is to *exteriorize* or *alienate* it." What he says is important and true, but it cannot be regarded as an answer to his question: why, when I attend *to* something, do I destroy its meaning? The answer is of considerable importance, for neurosis is a form of alienation, a loss of meaning. To understand the precise mechanism of this loss would be to carry psychology an important step beyond Freud.

In short, we need a more precise understanding of the "interference" mechanism.

Such an understanding has begun to emerge in the past decade or so as the result of an apparently unrelated discipline: split-brain research. We shall see that it can, in fact, be regarded as the key to understanding the relation between the conscious and the unconscious.

For more than a century, surgeons have known that when the left side of the brain is damaged, the speech faculties are affected, whereas damage to the right side prevents recognition of faces. As long ago as 1864, the neurologist Hughlings Jackson noted that a patient with a right-hemisphere tumor ceased to recognize people and places, and he made the suggestion that the left hemisphere governs speech while the right governs recognition. More recent researches—notably by Roger Sperry of the California Institute of Technology, and Robert Ornstein of the Langley Porter Neuropsychiatric Institute—have shown that, basically, the left cerebral hemisphere governs rational thought, while the right governs intuition. Damage to the left side impairs the verbal faculties; damage to the right impairs artistic creativity. In crudely simplistic terms, the left is a scientist, the right an artist.

In evolutionary terms, this development is fairly recent. Of man's three brains—reptile, mammal, and human—the reptile brain, at the base of the skull, is the oldest, developed by our fishy and saurian ancestors. The second, which includes the cerebellum, was developed when reptiles developed into mammals. Together, these two portions constitute the "old brain." Our third brain is the most recent evolutionary development, the cerebral cortex, encased in the top of the skull. In man, its development has been so swift and spectacular—a mere half-million years—that some scientists like to speak of "the brain explosion." This is our thinking brain, the part that controls the will and our waking consciousness. This is the "new brain" that we are now discussing.

Oddly enough, the left side of the brain governs the right side of the body, and vice versa. But apart from this division of function, there seems to be close cooperation between the two halves. They are linked together by several knots of nerve fiber, the largest and most important being known as the *corpus callosum,* or cerebral commissure.

In the late 1930s, scientists discovered that if this commissure is severed, it seems to make no obvious difference to the functioning of the brain. However, it appeared to benefit epileptic patients, reducing the frequency of the attacks; apparently the operation prevented some kind of electrical feedback between the two hemispheres. In the early 1950s, Sperry and his team discovered that split-brain animals were unable to transfer learning from one side of the brain to the other; if each eye was covered in turn, the animal could learn two diametrically opposed solutions to the same problem. But it was in human beings that the most interesting results were observed. If a split-brain patient banged into some object with his left side (connected to the right brain) he failed to notice it; he paid attention only if he banged into things with his right side. Told to tap his left foot, he was unable to do so, but he had no difficulty in obeying a command to tap his right foot. He had considerable difficulty writing words with his left hand. It began to look as if the right side of the brain was deaf and dumb.

Gradually, a fascinating pattern began to emerge. If a split-brain patient is shown an apple with the left side of the brain, and an orange with the right, and then asked what he has seen, he replies, "An apple." Asked to write down what he has seen with his left hand, he writes, "An orange." Asked what he has just written, he replies, "Apple."

In fact, the split-brain experiment reveals that we have two people living inside our heads, one in the left and one in the right hemisphere. They are like neighbors whose houses are connected by a covered passageway, so they are in constant communication, but who live and sleep each in his respective section. Another experiment underlined the same point. If the right eye (connected to the left brain*) is covered, and alternating red and green lights are flashed in the other eye, the patient has no idea what color he has just seen. Therefore his guesses ought to be exactly what is expected from chance. In fact, the results are well above chance. The patient would make the wrong choice—"Red"—then jerk as if someone had nudged him in the ribs and say, "No, green." The "dumb" hemisphere had heard the incorrect guess, and somehow managed to kick the ankle of its better half.

From our point of view, there are important advantages to be

* In fact, the right half of each eye is connected to the left brain, and the left half of each to the right, but for simplicity, it is easier to speak of the left and right eyes.

gained from thinking in terms of these "two selves." It seems to correspond to a real division in the psyche, between the receptive (right) and aggressive (left), the yin and yang of Chinese philosophy. At the same time, it is important not to take the distinction too literally, that is, too anatomically. Split-brain research is a relatively new field of exploration, and tomorrow's discoveries could contradict what we appear to know today. The biologist Stan Gooch is convinced that the true distinction is not between right and left, but between the cerebrum (i.e., the combination of right and left) and the cerebellum, part of the "old brain." But from our point of view, these problems can be ignored. The important revelation is that we have two people living inside our heads, and that the one who inhabits the left side of the brain calls himself "you." He seems to be quite unaware that, only a few centimeters away, there is another being who also believes himself the rightful occupant of your head. Once we have been handed this important clue, we can pursue it with the aid of self-observation. Whether split-brain research confirms these observations in detail is beside the point. What matters is that Sperry's discovery corresponds so closely to what we already know about man's curious self-dividedness, and provides a foundation for some fruitful insights.

We may begin by making the assumption that Freud's "ego" is the "self" that inhabits the left hemisphere. When only the right side of a split-brain patient was shown an "indecent" picture, she blushed. Asked why she was blushing, she replied, "I don't know." It was true; her "ego" didn't know, and her right brain had no way of telling it. This also clearly suggests that the right brain is, to some extent, what Freud meant by the "id" or the unconscious. At least, it seems safe to assume that the "I" that blushes is also the "I" that stammers or faints or produces a sudden desire to rush to the toilet—like the female pianist described by Freud. For practical purposes, then, we may identify that right-brain "I" with the Freudian unconscious; it seems fairly clear, at least, that the right brain is the gateway to the unconscious. That other "I" is less vocal and aggressive than the rational "I," but its roots go deeper, and its powers are far greater. In *The Dragons of Eden,* Carl Sagan calls this "other self" "the silent watcher," and suggests that we are often conscious of it in dreams, or in certain drug experiences. He tells how a friend became aware of the "watcher" when he was smoking marijuana, and addressed to it the question "Who are you?" The answer came back: "Who wants to know?"

By simply reflecting on our mental processes, it is possible to observe the different functions of the left and right halves. The left-ego is not only the part that deals with language and everyday logic, it is also the part of me that "copes" with the external world. Its attention is turned "outwards." This immediately suggests that the "other self," in the right hemisphere, looks "inwards." And this again seems to be confirmed by the fact that it is the right that appreciates music. When we enjoy music, we sink "inside ourselves"; we may even close our eyes to prevent the external world from distracting us. The left side copes with everyday existence, it is rational; the right side is contemplative, intuitive.

The odd thing is that although the person I call "I" lives in the left hemisphere, what might be called "my personal center of gravity" *can* move about to some extent. In musical appreciation, in meditation, in close contact with nature, "I" become nonverbal. I seem to sink deep into myself, and the everyday "me," constantly reacting to problems and anxieties, seems to be *another* person, a stranger.

I note another thing about these moods of "inwardness." They renew my energies. If, for example, I have done a long day's driving, my left-brain ego has been kept constantly on the alert to prevent accidents, and I may sink into a purely "automatic" state. I feel exhausted, yet cannot afford to give way to my fatigue until I am safely home. Yet if, as I begin to sink into that state of bored fatigue, I happen to switch on the car radio, and find myself deeply interested in the program, I experience a magical return of my energies. I sigh and relax, and as I do so, I feel the first trickle of energy that tells me that my inner-tanks are beginning to refill. All of which suggests clearly that the right somehow "creates" energy, while the left "spends" it.

When we are healthy, the left and right work in harmony, like two men at either end of a double-handed saw. If, for example, I am setting out on a holiday, my mind is in a state that could be described as optimistic alertness. There is an indefinable air of *reality* about everything. As I stand on the station platform, I am aware of the sunlight, the slight breeze, the smell of paint from the bench, the glossy surface that reflects the sun, the half-dozen shades of green in the trees opposite . . . In short, I am not merely seeing, but am also responding to what I see. There is no "lag" between my perception and my response. Left and right are in harmony.

This is because "I" am interested in what goes on around me, and my hidden partner responds by sending up energy. But if I am engaged in some routine task, and my interest flags, then a "perception gap" appears. I no longer respond immediately. I see things, and my response comes a fraction of a second later, like a delayed echo. One interesting experiment revealed that when the left brain is engaged in routine calculation, i.e., adding a column of figures, the right brain displays sleep rhythms—alpha waves. The right has no part to play in mechanical calculation, so it goes off duty. In the same way, if I watch television for too long, or try to finish a long book in a single sitting, my ability to feel and respond seems to drain away. I experience a sense of unreality; I *see* things, but my ability to respond (the right brain) has fallen asleep, or become sluggish with boredom.

And this, clearly, is the basic mechanism of neurosis. If we spend too much time in a state of tension, like an overworked housewife or businessman, or boredom, like a worker on a production line, the right ceases to do its proper work of backing up the left, and the "perception gap" widens. Our responses lose their variety, and become limited to certain habits—lighting a cigarette, watching sports on television. There is a diminution in our sense of reality. This, in turn, produces a loss of *interest* in the reality around us—the familiar feedback effect. The American neurologist J. Silverman noted that long-term patients in mental hospitals, and prisoners serving long sentences, showed "diminished field articulation and diminished scanning"—that is, they *saw* less.[2] We "scan" the world, that is, we notice things, in order to interact with our environment and to change it. If the environment remains unchanged year after year, the need to interact vanishes. We "put less" into perception, i.e., the right becomes bored and lazy, and so sees less. In effect, the mind has become a stagnant pond, and the stagnation can breed all kinds of germs: neuroses.

It can be seen that this corresponds very closely to Freud's picture of the mechanism of neurosis. But there is a basic difference. According to Freud, it is the unconscious that incubates repressions and hatches them into neuroses. We can see that the conscious mind is as important as the unconscious in the mechanism of neurosis—*precisely* as important, since the two stand in the relation of two tennis players, each playing an equal part in the negative-feedback process. However, the starting point of the neurosis is not sexual repression, but that initial failure of the right to back up the left.

All this enables us to see why, although Reich remained a lifelong Freudian, he came closer than Freud to an understanding of the mechanism of neurosis. Reich believed that neurosis is a form of stasis, sexual stasis. In fact, neurosis *is* a form of stasis or stagnation. The ego becomes separated from its source of power and energy, just as Reich believed. Reich recognized that the central problem is to start the energy flowing again. Like D. H. Lawrence, he believed that sexual experience is one of the most effective ways of bringing this about, and again, he was correct. Human beings who have lost contact with their wellspring of vitality need to be *galvanized* by a sense of excitement or emergency; the strength of the human sexual impulse makes it a highly effective means of galvanizing the unconscious mind into a state of wakefulness.

This observation draws attention to another interesting aspect of the relation between the "two selves." Sperry noted that the right hemisphere has no sense of time; it ambles along at its own comfortable pace as if clocks had never been invented. The left, on the contrary, always seems to be in a tearing hurry. Its task is to scan the world at lightning speed. In effect, it is a high-speed camera that takes a series of monochrome photographs. It is the task of the right brain to give this flat world a third dimension, to give it color and reality, but it must be allowed to do this in its own good time. If the left is in too much of a hurry, the right shrugs and lets the distance between them increase. In effect, the left and right are like two hikers, one of whom habitually walks at twice the speed of the other.

But if we are to stay mentally healthy, they must be persuaded to walk at the same speed, and this can obviously be done in two ways: either by persuading the left to slow down to the same speed as the right, or persuading the right to increase its pace to the same speed as the left. We can do the first by relaxing, meditating, listening to music, enjoying nature, in fact, by becoming "absorbed" in anything. Drugs and alcohol have the same effect, plunging us into a more relaxed world of nonverbal consciousness. The second method demands an increasing rhythm of excitement—like the ritual dancing practiced by the ancient Greeks or modern African tribes. Civilized man induces excitement by many methods, from watching his favorite football team to driving a fast car; sometimes he uses the altogether more dangerous expedient of starting wars. Graham Greene has described how he used to shake himself out of moods of depression by playing Russian roulette with a loaded revolver.

Sex has the advantage of both methods. It causes excitement; but the intensity of pleasure also causes the left to "slow down" in order to enjoy the experience to the full. It is therefore, as Reich realized, one of the most effective methods of promoting cooperation between the "two selves."

Yet Reich's determined reductionism diluted the value of his insight. His obsession with the sexual impulse prevented him from seeing beyond it; the result is that there is something oddly limited and disappointing about his concept of health. A healthy man or woman is free from sexual stasis. But there is something trivial about this definition. Did Leonardo have to be free from sexual stasis when he painted *The Last Supper*? Or Handel when he composed the *Messiah*? Or Tolstoy when he wrote *War and Peace*? The human spirit is capable of so much more than mere "health," and Reich's psychology has no room for these "higher reaches of human nature."

Reich's sexual reductionism is the cause of a more fundamental error. Like D. H. Lawrence, he was inclined to see sexual release as the ultimate cure for man's self-division—the natural antidote to what Lawrence called "head consciousness." This seems to imply that man would be better off if he could suppress "head consciousness" and replace it with something more instinctive and primitive, a kind of "genital consciousness." This attitude shows a failure to grasp the relationship between "head consciousness"—the left hemisphere—and its instinctive partner. It is true that "head consciousness" can lose contact with its source of vital energy, but its real purpose is to act as intermediary between "instinctive consciousness" and the world. It does this by turning the intuitions of the right hemisphere into words, and expressing them in the form of relationships. For example, my business as a professional writer is to translate insights into language. When I first started writing in my early teens I found that the words often killed the insights. My clumsy attempts to express myself produced sentences that clanked and groaned like rusty armor. These struggles left me discouraged and exhausted, with the feeling that intuitions ought to be left alone, not forced into the straitjacket of language. But I persisted, largely because there seemed to be no other way. And eventually, to my delight and astonishment, I discovered that I was getting better at it. The intuitions were no longer being squashed out of shape or buried under top-heavy definitions. Moreover, if I expressed some insight with unexpected neatness and precision, the excitement would lead to a flood of further intuitions. It was as if the right brain became excited at seeing its feelings expressed so well, and shouted "Yes, yes, that's it"; and the left, delighted with this approbation, caught the new intuitions as fast as they flew out of the subconscious and turned them into more neatly chosen words. In moments like this, it suddenly became clear that "head consciousness" was nothing to be ashamed of; it could, under the right circumstances, enter into a highly fruitful relationship with the intuitive-self, and open up immense new horizons of possibility.

It was then that I observed that this ideal cooperation between left and right created a deeper sense of *reality* than we otherwise experience: a sense to which I later applied the label "Faculty X." This refers to those curious flashes of intensity in which we suddenly become aware of the *reality* of some other time or place—one of the best-known examples being that passage in *Swann's Way* in which Proust describes how the taste of a cake dipped in herb tea suddenly brought back the reality of his childhood in Combray.

William James touches on another aspect of "Faculty X" in the *Varieties of Religious Experience,*[3] when he remarks that an athlete may play a game with technical brilliance, until one day he is carried away by excitement, *and the game plays him*. "In the same way, a musician may suddenly reach a point in which pleasure in the technique of his art entirely falls away, and in some moment of inspiration, he becomes the instrument through which music flows."

These are the moments when the feedback between right and left builds up to a new intensity, and can be recognized as the basic mechanism of our mental evolution. Such insights make us clearly aware of what is wrong with the psychologies of Freud and Reich. They conceive the human mind on the model of the human body. If the balance of my physical health is upset by an infection, the doctor's task is to destroy the infection and restore my normal equilibrium. But if the balance of my mind or emotions is disturbed, it is not enough to restore it to equilibrium. Where the mind is concerned, equilibrium is another name for stagnation, and mental stagnation is the ideal breeding ground for neurosis. Man is only truly healthy when he is moving forward, evolving, struggling to increase the feedback between the "two selves." In short, the human psyche is a dynamic, not a static, system.

In theory, Reich accepted the static model. But his intuition led him in another direction: towards a dynamic, or evolutionary psychology. And Freud's own intuition was acute enough to recognize a dangerous rebel when he saw one. This was the real cause of the breakdown in their relationship.

CHAPTER FIVE

Reich returned to Vienna from Davos in the early summer of 1927, and resumed his psychoanalytic practice and work at the clinic. To the casual observer his life seemed back to normal. Inwardly, however, everything had changed. Reich had lost the battle to convert the psychoanalytic movement to the genital theory, and, therefore, a break was sooner or later inevitable. But Reich was not the man to stand around waiting for it to happen. He was prepared for new beginnings, new alliances.

The events that would change his life had, in fact, already taken place. In January 1927, at the small town of Schattendorf on the Hungarian border, there had been a violent clash between political opponents. Left-wing Social Democrats were holding a meeting when they were fired on by reactionary forces; an old man and a child were killed in the shooting, and three of the reactionaries were charged with murder. It was an explosive issue, for Vienna was a leftist stronghold, and the government of Austria—under the Christian Socialist Ignaz Seipel—was distinctly right-wing. For the past five or six years, the administration of Vienna had been carrying out an ambitious plan of "soaking the rich" and using the money to finance a social revolution: workers' housing projects, adult education, health clinics. The church and the peasantry—represented by Seipel—had no patience with these attempts to Bolshevize the ancient kingdom of Austria. So the two factions observed the trial of the political killers with interest, and the government was delighted when, on July 14, they were found not guilty and released.

The workers regarded the acquittal as a calculated insult; a mass rally turned into a riot and the Palace of Justice was burned. The police fired on the crowd; eighty-five workers and four policemen were killed.

Reich watched the slaughter. He had followed a crowd of protesting workers to the Palace of Justice, which was on fire by the time they arrived. Mounted policemen were trying to disperse the mob, and ambulances were moving in to carry away those who were trampled underfoot. Reich rushed home to fetch Annie. If they had intended to join the marching workers, they were soon discouraged. From behind a tree, they saw a line of police advance on a crowd of demonstrators; then the officer gave the order to fire. The crowd scattered, and bodies lay outstretched on the ground. Reich decided to go home.

The following day, the Social Democrats ordered a general strike; but it only lasted four days. Seipel had achieved what he wanted—a decisive defeat for the left. It was not as decisive as the slaughter that followed the Spartacist revolution in Berlin in 1919; but it meant that the leftists were on the defensive and they remained so until they were bloodily destroyed or driven underground by the Dollfuss government in 1934.

Reich, understandably, was on the side of the leftists. It was not simply that his clinic stood to gain from their social welfare schemes; he was also emotionally involved in the plight of his poorer patients. In *The Function of the Orgasm* he describes the case of a pretty working-class girl who had become completely mute. Under hypnosis she recovered her voice, and was able to tell her story. Her husband had deserted her, and she and her three children were on the point of starvation. Ten hours' work a day sewing brought her only just enough to live on. She began to experience compulsions to murder the children, and a desire to hand herself over to the police to protect them. Fear of being hanged made her throat constrict and made her mute.

Reich was able to help her over the worst difficulties. The eldest children were placed in a "good institution," and Reich collected money for the mother. But it was only a partial solution; she used to come to Reich's house and make demands, threatening to murder the baby. When Reich went to see her at her home, he was horrified by the squalor, and became suddenly aware that this woman had nothing in her life but misery, loneliness, and drudgery. Reich was faced with the problem of how human beings could continue to live such hopeless and squalid lives year after year. He could now understand how the mother had been tempted to murder her children: she had never had a chance. She had been an orphan, brought up in the same squalor—living six to a room. She had been sexually assaulted several times by adult males, and experienced an immense longing for a mother's protection. As an adult, she was sexually frigid, which may explain her husband's desertion. Now she saw her children condemned to the same life that she had led. Psychoanalysis might cure the constriction of the throat, but it could do nothing to make her life more bearable. Reich adds that in spite of this misery, she read books, some of which she borrowed from him.

It is easy to understand why Reich supported the left-wing government of Vienna, but rather more difficult to grasp how he came to be converted to orthodox Marxism, for Marxism is basically a form of materialism—dialectical materialism. (Dialectical means simply that matter is in a continual process of change and development due to the clash of opposites.) Reich had started his career fascinated by the vitalism of Bergson and Driesch. He was attracted to Freud because the libido seemed to be another name for this basic principle of evolution. For the Marxist, terms like "the life force," "spirit," and "God" represent bourgeois misunderstandings of the dialectical process. The party line on psychoanalysis was that it was another typical product of bourgeois thinking. Society was rotten because capitalism was decadent, not because of sexual repressions. According to Marx and Engels, all ideas and beliefs have a material origin, in fact, an economic origin. There is no point in asking whether there is any "truth" in Aquinas' *Summa Theologica*; it is simply a typical mental prod-

uct of the monastic period, as the excreta in the monastery lava-
tories were a physical product. The same thing applied to psychoanalysis.

How could Reich reconcile this kind of crude reductionism with
his own psychological insights? He was turning away from orthodox psychoanalysis because he was repelled by Freud's pessimistic
reductionism, his insistence that man is a helpless puppet of his
subconscious urges. But Marxian materialism was even more arid
and bleak. According to Marx, society is governed by the brutal
push-and-pull of Darwinian selection. The capitalists own the
wealth and means of production because they have taken them by
force; obeying the same material law, the workers should take
them back again. *This* was the force behind evolution, not the libido, the secret sexual energies that express themselves through
joy and tenderness.

The answer to the contradiction, as it emerges in Reich's writings—particularly the essay *Dialectical Materialism and Psychoanalysis* (1929)—is that Reich was not too concerned about these
"theoretical" disagreements between Marxism and psychoanalysis.
Quite simply, he felt that Communism could become the ideal instrument for the propagation of his own views on "sex economy."
It was clear that, where his own career was concerned, psychoanalysis had turned into a blind alley. His views might be toler-
ated, but they could never make real headway in the face of
Freud's new theory of the death-instinct and the superego. In retrospect, we may feel that Reich would have been wiser to follow
the example of Jung and Adler, and simply take himself off into
the wilderness, to attempt to create his own variant of psychoanalysis. But then, for better or worse, Reich was never a true
loner. He had the courage of the pioneer, but he liked to be surrounded by people, to feel himself part of a movement. There was
a great deal of "other-direction" in Reich (to borrow David Reisman's term); we can see this in Ilse Reich's story of the way he
used to don a spotlessly white laboratory coat and play the great
scientist when he had to receive a visitor. Besides, as we have
seen, Reich had a powerful streak of opportunism. This is not
necessarily to his discredit; a man of genius who is not an opportunist may end by being neglected. Reich had risen to eminence as
a psychoanalyst; now he saw the possibility of becoming the psy-

chological theorist of the greatest revolutionary movement in the
world. It must have struck him as entirely logical and reasonable
to embrace Communism. At the very least, it was an immensely
exciting gamble.

Reich lost no time in putting his new resolve into practice. The
day after the burning of the Palace of Justice, he joined a medical
group called *Arbeiterhilfe* (Workers' Help) which was affiliated to
the Communist Party. He hurled himself into his new activities
with typical dynamism, lecturing to workers' groups, distributing
leaflets, taking part in demonstrations, and devouring the works of
Marx and Engels. In his lectures, he could point to Soviet Russia
as an example of a society that was moving towards sexual freedom: male dominance of the family was being undermined by
new laws; divorce and abortion were easier to obtain; the antiho-
mosexual laws were rescinded (they were reintroduced in 1934),
and in the new Soviet society, sex outside marriage was no longer
considered immoral. All this suggested that Russia was carrying
out the sexual reforms that Reich himself advocated.

Combining these observations with his orgasm theory, Reich
constructed his own blueprint of the ideal society of the future.
The workers, he said, were condemned to sexual misery by capitalist society. It was not simply a question of the inhibition of the
sex instinct by bourgeois morality. It was also the problem of
abortion and venereal disease and overcrowding. This latter factor, Reich emphasized, was one of the basic problems for the
worker. Privacy is essential to full sexual enjoyment. Besides,
when parents are forced to copulate in the same room as their
children, the children are likely to develop sexual traumas, while
the less sensitive ones may experiment with incest. All this is the
fault of capitalism, said Reich, for it is in the interests of the
bosses to encourage fertility among the workers; they need a high
birth rate to ensure their control of the labor market.

After a half century of increasing sexual freedom, this part of
Reich's argument still carries a great deal of force and conviction
—no healthy society can be based on unwanted pregnancies. It is
Reich's analysis of the "compulsory sex morality" that now seems
altogether less convincing. According to Reich, the idea of premarital chastity is a bourgeois invention. It applies far more
strongly to women than to men because in a capitalist society, the

laws of inheritance are of enormous importance. So a woman is expected to be a virgin until she marries, and strictly faithful to her husband thereafter. But this fills society with frustrated young men, who are forced to satisfy their needs either through adultery or by turning to prostitutes. Moreover, strict sexual morality gives sex the additional allure of the forbidden, which in turn gives rise to sexual neurosis and perversion. The answer, said Reich, must lie in the rejection of the compulsory sexual morality, in regarding sex as something healthy and delightful. When Reich came upon the studies of the anthropologist Bronislaw Malinowski, he was enthusiastic; they provided him with just the ammunition he needed. Malinowski had studied the Trobriand islanders of Papua, New Guinea, and observed that their sex lives were completely free of inhibition (the incest taboo being the only exception), and that as a consequence they seemed to be a perfect example of mental health. Sexual neurosis was unknown among them; there was no sexual perversion, and little or no violence. Child-beating was regarded as a disgrace. In short, they seemed to be a living example of Rousseau's Noble Savage. Apply these principles to the socialist state of the future, said Reich, and we would be halfway towards a real Utopia.

In retrospect, these arguments seem unduly optimistic. No doubt the compulsory sexual morality of the Victorians produced many unhealthy effects, but its gradual disappearance has not produced the social and psychological revolution that Reich leads us to expect. There are Scandinavian countries where sexual education in schools is detailed and precise, where pornography is openly available, where teenagers sleep together as a matter of course; but their rate of mental illness is as high as that of less enlightened countries like Great Britain and a great deal higher than that of countries dominated by the Roman Catholic Church's proscriptions, where the compulsory sex morality still exerts its grip. No sensible person can doubt that modern sexual freedom is preferable to the pruderies and inhibitions of the Victorians; but there is no sign that it has brought Reich's Utopia any closer. The inference seems to be that the "compulsory sex morality" is a rather less important cause of human misery than Reich supposed, or that there are a great many other causes that weigh more heavily.

This is, of course, precisely what we would expect from the observations of the last chapter. Neurosis is basically a *strain* between the rational self and the instinctive self, with the rational self continually interfering with the natural flow of instinctive activity. It can be caused by *any* type of anxiety that leads the rational self to over-react. Sexual frustration is only one of many possible forms of anxiety. Neurosis *can* be cured by sexual satisfaction, but this does not mean that sexual satisfaction is a universal panacea, or that a sexually satisfied person is not just as subject to other kinds of anxiety.

There is another, more serious objection to Reich's "sexual politics," and it applies equally to his new political beliefs. One of the chief problems of human nature is a certain element of "cussedness," what Poe called "the imp of the perverse," and what Fichte meant when he said: *Frey seyn ist nichts; frey werden ist her Himmel* (To be free is nothing; to *become* free is heavenly). Such is the perversity of human nature that we seem to experience our freedom only when it is threatened; in circumstances where we *ought* to feel free and happy, we often look around for minor anxieties to occupy our attention. And this odd preference for anxiety underlines a basic characteristic of human nature: that we operate at maximum efficiency only when we are loaded down by a certain *weight*—of interest, of responsibility, even of anxiety. This is only to say that man is basically a purposive animal; a man with a strong sense of purpose does not become neurotic. A man without a sense of purpose is likely to become neurotic even if he has no real problems. Any scheme for improving the human lot which merely concentrates on *removing his problems* will leave him as dissatisfied as ever.

All this is not to say that such schemes are futile; only that anyone who believes them to be an *ultimate* solution to human problems is being naïve and short-sighted. And anyone who reads any of Reich's "sex-pol" writings, from *Dialectical Materialism and Psychoanalysis* to *The Invasion of the Compulsory Sex-Morality,* will see that this is precisely what he believed. The conclusion must be that Reich's belief that sexual freedom would bring some enormous basic change in human society was overoptimistic.

But then, Reich's true talents did not lie in the field of abstract thought; he was a man of action, and during the next two or three

years, he was carried along by such a headlong rush of activity
that it is surprising that he found any time to write. He continued
his work at the technical seminar, and remained an active member
of the Psychoanalytic Association. In 1928 he also became the
vice-director of the Psychoanalytic Polyclinic, the institution that
gave free treatment to workers. He continued to be a member of
the Workers' Help organization, and in 1928 became a member of
the Communist Party. As if all this were not enough, in January
1929 he formed a Socialist Society for Sex Consultation and Sexo-
logical Research, to give free information and advice on sexual
problems. Here his attitude remained uncompromisingly revolutionary, advocating that unmarried teenagers had as much right to
contraceptive advice as married couples, and that any woman who
was unwilling to be pregnant should have a right to an abortion.
In Roman Catholic Austria, these views provoked understandable
hostility, and this may have contributed to Reich's increasing dis-
satisfaction with Vienna, and his decision to move to Berlin.

The essay *Dialectical Materialism and Psychoanalysis,* the chief
product of these years, was basically an attempt to justify psychoanalysis in the eyes of the Marxists, who still regarded it as a
product of bourgeois decadence. This was not an easy task, since
psychoanalysis is basically a doctrine about the mind—particularly
about the unobservable "unconscious" mind—and Marxism is basically a doctrine about matter. Reich was attempting to bend both
of them so they met in the middle. Where Marxism was concerned, this had to be done cautiously, since he had no desire to
appear a heretic. Reich's line was simply that the crudest form of
Marxism, which attempted to reduce all ideas to economic
processes, was untrue. Marx never attempted to deny the reality of
the psychological process, he explained anxiously. And if the
"material reality" of these processes is recognized, then it follows
that a materialistic psychology *is* possible. Having negotiated this
major obstacle with considerable skill—and a masterly ambiguity
in the use of such words as "material" and "organic"—Reich proceeds to the major task of demonstrating that psychoanalysis is a
"materialist" psychology. This is not particularly difficult, since
Freud had taken so much trouble early in his career to place psychoanalysis on an "objective" foundation. Reich lays all the emphasis on Freud's libido theory, and even adds that, according to

Freud, the source of the libido lies in chemical processes, which are not yet properly understood. In short, Reich presents a version of Freud that Freud would have indignantly disowned. In order to escape the accusation of deliberate misrepresentation, Reich offers a paragraph on the subject of the later theory of the death-instinct, then goes on to dismiss it as "a hypothesis beyond the clinical sphere" which has opened the door to many "futile speculations." Reich continues that he is opposed to the new hypothesis regarding instincts, feeling instead that the destructive instinct also stems from the libido. And, having laid that awkward question to rest, he is now free to expound psychoanalysis with his own personal emphasis.

In fact, the essay is so short, a mere fifty pages or so, that there is no need to tread on thin ice; an explanation of Freud's theories of repression, the unconscious, the libido, etc., takes up most of the space, and although dialectical materialism is placed first in the title, there is little or nothing about it in the essay. Reich's chief aim seems to be to convince his Marxist colleagues that psychoanalysis, like Marxism, is a beleaguered movement rejected by the bourgeoisie, and fighting for its life against subtle internal enemies. He attacks Jung, Adler, and Rank as victims of sexual repression, whose personal hang-ups have driven them to try to desexualize psychoanalysis. Repeatedly, says Reich, sexual repression has fought against psychoanalysis and won. Even Freud has become untrue to his original vision, with his abandonment of the libido theory. Psychoanalysis, says Reich, is now suffering the fate that overtook Marxism when the Reformed Socialists got their hands on it—death by exhaustion of meaning. Reich then goes on to make a statement that reveals the glaring absurdity of his whole argument: "Official science will continue to have nothing to do with psychoanalysis because its class limitations prevent it from ever accepting it." In fact, by 1930, official science was well on its way to embracing psychoanalysis, and in America, the country where it gained its most enthusiastic following, class limitations showed no sign of preventing capitalists accepting it.

Reich's essay would certainly have caused a further deterioration in his relations with Freud if it had been published in Vienna. In fact, it appeared in Moscow, in both German and Russian, with the title *Under the Banner of Marxism*; only an excerpt appeared in Vienna in the *Almanach of Psychoanalysis*.

In September 1929, Reich went to Moscow to lecture on the prevention of neurosis, and to study Soviet methods of child care. In *Wilhelm Reich,* David Boadella states that Reich's name became well known in Moscow after publication of his essay, and that he was invited to Russia; Ilse Reich states that Reich "arranged with some Russian colleagues for a lecture tour," and this sounds the more likely version. From the beginning, Marxists showed themselves unwilling to accept Reich's "materialist" version of psychoanalysis. When Reich republished the book in 1934, after his expulsion from the Communist Party and the Psychoanalytic Association, he admitted wryly that everyone involved had disowned his ideas. He adds that both the Freudians and the Marxists had offered him the same choice between psychoanalysis and Marxism. But the Moscow trip seems to have been a success; with the publication of his essay, and his lectures at the Communist Academy and the Neuropathic Institute in Moscow, it looked as if Reich was establishing for himself a new position as the chief sexual theorist of the Russian Communist Party.

Back in Vienna, Reich had to recognize that his involvement in revolutionary politics was making his position in the psychoanalytic movement completely untenable. Federn, who was, after all, himself a socialist, was now showing open hostility. When Reich presented a paper at the Psychoanalytic Association in April 1928, Federn, as chairman, declared that its contents were utterly commonplace, and proposed that the paper should not be debated; Reich wrote an indignant letter to Freud. But Freud himself had little sympathy for Reich's revolutionary views. In *Freud and His Followers,* Roazen states: "Politically, Freud was moderate and pro-establishment, and by the 1930s he was supporting a reactionary regime in Austria." This is not entirely accurate. Jones says that Freud sympathized with the progressive reforms of the Viennese government, but that he never voted either for the socialists or for their opponents, the Christian Socialists. But, when the small Liberal Party put up a candidate in Freud's district, Freud voted for him. In 1919, he surprised Jones by saying that he had been half convinced by the arguments of an ardent Communist; the Bolshevist told him that the coming revolution would result in some years of misery and chaos, then in universal peace and prosperity. Freud replied: "I believe the first half . . ."

It seems clear, then, that Freud was innately conservative with mild liberal tendencies. Reich told Eissler that "Freud wanted nothing to do with politics." (He added the strange comment that he himself had no desire to get involved in politics, but had been trapped into it.) On December 12, 1929, their views finally came into head-on collision at a meeting of the Viennese group at Freud's home. Reich delivered a paper on the prevention of neurosis—probably the same one he had delivered in Moscow—which argued that neurosis could be prevented if the family and society could be fundamentally reorganized. In the conversations with Eissler, he summarizes his views in a single clear image: a stream must be allowed to flow; if it is dammed, it will sooner or later overflow its banks. And if the stream of bioenergy is blocked, it, too, will overflow, producing neurosis, perversion, and delusions. The answer lies in removing the blockage and allowing the stream to flow naturally. This, says Reich, requires major changes in the rearing of children and in education.

The lecture not only stirred Freud to passionate opposition, it also had the interesting effect of causing him to think deeply about his own view of neurosis, for Reich was attempting to convince him that the orgasm theory *was* his own view. And *if* Freud's sexual theory admits that neurosis is caused by sexual stasis, and *if* the orgasm is the obvious cure, then Reich was certainly drawing the logical consequences of Freud's own theory.[1]

That sounded thoroughly plausible, for indeed, Freud *did* regard neurosis as a kind of blockage. Then why could he not agree that it could be cured by a good orgasm? Freud struggled to formulate his views that evening; he told Reich that "Culture takes precedence," that is, that neurosis is basically a cultural phenomenon. But how could such a view be reconciled with the sexual theory? The problem so obsessed Freud that he went on to write a book in answer to Reich—*Civilization and Its Discontents*. He must have started writing it immediately after that evening, for many sentences in it were actually spoken at the meeting.

We have already mentioned the basic thesis of *Civilization and Its Discontents*: that civilization is based on the denial of man's natural instincts. But it is the logical implications of this theory

that are so startling. It is not only a rebuttal of Reich's theory of
social revolution, but also a denial of Freud's own sexual theory.
This can be seen if we translate its thesis into terms of split-brain
research. Animals are dominated by their instincts; they have no
"rational self." This means that, apart from instinct, they lack any
sense of purpose or direction. To judge by its brain size, a cow
could easily master the technique of opening a farm gate; but it
sees no reason to do so.

Man has developed the left side of his brain, which is essentially
a *brake on instinct*. It can instantly veto any impulse that ema-
nates from the right; interrupt any instinctive process, from eating
to copulation, from sleep to digestion. Neurosis is basically the result of this continual interference. With so many complicated inhibitions, the instinctive self can no longer operate normally. The
"natural man" is strained and filtered through a process of
thought, and sometimes the brake can jam completely, locking the
whole mechanism. This is Reich's "stasis."

But then, and here we come to the heart of the matter, neurosis
is a fairly small price to pay for the advantages of the inhibitory
mechanism. Consider the process of driving a car; it is a complex
and subtle mixture of inhibition and relaxation; the right side of
the brain—the habit mechanism—does most of the driving, but with
continuous interference from the left, the "look-out." And if driving a car is a complex co-operation of the two halves, what about
writing a symphony or a poem? Mozart's Jupiter Symphony
sounds like a spontaneous, bubbling outburst from the right side
of the brain; in fact, we know it was shaped at every step by the
left side. Dante's *Commedia,* Goethe's *Faust,* Beethoven's Ninth
Symphony, required a subtlety of interaction a thousand times as
complex as driving a car. Civilization, culture, *is* the cause of neurosis, or rather, neurosis is one of its inevitable consequences. So to
imagine that neurosis can be cured merely by an orgasm is crude
and shallow nonsense, a failure to grasp the purpose of the inhibitory mechanisms.

In a sentence: neurosis is the outcome of the inhibitory mechanisms that man has developed to create civilization.

But Freud's earlier sexual theory had stated that neurosis is *always* caused by sexual repressions and traumas. He had not sim-

ply contradicted himself; he had virtually consigned the sexual theory to the scrap heap.

Perhaps the most astonishing part of the story is that nobody noticed, probably because Freud pointed out that the sexual instincts—along with all the others—are repressed by civilization. Nevertheless, it remains basically clear that in answering Reich, Freud had at last recognized that neurosis *is* the negative part of the evolutionary process.

Oddly enough, Reich is also correct when he says that Freud really agrees with him. For Freud is not, for one moment, denying that neurosis can be cured by sexual fulfillment, a satisfactory orgasm. He is only stating that sex is not the only source of neurosis: that there are a thousand other sources, and that they are inherent in civilization. Freud had put his finger on Reich's central weakness—*a weakness for which he, Freud, was basically responsible:* his crude and simplistic view that all neurosis is sexual in origin. And in reacting against Reich's view, Freud himself had disowned the sexual theory.

What is perfectly clear is that Freud's attempt to explain himself more clearly failed to influence Reich. The "elephant's child" was too firmly set on his own path. He noticed that Freud had abandoned the sexual theory—he says as much in the talks with Eissler—but he assumed it was due to timidity and the influence of his disciples. That meant, as Reich correctly inferred, that he, Willy Reich, was now the sole guardian of the sexual theory in its original pristine dogmatism.

The realization does not seem to have bothered him unduly. There was no reason why it should. It now looked as if Reich was beginning to achieve a position on his own account. He was virtually the psychological spokesman of the German Communist Party. If Freud thought him a heretic, there were many younger psychoanalysts who were convinced of his correctness. In spite of the controversy that surrounded him, his private practice continued to flourish, for the simple reason that he was a fine clinical psychotherapist. And if Reich was ever disturbed by the controversy, he must have reflected that Freud's early career had been just as stormy. No, the position was, on the whole, highly satisfactory. The only minor problem was that Vienna was not really large enough to hold two men of the stature of Freud and Reich.

It was, in fact, Reich's skill as a psychotherapist, rather than his orgasm theory, that was responsible for his steadily increasing reputation among the younger analysts. Ever since 1926, Reich had been developing a new and highly effective method of attacking neurosis. It was more positive and direct than ordinary psychoanalysis, and it had the enormous advantage of being a great deal quicker. This was the technique of "character analysis."

According to Reich, neurosis was due to deep-seated inhibitions, or "resistances" (Freud called them repressions). The therapist's problem was to get at these resistances. The Freudian method was to persuade the patient to talk freely; but this was based on the assumption that he wanted to do so. Reich's clinical experience led him to feel that this was a mistake. The psychotherapist's task is, in effect, to strip the patient bare. But most people have a natural dislike of being stripped bare, especially in a cold climate. It is natural, said Reich, that the patient should feel a certain defensive hostility towards the psychotherapist. Therefore, said Reich, the starting point should surely be to break down this mistrust, so the patient could become truly cooperative. The patient should be encouraged to be critical towards the analyst, even to express open hostility. It was a matter, says Reich, "of really freeing the patient's aggression and sexuality." If the aggression could be freed first, the sexuality would follow. The analyst's job was not to establish a polite, cooperative relationship with the patient—this might conceal deep resistances—but to poke his tender spots and encourage him to express suffering and rage. Gradually, says Reich, he began to understand the inherent animosity which is always present in patients. If the psychoanalyst declines to allow himself to be deceived by apparent co-operation on the part of the patient, and instead attacks his character defenses, the patient will invariably lose his temper. In effect, the method was to criticize the patient—or at least to try to make him see himself in a critical light. If the psychoanalyst could hold a mirror up to the patient, enabling him to perceive his own evasions, his attempts to impress or placate the analyst, the patient would give in to rage. And this was the first step in breaking down the resistance.

And these resistances, Reich came to believe, are never simple or straightforward; they exist layer upon layer, like geological strata. In *The Function of the Orgasm,* Reich had explored Semon's idea of "engrams," memory traces of unpleasant experiences, like scars on the psyche. Every time we have been deeply hurt or upset, and have been forced to accept the experience passively, the result is a piece of psychic scar tissue, which has less "feeling" than the surrounding tissue. Eventually, these patches of scar tissue come to form a kind of armor. The function of the armor is to protect against further hurt. But it also has the effect of keeping out pleasure. Reich found that people reacted with violent hatred to attempts to pierce the armor and alter the neurotic equilibrium that had been achieved with so much difficulty. But if the patient was to be cured, he had to be persuaded to strip off his armor, or at least, to stop cowering inside it.

Therefore Reich had developed new clinical methods, designed to pinpoint the resistances. Instead of sitting at the head of the couch, staring at the patient's feet, the analyst should sit where he could look the patient in the face. His task was then to watch like a hawk, trying to recognize resistance in its many forms—silence, anger, sarcasm, "Freudian slips," even excessive politeness and co-operation. In *The Function of the Orgasm,* Reich mentions a typical case of such resistance: a passive-feminine youth who suffered from hysteria, impotence, and an inability to hold a job. The patient was overly polite, and readily discussed his intense attachment to his mother. Normal psychoanalysis would have proceeded immediately with an exploration of the patient's Oedipus complex; Reich, instead, kept on pointing out that his politeness was a defense against the analyst, until the patient finally became openly offensive. Reich provoked him further, destroying his defenses and releasing the hatred. This, in turn, released anxiety, and Reich eventually became convinced that he was dealing with a case of destructive hatred of the father, based upon a desire to castrate him, while being afraid, at the same time, of being castrated by him.

It is the final sentences of Reich's account that give rise to doubts. He claims that when the patient's femininity had been removed, his incest desires were able to express themselves, which resulted in renewed ability to experience erection—though without orgasm. In short, he failed to cure the patient, although he managed to improve his condition. But if Reich's method was so superior to Freud's ("to interpret the material in the order in which it

appears"), why this poor result? The answer becomes clear from
the more extended version of the case offered in Reich's book
Character Analysis (1933), regarded by many as his most important work. Here we see that, in spite of the new "characterological" insight, Reich's approach remained basically Freudian. At the beginning of the analysis, Reich decided that the
trouble lay in an Oedipus complex, which has given the patient a
definite homosexual orientation. (When asking a favor, he would
stroke Reich's arm.) There is endless analysis of dreams, all interpreted sexually. For example, the patient has a dream that the
apartment is surrounded by criminals; he escapes in disguise, but
is stopped and searched by the gang leader. As the leader comes
upon a piece of incriminating evidence, the dreamer finds a revolver in his pocket and fires it. Suddenly, he feels master of the
situation. The leader of the gang changes into a woman, and the
dreamer picks her up and carries her into the house.

This, says Reich mysteriously, indicates the incest motif. Moreover, the patient's disguise is an allusion to his "masquerading in
the analysis." He pays no attention to what seems to be the major
content of the dream: the dreamer's final act of courage that sets
him free and gives him back his masculinity, a clear indication
that the patient's unconscious mind is fighting back. In the Freudian tradition, Reich is interested only in the dream's negative content. Throughout the analysis, he continues to ignore these positive indications. The patient dreams that his brother climbs into
his apartment with the intention of killing him with a sword; but
the patient is too quick, and kills his brother. He dreams that a
pickpocket is about to take his wallet, but he feels it happening
and prevents the theft. He dreams that he is on a train that is
about to crash, but he manages to jump clear. Reich continues to
interpret all this in terms of incest desires and fear of castration.
When the patient dreams of a girl lifting her skirt, and he turns
away in embarrassment, Reich explains that he is afraid of the female genital because it looks like an open wound, and that he
must have been frightened as a child by his first sight of it. (The
patient found this plausible, but could not recall any such experience.)

Understandably, then, Reich failed to cure the patient, for he
remained totally convinced throughout that the trouble lies in fear

of castration, and in some "primal scene" in which he was frightened by the sight of an exposed vagina. The only evidence he offers for this "Oedipus" interpretation is that the patient admitted rebellious feelings towards his father, who was suffering from venereal disease, and often solemnly warned his son against sex. Yet the evidence that Reich presents seems to explain the case without the need for Freudian explanations. The patient's heredity was poor; one grandfather also suffered from venereal disease, the other grandfather committed suicide. An uncle committed suicide; another was a nervous wreck; a great aunt was mentally unbalanced; his mother was neurotic and overanxious. Understandably, the patient grew up nervous and afraid of life, subject to attacks of anxiety. Before the neurosis began he brooded on the end of the world, and on the possibility that he suffered a hereditary taint of venereal disease. These fears were brought to a head by attending a hygiene exhibition—presumably with lurid photographs of the effects of venereal disease. Not long before this, he had been with a prostitute, but had been impotent. All of which seems to suggest that the problem originated in his fear of venereal disease, and of insanity, brought to a head by the experience with the prostitute and the hygiene exhibition. The material about the incest desire and castration complex is totally irrelevant—and failed to play any part in the "cure."

How should the case have been treated? The patient's dreams suggest that a more profitable starting point may have been his own "will to health." This is almost certainly the line that would have been pursued by an "existential" analyst like Maslow or Frankl. One of Maslow's own early cases may be cited as an illustration. In 1938, he treated a girl who complained of depression, sexual frigidity, insomnia, lack of appetite, a sense of meaninglessness; she had even ceased to menstruate. Maslow found out that she had been a brilliant psychology student at college, but could not afford to go on to graduate studies. She had taken a well-paid job in a chewing gum factory as subpersonnel manager, and was able to support her unemployed family, who were victims of the depression of the 1930s. But after a year, she was prostrated by boredom and a sense of wasting her life; hence the symptoms. Maslow suggested that she continue her graduate studies at night school, and the symptoms quickly vanished.

If Maslow had been presented with Reich's case of the passively feminine patient, he may well have attempted the same approach, trying to find out whether there was any possibility of creative expression, and generally attempting to give the patient confidence to take a less passive role towards his own capacities. He would almost certainly have recognized the will-to-health manifested in the patient's dreams, and done his best to strengthen this by making the patient fully conscious of it, and generally attempting to induce a more positive and optimistic frame of mind. As far as one can tell, Reich seems to have achieved his partial cure by stimulating the patient's aggression, and thereby attacking his passivity—the root of the whole problem.

On the other hand, it is clear that, once again, Reich's instinctive insight has carried him beyond Freudian analysis. He himself recognizes this when he says that a Freudian analysis would have resulted only in an intellectual knowledge of the patient's problems, whereas the real problem is "to alter the patient *dynamically*." Yet the insight is only partial. Although he recognizes that the cure must be "dynamic," his Freudian training causes him to see the problem in static terms, as if the patient is a corpse lying on a table, and the analyst's problem is to find the diseased organs. He seems unaware that one of the fundamental causes of the neurosis is the passivity, the *abnegation of will*. In existential terms, one could compare the patient to a boat that is shipping too much water because the pumps have ceased to work. The problem is not even to find out why the pumps are not working; it is to *start them*.

Other cases described in *Character Analysis* make it clear why older analysts, like Federn, were so suspicious of Reich's "characterological" approach. To read some of them in detail is to feel that Reich had turned psychoanalysis into a battle of wills, an expression of his own pugnacious character. At the same time, it is possible to see why Reich was well qualified to be a psychotherapist: he obviously becomes absorbed in this game he is playing with the patient, determined to win; so he shows endless patience. Some of the cases read as absorbingly as short stories. He describes, for example, a patient suffering from inferiority feelings, who treats the whole analysis with a kind of fatalistic boredom. His childhood had been unhappy, and he is a thoroughly inadequate personality. His attitude to the analysis is of passive resistance. Reich sensed that his attitude towards the analyst was basically hostile: a feeling that even if Reich was more dominant and potent than he was, he (the patient) nevertheless possessed higher ideals. He detested the thought of anyone being superior to himself, and felt an immediate urge to attack them. For Reich, the climax of the analysis came when the patient admitted that he had often compared his own penis with his brother's larger one, and envied his brother's superior endowment. For the reader, the interest lies in the will-to-power battle between analyst and patient. Reich explained ruthlessly that the patient was attempting to overcome his impotence in a typically neurotic manner. He was trying to compensate by making himself feel superior in the intellectual realm. He was resisting the analysis because he was convinced he was cleverer than anyone else. If the analysis succeeded it would destroy not only the neurosis, but this secret sense of superiority. But the result of the analysis is anticlimactic. Reich says merely that after a few months of persistent work on the patient's ego-defense, he was able to "raise the ego" to a level at which it was able to assimilate the repressions—a claim whose inexact form suggests that the patient remained uncured. (When a cure is successful, Reich has no hesitation in saying so.)

In another case, the patient (again male) resists the analysis with a "vaguely ironical" smile that is used to conceal his hostility. Again Reich's technique consisted of frontal attack, continually drawing attention to the smile. In this case, the patient continued to resist and to deride analysis for six months, so that unusual patience was necessary. Another patient is characterized by an aristocratic dignity of manner, which never changes. With typical bluntness, Reich tells him that he is play-acting an English lord, whereupon the patient admits that he is deeply ashamed of his father, a Jewish shopkeeper, and has always fantasized about being the son of a lord. This lordly behavior conceals sadistic and homosexual tendencies that are at the root of his problems. By refusing to be taken in by the defense, Reich persuaded him to drop it, and to speak frankly about his problems. These cases demonstrate that Reich possessed in abundance what Freud seemed to lack: a kind of novelist's insight into character, which enabled him to put his finger on hidden weaknesses. At the same time, there can be no doubt that this insight sprang, at least in part, from Reich's own defensiveness and aggressiveness. In reading his own lengthy accounts of these cases, it is impossible not to observe that he derives considerable ego-satisfaction from sitting behind a desk and attacking the ego-armor of his patients. It is also clear why he was never able to complete his training analysis; he had an intense dislike of being on the receiving end.

After that frustrating meeting at Freud's house in December 1929, Reich must have realized that he had no future as a member of the Vienna circle. For three years, Freud had been consistently rejecting Reich and his ideas. In December 1926 he had rejected the whole idea of character analysis, as well as Reich's observation (derived from the cases of cardiac tension) that anxiety is the result of suppressed sexual excitement. (Freud said that anxiety was derived from deep unconscious problems, and that it *caused* sexual repression.) In totally rejecting the orgasm theory he had, in effect, expressed his disagreement with all Reich's most basic insights. Reich's remarkable capacity for self-deception might enable him to believe that Freud was really on his side; but in practice, he could see that the Vienna circle regarded him as a thorn in the flesh. They not only felt that his ideas were mistaken; they felt that Reich himself was a thoroughly undesirable character. He was becoming increasingly well known as a Communist agitator, always joining in marches and demonstrations. In October 1928, he was one of the leaders of a group of two hundred fifty Communist workers who demonstrated against a mass meeting of Fascists and Social Democrats at Wiener-Neustadt; the Viennese police managed to round them all up before they reached their objective, and sent them on the next train back to Vienna. The aggressive Reich was furious at the docility of the workers in the face of police authority; he was unable to understand why they never took to the streets and smashed shop windows in the wealthy streets of Vienna. Typically, Reich failed to recognize that he belonged to a dominant minority of human beings, while most of his comrades belonged to the nondominant majority; he was inclined to believe that sexual repression had robbed the workers of their natural aggression.

As far as Freud was concerned, Reich's political views were his own business; but this attempt to represent himself as a liaison-man between psychoanalysis and Communism was a different matter. In the eyes of the Vienna group, the Communists were revolutionary hotheads, and association with them could only discredit psychoanalysis. If Reich had stayed in Vienna, he would probably have been expelled from the Psychoanalytic Association a great deal sooner. Fortunately, he read the warning signs, and moved to Berlin in September 1930. Just before he left, Reich went to see Freud for the last time, and the hostility came out into the open. "He was very sharp, and I was sharp too," Reich told Eissler. Reich expressed his views about the social cause of neurosis, particularly in the family. Freud told him that his ideas had nothing to do with "the middle road of psychoanalysis." Reich replied that he remained convinced that the best way to prevent neurosis is to do away with social misery. Freud must have felt that he had heard all this before. He became angry, and told Reich: "It is not our business to save the world." Twenty years later, Reich admitted ruefully to Eissler that he now agreed with Freud. Reich left after an hour and a half. When he looked back from the street, he saw Freud striding up and down the room "like a caged animal." It was the last time he saw him.

Reich's ostensible reason for going to Berlin was to make the third attempt at his training analysis, this time with Sandor Rado. The analysis was still incomplete when Rado went to America six months later, but it is doubtful whether it would have been completed even if Rado had remained in Berlin, Reich saying that Rado was "jealous, awfully jealous." Annie Reich expressed the opinion that Rado's desertion contributed to Reich's personal deterioration; but this seems to suggest that some degree of reliance and intimacy grew up between them, and Reich's comments on Rado contradict this notion.

The Berlin period was among the happiest of Reich's life. The atmosphere there was altogether less claustrophobic than in Vienna. The psychoanalytic movement was flourishing—the Berlin Psychoanalytic Institute had been founded in 1920—and so was the workers' movement. Karl Abraham, one of the "old guard," had been active in Berlin, but he had died in 1925, so most of the Berlin psychoanalysts—Rado, Franz Alexander, Hanns Sachs, Erich Fromm, Siegfried Bernfeld, Otto Fenichel, George Grod-

deck, Melanie Klein—knew Reich only slightly, if at all. They were
prepared to accept him as a gifted psychoanalyst with interesting
political views. At least three of the Berlin group—Fenichel,
Bernfeld, and Fromm—were Marxist in outlook. After the hostility
of Vienna, Berlin must have seemed an ideal haven. Fenichel was
one of the younger analysts who had responded to Reich's work
with enthusiasm; he and Reich now proceeded to gather together a
group of psychoanalysts who were also Marxists. In November
1930, Reich delivered his lecture on the prevention of neurosis to
the Berlin Association of Socialist Physicians; it was a great success. A series of lectures at the Marxist Workers' Center aroused
such enthusiasm that Ilse Reich heard about them in Paris four
years later.

Reich, then, seemed to have "arrived." The bad old days were
over. The operation of changing horses in midstream had been su-
premely successful; the Marxists accepted him as a psychoanalyst
and the Berlin psychoanalysts accepted him as a Marxist. Freud's
approval was no longer important. By 1931, it looked as if Reich
had achieved the position of security and distinction that had so
far eluded him.

The basic unit of the Communist Party is the "cell"—a leftover
from the days when the Party was outlawed and members had to
operate in small fighting units. In hostile countries, cells are small
—three to five people—but in Germany, where the Party was legal,
they were larger. Reich was appointed to a cell of about twenty
members in an apartment building known as the Red Block—presumably because it was inhabited mostly by leftists. The Red Block
was in the Bonner Platz; the cell meetings seem to have taken
place in the Wilmersdorferstrasse. Most of the members were artists and writers.

Arthur Koestler, who became a member of the same cell in
1932, has described its activities in his autobiography *The Invisible Writing*, and in his contribution to a book called *The God
That Failed*. The leaders of the cell were two unsuccessful writers,
Alfred Kantorowicz and Max Schroeder, both easygoing, likable
men—Koestler says of Schroeder that he was a "lovable type of
Munich bohemian, who had found in his devotion to the Party a
compensation for his literary, sexual, pecuniary, and other frustra-

tions." Cell meetings started with a political lecture from Kantoro-wicz, based on a briefing at the Party District HQ. "This was fol-lowed by a discussion, but a discussion of a peculiar kind. It is a basic rule of Communist discipline that, once the Party has de-cided to adopt a certain line regarding a given problem, all criti-cism of that decision becomes deviationist sabotage. In theory, discussion is permissible before a decision has been reached; in practice, decisions are always imposed from above, without previ-ous consultation with the rank and file . . . So our discussions al-ways showed a complete unanimity of opinion."

Koestler gives an example of the kind of matter on which the party allowed no discussion. When he first joined the Party, Koestler wondered why, with the increasing menace of the Nazis, the Communists could not come to an understanding with the So-cial Democrats? Why did they persist in calling them "Social Fas-cists"—"which drove them mad and made any collaboration with them impossible"? Koestler's instructor explained that the Party wanted nothing more than to establish a united proletarian front with the Social Democratic masses, but that it had to start at the bottom, not the top; the Social Democratic leaders were traitors who would betray any agreement. After five minutes of this, Koestler felt rather foolish, and accepted the Party's anti-Socialist line with enthusiasm. But his original view proved to be right; Hitler found it easy to defeat the left because they were divided.

There is something absurd in the idea of Wilhelm Reich taking his place as a cog in this party machine, and quietly listening to lectures on the party line from his cell leader. Reich was not that sort of man; if he had joined the Roman Catholic Church he would not have been satisfied until he became Pope, or at least, a cardinal. Neither was he one to take his orders from Moscow. Reich had to be a leader or nothing. The moment he arrived in Berlin, he began working to seize the initiative. Just before leaving Vienna, he had lectured at the Third Congress of the World League for Sexual Reform—formed in 1928 by Dr. Magnus Hirschfeld—on "The Sexual Misery of the Workers," and had been appointed to a four-man committee to create a political plat-form on the League's views. Reich worked out a manifesto, which he submitted to the "agitprop adviser" of the KPD (German Communist Party). The Party liked the manifesto, but Hirschfeld's World League thought it too communistic and rejected it. Whereupon Reich suggested that the Communist Party should found an organization for sexual reform. The idea found immediate favor, for the Party felt that such a movement would attract new members. The Party handed over the matter of organizing the "Sex-pol" movement to its cultural branch, led by two men named Bischoff and Schneider whom Reich later described as "stooges of the Moscow dictators." Reich was appointed one of the leaders of the Sex-pol movement. He immediately produced a new manifesto, which declared that sexual repression was one of the most valuable weapons of the capitalists, and that sexual freedom would be a vital step in the overthrow of capitalism. The Church, the bourgeoisie, and the government were all in this conspiracy to keep the workers cowed and guilt-ridden. In Soviet Russia, according to Reich, marriage and family were gradually fading away —an opinion he would later regret.

The German Association for Proletarian Sexual Politics held its first congress in Dusseldorf in the fall of 1931; eight other associations for sexual freedom joined the movement, swelling its ranks by about 20,000; before the year was out, groups in other German cities had increased the number to 40,000. Since the German Communist Party (the largest in Europe) was only 124,000 strong, Reich's movement had added to its membership by almost one-third. Understandably, he was highly regarded by the Party executive. As the movement continued to attract large numbers of young people, Reich suddenly found himself in demand on platforms all over Germany.

This success was his undoing. He was becoming a spokesman for a large part of the German Communist Party, but his views were too individualistic to represent any party. Various writers have given different reasons for his fall from favor. James Wyckoff, in *Wilhelm Reich, Life Force Explorer,* states: "But Reich's success in recruiting people to what he called his 'sex political' platform worried the Communist Party leaders, who feared that sexually happy members might not adhere to the political party line." Ilse Reich explains that "they feared that diverting interest to mental hygiene problems would weaken the revolutionary ardour for the party . . ." The truth is a great deal plainer. As the implications of Reich's views became clearer, the Party realized that it had no desire to be identified with a movement for sexual freedom. Reich's views on the wickedness of the bourgeoisie and the Church were all very well; but what he was saying, basically, was that there was no harm in boys and girls getting the maximum pleasure from their bodies. Interpreted more freely, this meant: Get your clothes off and make love, or, to be more precise: Get your clothes off and fuck. This was obviously why so many young people were drawn to the Sex-pol movement. It was not their interest in the implications of Malinowski's work among the Trobrianders, or Reich's belief that the marriage and divorce laws needed liberalizing. It was their hopeful expectation that a meeting of the Young Communist League might end with a pleasant sexual encounter with a member of the opposite sex. This was also the reason that the Communist Party began to feel misgivings.

The point is of central importance, not only to an understanding of Reich, but to that of the hostility he aroused. It is important to grasp precisely what was wrong with Reich's formulation of his ideal. As an immensely vital and highly sexed individual, Reich felt that he deserved uninhibited sexual expression, and, like any sexually successful individual, his attitude towards sex was healthy and frank. Under different circumstances, he might have become another Casanova or Frank Harris, practicing sexual freedom without necessarily preaching it, but his conversion to Freud enabled him to link his natural inclinations with his philosophical convictions. Reich was an intensely serious and idealistic individual, but there is no contradiction between intellectual seriousness and sexual athleticism—the Protestant philosopher Paul Tillich was a serious theologian as well as an insatiable adulterer. Reich's mistake lay in trying to generalize his personal convictions into a social theory—a mistake that had been made a century earlier by the poet Shelley. It was this curiously idealistic approach that led to his downfall.

What Reich failed to recognize is that our culture is not homogeneous. People are seldom aware of what their next-door neighbor is doing or thinking. We speak of the permissive society of the second half of the twentieth century without realizing that there are millions of individuals who are still living in the middle of the Victorian age. In most American big cities it is possible to buy hard pornography and to see films showing sexual acts; yet an enormous percentage of American adults, perhaps the majority, would be outraged if taken to see a blue movie, or offered a magazine showing men and women making love. People live in individual life-worlds like watertight compartments. A puritanical old maid may buy her daily newspaper at a bookstall that sells pornographic magazines, and not even notice them. She may sit in the beauty parlor and listen to women discussing a homosexual play that was presented on television without really taking in what they are saying. It is all unreal, part of an alien world. This is why bookshops are able to sell the works of Sade or Genet without interference. Those who want to read them do so; those who don't are hardly aware of their existence.

This is why a society may be thoroughly permissive when it comes to allowing its members to "do their own thing," yet savagely intolerant when it comes to generalizing these ideas. An individual may preach what he likes, provided he allows the others the choice of ignoring him. There is nothing to prevent a man from placing a soapbox on any corner and preaching cannibalism or sexual perversion provided he makes it sound reasonable; those who don't want to listen will walk on. But if he protests that the television companies will not allow him time on the air to bring his views to the masses, the result will be universal outrage, and demands for his imprisonment. This is because he is violating a basic social taboo: he is trying to force his way into their heads, and this arouses the same kind of resistance as if he tried to force his way into their homes.

Reich's views on sexual freedom reveal another curious blind spot. For better or worse, most young and healthy males are promiscuous. Adolescent males would cheerfully have intercourse with ten different women a day, every day of the year. They are in a more or less continuous state of sexual arousal. This means that their desires are basically unsatisfiable in *any* kind of society. Since most women are less promiscuous than men, the male is bound to experience some sense of sexual deprivation, even if he has a dozen mistresses. Reich's views on sexual freedom presuppose that male sexuality is basically "reasonable," like that of the female, but most of us realize instinctively that this is untrue. An American judge, in sentencing a particularly brutal sex murderer, once made the interesting observation that the male sexual urge is

out of all proportion to any useful purpose that it serves—a remark
that is profoundly anti-Reichian in spirit, for Reich assumes that if
society could outgrow "Victorian" sexual taboos, sexual frustration would vanish, and human beings would cease to be neurotic.
If the judge is right, Reich was simply underestimating the power
of the sex instinct.

Whether or not Reich was correct, there can be no doubt that
most human beings are instinctively on the side of the judge. They
feel that human sexuality is not a subject that fits into tidy logical
categories. We may agree with Reich that sexual repression is bad
for us, that sexual ignorance is disastrous, that healthy human
beings regard sex as a pleasure rather than a transgression. Yet
somehow, it still does not seem to follow that sexual freedom will
transform society. There seems to be something simplistic and
over-rational about this view.

But this is not why the Party comrades came to reject Reich's
sexual views. Their reasons were expressed in various criticisms
and arguments at the time.[2] One leading official of a youth organization commented: "Reich wants us to turn our Association's gymnasia into brothels. We are to turn our young people towards sexual matters instead of diverting their attention. We don't like to
talk about sex too much, but otherwise we're not against it." The
accusation that Reich wanted to turn the gymnasia into brothels is
unfair, but it makes his point. From the Party's point of view,
Reich *did* like to talk about sex too much. The *Deutsche Volkszeitung* meant basically the same thing when it called Reich "an
unrecognized erotic hermit in the sexual wilderness." A Communist doctor remarked: "He concentrates on orgasm, but orgasm
disturbances play only a secondary part within the proletariat."
Another one makes the point even more clearly when he says: "In
my talks, I dealt with sexual questions for ten minutes at the most,
and with political questions for one and a half hours." The basic
objection becomes clear: not that Reich is wrong about sex, but
that he *overemphasizes* it, until a relatively trivial matter is made
to seem far greater than it should be. A religious leader might
have raised the same objection—not on moral, but on spiritual
grounds: that there are far more important things in life than sex.
The Communists were making the same objection in their own
terms. They saw the really serious matter as the struggle between

the workers and the capitalists—a struggle that, in their eyes, was as momentous as the battle of Armageddon. Reich's belief that "orgastic potency" had an important role to play seemed to be trivializing the issue. Reich's opponents—whether Christians, Communists, or ordinary sceptics with no axe to grind—all expressed basically the same objection: sex may be important, but it's not *that* important.

Reich, of course, was incapable of understanding such an objection. He had committed himself to Freud's theory that sex is the most important and basic impulse in the world, in fact, the *only* basic impulse. Given that dogma, the rest followed. His opponents could only feel that he was something of a crank, a man who had fallen into the error of wildly exaggerating the importance of one single facet of human existence.

It is unnecessary, then, to look for sinister conspiracies to explain Reich's dissensions with the Communist Party, and equally unnecessary to accept Reich's explanation that "emotional plague" was to blame. The Communists simply felt that all this talk of sex was *not* what Communism was about. Reich's earlier arguments about the misery of working-class women, the problems of abortion, the need for better marriage laws, had deceived them, and made them feel that he was basically a Communist. Now, as the Sex-pol movement expanded, and Reich talked earnestly about orgastic potency and genital personalities, they felt they were seeing him in his true colors, as someone who wanted to push civilization towards decadence. While Magnus Hirschfeld's World League for Sexual Reform was concerned with removing the stigma from the idea of sexual deviance, as far as the Communists were concerned, world revolution had nothing to do with allowing homosexuals and masochists to practice their deviations with public approval; it could only confuse the issue. And the same was true of Reich's talk about sexual freedom. It was a red herring that had been dragged into the proletarian struggle by a vociferous propagandist. A doctor remarked: "We Communist doctors are principally to blame that [the cultural section of the KPD] came under Reich's ideological influence. We others made no effort. He, in contrast, acted very energetically." They felt, in fact, that he was an opportunist who had tried to use the Party for his own ends. Fortunately, he had been discovered in time. Bischoff and

Schneider, leaders of the cultural section (IFA) did their best to repair the damage by putting every obstacle in the way of Reich's *The Sexual Struggle of Youth*. Reich borrowed money, founded his own press, the Verlag für Sexualpolitik, and brought it out himself, together with several other pamphlets on the same subject. In doing so, he was pouring oil on the flames; Bischoff and Schneider were, technically, Reich's superiors in the Party; by going over their heads, Reich had committed a breach of Party discipline. It made no difference that he felt he was in the right, and that he said so in a letter to the Executive Committee. Reich was too politically inept to realize that he was making things worse. Party discipline was in many ways like the monastic discipline of the Middle Ages; to defy the Abbot was not only to oppose the authority of the Church, but of God. Reich had showed his cloven hoof, and revealed once more that he was simply not of the stuff of a good Party member. So although the Sex-pol organizations received his new offerings with enthusiasm, and the French Communist Party accepted *The Sexual Crisis* for publication, the Executive Committee had to face up to the recognition that their distinguished recruit was more trouble than he was worth.

Unaware of the gathering storm, Reich continued his work for the sex hygiene clinics, wrote prolifically, read Engels and Malinowski, and studied the increasing influence of Nazism with horrified fascination. It seemed to him to provide obvious confirmation of his theories. These jack-booted young enthusiasts, marching to the Horst Wessel song, were in the grip of a vague, mystical longing for freedom and heroic adventure. This longing, said Reich, was the result of the *unnaturalness* of modern civilization. It was a craving to return to more natural means of self-expression—in particular, to genital self-expression. When human beings have been forced for thousands of years to deny the basic laws of their own nature, and, in so doing, have built up a kind of counternature, they are bound to feel a sense of superstitious horror at the very idea of behaving naturally. Ergo, Fascism was basically a form of frustrated sexuality. It was in the interest of dictators like Mussolini and Hitler—and Reich would soon include Stalin on the list—to encourage "the compulsory sex-morality," because frustrated young people were ideal recruits to Fascism.

The idea is deployed at length in Reich's largest and most im-

portant sex-political work, *The Mass Psychology of Fascism,*
where it is expanded to some four hundred pages. It is perhaps
Reich's most brilliant piece of polemical writing. Yet here again, it
is difficult not to feel that he has made one of those curious errors
of judgment and overshot the mark. The argument that Fascism is
based on repressed sexual energy *sounds* plausible because we
know that many Nazis were sadists. But when the argument is expanded to book-length, its weaknesses begin to appear. Was the
ordinary young German soldier really a product of sexual repression? In order to believe this, we have to accept Reich's thesis that
man has been repressed for thousands of years by civilization until
he has been twisted into a completely unnatural mold. And if we
can accept this pleasantly romantic view—man the noble savage,
corrupted by his own success—we then need to be convinced by
the second part of Reich's argument: that the answer lies in sexual
freedom. The argument is a little too schematized and oversimplified. Who was responsible for the original repression? The
Church and the aristocracy, who wanted to impose their authority.
The "genital character"—that is, the kind of human being who
enjoys sex without neuroses—is naturally hostile to authority, so
that it was in the interest of the Church and the capitalists to incubate neurosis by trying to give everyone a guilty conscience. The
mystical and religious emotions expressed by St. John of the Cross
or El Greco are another form of repressed sexuality.

The truth is that there is no evidence whatsoever that Fascism is
based on repressed sexuality, or that Hitler and Mussolini tried to
create sexual guilt. If Hitler expected the drum-majorettes in the
Youth Movement to be virginal, it was not because he thought sex
was wicked, but because he believed that promiscuity springs out
of boredom and lack of purpose, and that Nazi ideology should
remedy that undesirable situation. Hitler's few remarks on sex in
his *Table Talk* suggest that he agrees with Reich. He certainly
regards it as one of life's great events: "The revelation that her encounter with her first man is for a young woman, can be compared
with the revelation that a soldier knows when he faces war for the
first time. In a few days, a youth becomes a man." Neither had he
any prejudices about sex for the unmarried: "Rather than die an
old maid, it's better for [a woman] to have a child without more
ado! Nature doesn't care in the least bit whether, as a preliminary,

the people concerned have paid a visit to the registrar." Hitler also seemed to share Reich's suspicion of the Church: "The evil that is gnawing at our vitals is our priests . . ." Hitler is not precisely Reichian in spirit, but neither is he precisely puritanical. As for Mussolini, he seems to have regarded sex as one of the supreme pleasures of life, and to have had no objection to his soldiers sharing his view.

So the overall impression of *The Mass Psychology of Fascism* is of a man determined to oversimplify for his own purposes. Reich is basically an anarchist who hates all authority, and believes that sexual freedom is the answer to all mankind's problems. Like Freud, he has no difficulty in seeing everyone he dislikes as an example of sexual repression and neurosis. But since Reich himself is authoritarian and neurotic, it is hard to take him seriously.

There can be little doubt that it was this tendency to oversimplify, to attempt to force reality into the Procrustean bed of his own ideas, that Annie Reich had in mind when she said that he showed a deterioration during these years. She was to experience it at first hand when she joined Reich in Berlin (against the advice of Sandor Rado). Reich had so convinced himself that the family unit was the source of all evil that he delivered an ultimatum: either she consent to place the children in a Marxist children's commune, or they would have to separate. Overwhelmed by Reich's dominant and inflexible personality, she agreed, although it went against all her natural instincts, and she later had no doubt that it had been a mistake. The children, predictably, hated it; they had a natural resistance to being indoctrinated into Communist ideology. Annie Reich recalls an incident when Reich reprimanded them for singing a German song instead of a proletarian revolutionary song. And when she writes about this period, Ilse Reich admits his ruthlessness: "Something was either black or white, you were for him or against him, never a shade of grey permissible. And those close to him had to follow him or get out . . . It was this inflexible attitude of his . . . that again and again lost him friends and co-workers." The ordinary reader may feel inclined to put it more simply: that, where personal relations were concerned, Reich was a bastard.[3]

The marriage was, in fact, already drifting towards a breakdown, one crucial factor being Reich's meeting, at the May Day parade of 1932, with a ballet dancer, Elsa Lindenberg, who became his mistress. In February 1933, Reich's world suddenly began to collapse. The German Communist Party repudiated his views and banned his books; he was virtually "excommunicated." And on February 27, just after Reich returned from giving a lecture in Copenhagen, a Dutch ex-Communist named van der Lubbe fired the Reichstag. Hitler had been Chancellor for less than a month. During that time, the German Communist Party had been exhorting the workers to take to the barricades: "Fresh bullets in your guns! Draw the pins of the hand grenades!" "Our fight cannot be broken by machine guns or pistol barrels or prison. We are the masters of tomorrow!" There had been three attempts to burn public buildings only two days before the Reichstag fire. So when Hitler was called to the blazing building around midnight on February 27, he had no doubt that it was a Communist plot, and swore revenge. (In fact, it now seems fairly clear that van der Lubbe acted alone.) The following day, Hitler persuaded President Hindenburg to sign a decree suspending various civil liberties; it was virtually martial law. With an ease that shocked other Communist Parties of Europe, the German Communist Party was suppressed. The trial of various Communists for the Reichstag fire proved to be a public defeat for the Nazis, largely because of Goering's incompetence as one of the prosecutors (he was Minister of the Interior). Four Communist leaders were acquitted; only van der Lubbe was sentenced and executed. But that was in September 1933; by that time, the Communist Party had ceased to exist in Germany.

Reich returned to Berlin the day after the fire, February 28. He was not among the 1,500 intellectuals and Communist officials who were arrested, but this was mainly because he moved to a hotel under a false name. On March 2, an article attacking his *Sexual Struggle of Youth* appeared in the Nazi press. The children were sent back to Vienna to stay with relatives; Annie Reich moved in with friends. Although the possession of revolutionary tracts was punishable by death, Reich lent his car to some young comrades to transport Communist literature. If they were caught, they were to claim that they had stolen the car; meanwhile, Reich would report it stolen to the police. After they departed, Reich realized that they had not agreed on the street from which it was supposed to have been stolen. As hours went by without the return of the comrades, Reich considered the possibility of making for the frontier that night, but they eventually brought the car back— they had been delayed by a flat tire. When the attack on his book appeared in the Nazi newspaper *Volkischer Beobachter,* Reich fled for the Austrian border with his wife, but changed his mind before he crossed it, and waited inside Germany for a few days— reasoning that if he left, it might be more difficult to get back in. He went back to Berlin and registered in a hotel under his own name; the Nazis were unlikely to expect him to be so open. When he learned that his home had been searched for a second time, he finally decided to make his way back to Vienna leaving all his pos- sessions behind him. He left the country disguised as a tourist on his way to a skiing holiday.

By mid-March, he and Annie were back in Vienna. They were even living under the same roof, but the marriage was now finished. And so was the most successful and eventful epoch in Reich's career. From now on, the going would be mostly uphill.

CHAPTER SIX

Vienna may have been a haven from the Nazis, but for Reich it held no welcome. His former colleagues of the Psychoanalytic Society must have felt something like dismay at his reappearance; they had hoped they'd seen the last of him. And for Reich himself, this return was something of a humiliation; when he had left for Berlin, he had hoped that he'd left these dreary plodders behind to their timid mediocrity. Now he was back among them, without money or possessions, and with a reputation that had grown more unsavory in his absence. In the previous year, Freud had made an open gesture of hostility. Reich had submitted a paper on masochism to the *International Journal of Psychoanalysis*. According to Freud, this "culminated in the nonsensical statement that . . . the death-instinct is a product of the capitalist system." Freud reacted with an irritable letter to the publisher, saying that the article could only be published if it was prefaced by a statement that Reich was a Bolshevik, and that "Bolshevism sets similar limits to scientific research as does a church organization." Freud went on to imply that Reich was no better than a Jesuit: ". . . the publisher would have made the same comment if he had been pre-

sented with a work by a member of the SJ [Society of Jesus]."
Reich replied indignantly that the Party had never made the
slightest attempt to influence his scientific freedom, which, as we
have seen, was wishful thinking. Freud was finally persuaded to
allow Reich's article to appear without this introduction—some of
the socialist psychoanalysts in Berlin said it would be tantamount
to a declaration of war on the Soviets—but the article was immediately followed by another by Siegfried Bernfeld, attacking it and
implying that Reich's criticism of the death-instinct was an expression of the party line.

On March 16, 1933, Reich received a letter from Freud, who
was the director of the Psychoanalytic Press, telling him that they
could not honor their agreement to publish *Character Analysis*
"because of current political conditions." Reich's name had been
too much compromised by his political agitations. Reich wrote a
letter of strenuous protest to the publishers, in which he made
things worse by asserting that the truth was that analytic theory is
revolutionary and thus was a commitment to the workers' cause.
When this had no effect, Reich borrowed money and published the
book himself; eventually, it was to become known as his most important contribution to psychoanalysis.

In April, Reich gave a lecture to a group of socialist students,
as a result of which he received a letter from his old enemy Federn,
asking him to stop addressing left-wing groups. Instead of telling
Federn to go to hell, as might have been expected, Reich answered
soothingly that he intended to leave Vienna in two weeks, and that
if, during that time, he received any requests to lecture, he would
consult Federn. The calm answer failed to placate the Psychoanalytic Association—of which Federn was chairman—and Federn insisted on a written guarantee that Reich would not lecture. Federn
spoke to Annie Reich on the telephone, and suggested that Reich
ought to resign from the Psychoanalytic Association. But Reich
had his back to the wall and was fighting hard. He asked for a
frank discussion with the board of the Association; this took place
on April 21, 1933, and the board requested him to stop lecturing
and to stop publishing political works. Reich again tried to compromise; he *would* stop, he said, if the Association would take
a public stand about his own work. He was really asking for an
open debate, which might open the way to some sort of agreement

—or, at least, to an end to the conspiracy of silence about him. But the board had no wish to be drawn into scientific discussions with a man they regarded as an embarrassment; they really wanted him to shut up and go away.

Reich was perfectly willing to go away; he had enough political insight to see that Vienna would soon become a bad place for Jews; but even here, the Association put obstacles in his way. Two Danish doctors, both Marxists, expressed their interest in studying with him, and wanted him to go back to Copenhagen. Psychoanalysts to whom they mentioned this advised them against it; Reich's former Berlin colleague Max Eitington, now in Vienna, was particularly emphatic. The fact that Reich was also a Marxist would mean that there would be too much "identification." What this really meant was that Reich would be able to promulgate his own heterodox brand of psychoanalysis. Reich asked the Association's authorization to teach in Copenhagen; it was refused. The Danes were undeterred; Dr. Tage Philipson invited Reich to return with him to Denmark. And so, after only six weeks in Vienna, Reich set out on his travels once more—this time without Annie. ("She was sick," he told Eissler, "I just had to leave her.") Elsa Lindenberg, the ballet dancer, who had remained in Berlin to oppose the Nazis, would join him later in Denmark.

Luck had now turned against Reich. Reading his letters of this period,[1] it is impossible not to feel a certain sympathy. In spite of his touch of paranoia, there was something honest and naïve about him. He believed that his discoveries were in the true tradition of psychoanalysis, and that in certain respects, he saw deeper than Freud. Here, as we have seen, he was undoubtedly correct. He liked to see himself as "a working scholar," whose purely scientific work was being obstructed for spiteful personal motives; here again, he was to some extent correct. But he was quite incapable of grasping that the real cause for the hostility went deeper than envy, or irritation at his bad manners; his opponents felt, quite simply, that he had sold out, that he was a Moscow man, a party liner, a political Jesuit, or—to some—a Jew-boy on the make.

At this distance in time, we are able to see that there was a certain amount of justice on both sides, but that each was constitutionally incapable of seeing the other's point of view. When, in the previous year, Freud had spoken irritably about the Party dogmas, Reich had underlined the words and added: "[What about] Freud's dogma of the death-instinct." What he was saying was that psychoanalysis had become just as much a dictator state as Russia, and that the pot had no right to call the kettle black. The real problem was that Reich had been a pot before he became a kettle. He had originally been a vitalist, drawn into the movement because he thought that Freud's libido was another name for the élan vital. He admits that Freudianism originally repelled him; he lumped it together with Krafft-Ebing, and the others who made "sexuality seem bizarre and strange." What interested Reich, as he says, was the question: "What is life?" But he swallowed his aversion when he decided that Freud's concept of the libido allowed him to be a psychoanalyst *and* a "life-force explorer." The implication can hardly be ignored: Reich began his career as a doctor with an act of compromise. It could be argued that this was not particularly reprehensible, since the motive was honorable: to combine his interest in the problem of the nature of life with his career as a doctor. But at a fairly early stage, Reich had to recognize that Freud was not the type of person to allow his disciples much freedom of thought; the fate of Tausk and Silberer must have made this clear. And since Reich was not a reductionist by nature, the honest solution would have been withdrawal from the psychoanalytic movement. Reich decided against this; he reasoned that, after all, he agreed completely with Freud about the importance of sex. Yet Freud's formulation of the death-instinct theory in 1920 should have warned him that the compromise was unworkable; this was, in effect, Freud's repudiation of the libido. By then, Reich was too convinced that he was on the road to success, perhaps even as Freud's successor, to heed the warning lights. He kept his eyes tightly shut, and went on working at his own version of the libido theory, meanwhile concerning himself mainly with psychoanalytic technique, by way of convincing Freud that he was sticking to the party line. By 1926, it was obvious that Freud really had abandoned the libido theory, and that Reich and he no longer had the slightest thing in common; Reich's reason for compromise had been pulled from under his feet. The clash of December 1926 made it clear that Reich had been mistaken in hoping that there was room for his own genital (libido) theory in the movement; Freud would not permit the least dissent. This was basically the cause of the 1927 crisis; Reich was forced to recognize that all his calculations had gone wrong, and that he had, in effect, wasted the past seven years. He continued to hope that some compromise might be found; but his reception by Federn and other members of the "old guard" made it plain that *they* understood perfectly well what had happened. They were intent on forcing Reich to make an open break with the movement as had Jung and Adler. But Reich felt he had an even better solution; by flinging himself into the worker's movement, he could outflank Federn and the rest. Once again, he was faced with the necessity for a basic compromise, and with an even grosser form of reductionism. And again, Reich tried to repeat the tactics he had used eight years earlier. He made a few mental reservations about "vulgar Marxism" under his breath—like Galileo muttering *"E pur si muove"*—and declared himself to be an advocate of sexual freedom for the workers. His reason for becoming a Communist was as flimsy as his reason for becoming a Freudian in 1919: he decided that the kind of "open sexuality" that he wanted to see was an essential facet of true revolutionary freedom, as defined by Marx and Lenin. This turned out to be an error of truly mountainous proportions; the Party saw the ideal Communist as a "steel-hardened cadre," not as a naked Bacchanalian. In due course, the Party turned out to be as intractable as Freud and told Reich he could take his sexual freedom back to his decadent bourgeois friends in Vienna.

Then came the supreme irony: the Freudian party liners, for whom he had bartered his integrity in 1920, now accused him of selling out to the Communists. Reich was perceptive enough to see the unfairness of the charge—as his remark about Freud's own dogmatism shows—but not sufficiently capable of self-appraisal to recognize that if they were being unjust, it was largely his own fault. He had tried to compromise twice, and fallen flat on his face each time. The Psychoanalytic Association had rejected him and refused to allow him to teach, although it had so far ignored his challenge to expel him. So he was at last forced to do what he should have done at least seven years earlier—set himself up as a Freudian defector, as Adler and Jung had done.

Although he failed to recognize it at the time, the German

Communist Party had done him a favor by throwing him out. It was not really in Reich's nature to be a good Communist. His natural genius and dominance meant that he was temperamentally closer to Fascism, that is, he was an authoritarian élitist. The expulsion was a shock to his ego; but it freed him from the burden of trying to force himself into a mold for which he was completely unsuited. It is true that for the next year or so, self-respect—the desire for consistency—led him to continue to think of himself as a left-wing rebel. But it was largely a matter of habit; every contact with the Party deepened his disillusionment. In Copenhagen, he tried to persuade the Communist organization "Red Help" to assist Walter Kolbenhoff, a young emigrant with suicidal tendencies; but Kolbenhoff lacked papers, and the leftist bureaucrats showed themselves to be as unsympathetic as their capitalist counterparts. Ilse Reich comments that it was this incident that led to Reich's true break with the Party, but the evidence suggests that, with his usual selective caution, Reich omitted to inform his Danish comrades of his change of heart.

On May 1, 1933, the day he arrived in Copenhagen, Reich sent a letter to his ex-analyst Sandor Rado, now in New York, asking whether, if he came to America, the American Freudians would "allow him to stay alive." What was probably behind this was a desire to know whether Rado himself would take kindly to his arrival in America—Rado now being Freud's chief representative there. Presumably there was no reply, since Reich abandoned his plan to sail for New York. He told Eissler that Rado was hostile to him because "Emmy, his wife, and I had very strong genital contact with each other." He added that "full embrace" had never occurred, but that they had danced together a good deal. Rado might therefore be excused for not wanting to see Reich in New York.

For the first few weeks, his work in Denmark went well. He was allowed a temporary permit to work, and began to enroll students the day after his arrival. His personal warmth and brilliance ensured that he was soon surrounded by admirers. Since all European Communist Parties were separate entities, it made no difference to the Danes that Reich was persona non grata with the German left, and the Communist magazine *Plan* accepted an article on nudism for publication. Reich also made arrangements to have *The Mass Psychology of Fascism* published in Copenhagen. It appeared in August 1933, and its publication proved to be a major mistake. Reich's best plan would have been to keep a "low profile" and confine himself to teaching psychoanalysis. By publishing *The Mass Psychology of Fascism* he made the authorities aware that an extreme revolutionary had arrived among them. The book also had the curious effect of alienating the Danish Communist Party, which went to the length of "expelling" Reich on November 21, 1933. (The expulsion meant little, since Reich had never been a member.) Their objection was that the book was "counterrevolutionary," since it blamed the German workers for allowing Hitler to take over. Another reason for their irritation was that Reich's article on nudism had landed the editor of *Plan* in trouble with the authorities; it advocated that teachers and pupils, as well as parents and children, should see one another naked, and the Danes were scandalized. (The article was eventually included in Reich's book *The Sexual Revolution*.) The editor, Edvard Heiberg, was sentenced to forty days in prison. Predictably, when the question of the renewal of Reich's residential permit came up at the end of October, Zahle, the Danish Minister of Justice, decided that Reich was an undesirable alien.

Reich fought hard against the decision. Two of his closest Danish associates, Eric Carstens and Sigurd Neergard, joined with him in giving a public lecture on "The Struggle for Psychoanalysis," attended by an audience of six hundred, and a petition was sent to the Minister of Justice. This cunning attempt to change his ground failed in its purpose; Zahle had no objection to psychoanalysis, but he objected to Reich's political views and his sexual liberalism. Besides, Reich was in trouble with the police; two rival psychiatrists had lodged a complaint about a woman "patient" who had attempted suicide. In fact, the woman was not a patient—Reich had declined to treat her—but nevertheless, the two psychiatrists, Clemmenson and Schroeder, suggested that Reich should not be permitted to remain in Denmark, and the conservative press, delighted to attack the "decadent" theories of Freud, launched a smear campaign against Reich. He was attacked as a "so-called sexologist" who was "fooling around with our young men and women and trying to convert them to this perverse pseudo-science."

Carstens tried to stem the tide by asking various distinguished scientists—Einstein, Bohr, Malinowski, and, predictably, Freud—to support Reich. He told Freud that Reich had rendered the Danish Psychoanalytic Association "such valuable practical assistance . . . that we wish to keep him at all costs." He pointed out that the doctor who *had* been authorized by the International Association, a man named Harnik, was known to have suffered a psychotic breakdown from which he had still not recovered, and that this was causing the Danish psychoanalysts embarrassment. Freud replied on November 12, 1933, saying that while he acknowledged Reich's stature as an analyst, he rejected his politics; therefore he was unable to help. If Carstens had known anything about Freud's implacable vindictiveness to "renegades" he would not have wasted his time.

Reich now had genuine reason for his persecution mania; this *was* persecution. He was being attacked from all sides, and, once again, he was homeless and at a loose end. As a temporary expedient he decided to move to Malmö, the small town facing Copenhagen across the Öresund strait which separates Sweden and Denmark; here his students could continue to visit him. More important, so could Elsa Lindenberg, who was now working in Copenhagen as a ballet teacher and physical therapist (using Reich's techniques). Before settling in, he decided to go on a European tour in late 1933, perhaps hoping to find somewhere to settle permanently. He also had a specific reason for wanting to visit England; he wanted to consult Sir Almroth Wright, director of the Physiological Institute, about how to measure electrical charges in the skin. According to Reich, this aspect of his trip to London was a waste of time, since Wright told him it was impossible. But he also took the opportunity to call on Ernest Jones, and was received with unexpected friendliness. As President of the International Psychoanalytic Association, Jones might have been expected to regard Reich with suspicion; instead, he assured him that, in spite of his disagreement with Freud about the death-instinct, there was plenty of room for him within the framework of psychoanalysis. Reich attended some meetings of a psychoanalytic group at Jones' house; they were also friendly, but gave Reich no reason to feel that he would be welcome in England as a practicing psychoanalyst. His greatest pleasure on this English visit was in meeting Bronislaw Malinowski, the anthropologist whose works had had such a stunning impact on him in the early Berlin days; they formed a warm friendship that was later continued in America.

Reich rejected London as a possible home, mistakenly, in the view of A. S. Neill, who believed, probably correctly, that Reich would never have been persecuted in England as he was later in America. He went on to Paris, and for a while was attracted by the ambience of a German Trotskyist group who admired his *Mass Psychology of Fascism* and would have been glad to recruit him to their number. The Trotskyists were, of course, opposed to Stalin, and to Soviet domination of the Comintern (the Third International Organization of Communist Parties). Trotsky was calling for a Fourth International, free of Stalinist domination. For Reich to move among these anti-Soviet rebels was already an important step away from his former orthodox Communism. But he must have felt that they were too small and weak to be worth joining; it would have been an admission of his own fall from influence. Instead, he went on to Zürich to meet some Swiss sexologists, then rejoined his wife Annie and the children for a holiday in the Tyrol. Here he began to work on a pamphlet inspired by his discussions with the Trotskyists; it was called *What Is Class-Consciousness?* and was basically a criticism of the German Communist Party, in fact, of international Communism as he had known it. Reich pointed out that the "masses" are *not* class-conscious; they don't, for the most part, nurse a desire to shoot the bourgeoisie and take over the means of production. He mentions a friend who picked up two young hitchhikers; they were working class, and vaguely socialistic, but on the whole bored with politics; they were more interested in pretty girls. *This* is the reality, says Reich, and the Marxist doctrinaires, with their bureaucratic organization and endless talk about the dictatorship of the proletariat, are simply out of touch. On the other hand, his own Sex-pol movement had drawn thousands of such young people into the Communist Party.

Yet Reich knew that his point would be lost. *What Is Class-Consciousness?* could be regarded as his postscript to his years of Communist involvement, a kind of weary turning-away from revolutionary politics. It was also, perhaps, intended as his political justification before posterity.

Reich went on to Prague, where he renewed contact with exiled German leftists, then decided to revisit Berlin on his way back to Malmö. (He first took the precaution of ascertaining that German customs officials kept no lists of wanted persons.) The atmosphere there struck him as ominous, and when a man on the railway platform seemed to recognize him, Reich hastily turned away. In Germany, there could be no possible doubt that the revolutionary dream was over. It is true that the Reichstag Fire trial had ended in the acquittal of the four Communists; but this was a victory for German justice rather than Communist propaganda. (In his autobiography, Arthur Koestler tells how the Communists in Paris had published a book "exposing" the Nazis for being responsible for the Reichstag fire, then admits: "We had, in fact, no idea of the concrete circumstances.") Communist propaganda notwithstanding, the German Communist Party had ceased to exist by 1934, and Berlin wore a military air, as if in the reign of Kaiser Wilhelm. Reich was glad to get back onto Scandinavian soil.

Malmö proved to be worse than Copenhagen. It was little more than a large village, full of malicious gossip and a lively interest in other people's affairs. Reich felt that this place embodied the futility and boredom that bred Fascism. The inhabitants were still living in the late nineteenth century, it was the kind of suffocating atmosphere described in the plays and novels of Strindberg. It was still dominated by puritan morals; young people walked around the streets in groups, and the boys stared at the girls without daring to speak. Reich lived in a boarding house full of snobbish bourgeoisie. Elsa came to join him on weekends; students like Tage Philipson, J. H. Lennach, and Lotte Liebeck came over every other day on the steamer, a mere three miles. Lennach and Philipson were in hot water in Copenhagen for starting a birth control group, and advocating legal abortion. Finally, the Malmö police became curious about all this coming and going, especially as many of Reich's visitors were known as left-wing revolutionaries; one day in April 1934, they took a group of Reich's students to the police station for questioning, and Reich was summoned there. His best course would have been to explain politely that he was simply a doctor conducting his classes, but his ingrained dislike of bureaucracy made him irritable and rude. The police came to search his room, but when he found they had no warrant, he ordered them to leave. They contacted the Copenhagen police, who went to search Philipson's room in his absence. The two hostile psychiatrists in Copenhagen apparently provided the Malmö police with the kind of information they wanted. When Reich's visa came up for renewal at the end of May 1934, further permission was refused. Once again, it is difficult not to feel that Reich himself was partly to blame.

Fortunately, Reich's prospects were again looking more promising; in Copenhagen he had met a number of analysts from Norway, including Harald Schjelderup, head of the Psychological Institute at Oslo University; Schjelderup became one of Reich's students during his brief stay in Copenhagen. Nic Hoel, the wife of the Norwegian novelist and critic Sigurd Hoel had been a student of Reich in Berlin. These and other Norwegian friends suggested that Reich might find Oslo more sympathetic than Copenhagen or Malmö. At Reich's suggestion, a psychoanalytic conference was held at Oslo at Easter 1934; there Reich met Ola Raknes, who was to become one of his closest friends as well as his most influential disciple in Scandinavia.

There was no point in moving to Oslo at the beginning of the summer holidays; instead, Reich allowed Sigurd Hoel to persuade him to enter Denmark illegally; he spent the summer at a country house at Sletten, on the coast, under the assumed name of Peter Stein. There he completed *What Is Class-Consciousness?* and it was published in the *Journal for Political Psychology and Sex Economy* in June 1934, under yet another assumed name, Ernest Parell. Ilse Reich comments that Reich seemed to enjoy this kind of hide-and-seek under pseudonyms.

The children also spent the summer holiday with Reich in Denmark. The break was good for him; he was feeling refreshed when he took them back to Switzerland in August. But even now there were new clouds on the horizon. On August 1, Reich received a letter from the secretary of the German Psychoanalytic Association, explaining that they proposed to omit his name from a calendar listing the members of the German branch that would be issued to coincide with the Thirteenth International Congress of Psychoanalysis to be held in Lucerne at the end of August. The omission, said Carl Mueller-Braunschweig, was purely a technical matter, due to the present situation in Germany, and it would quickly be put right once the Scandinavian group was recognized at the Congress. Reich, who had planned to attend the Congress, dug in his heels and said he had no intention of "resigning," but there was little he could do. He arrived at the Congress on August 25, and was told that he would not be allowed to read his paper; he was, for the moment, no longer a member of any psycho-analytic body. A special meeting was called to consider his case under the chairmanship of Anna Freud; again he was asked to re-sign, and again he refused. An executive meeting was then held—which Reich, as a nonmember, was not allowed to attend—and Federn, Eitington, and Jones all had unkind things to say about him. Pressure was put on the Norwegian group not to allow Reich to become a member, it was hinted that they would not receive their recognition otherwise; to their credit, they refused. (They received their membership of the International Association in spite of this.) In effect, if not in actuality, Reich had been expelled from the International Psychoanalytic Association. (Jones later insisted that he had resigned.) His exclusion was not, then, a purely technical matter.

On the fourth day of the Congress, Reich was allowed to deliver his paper as a guest; it was on "Psychic Contact and Vege-tative Current," and it demonstrated once again that Reich never stood still. It was in this paper that he introduced the concept of "muscular armor," the notion that a neurosis is often accompa-nied by a rigidity in the muscles; so that, for example, a person suppressing a great deal of anger might develop a rigidity of the back and shoulder muscles, and poor circulation in the hands and arms. It was a development of the recognition of his Vienna days that neurosis often expressed itself in the form of physical effects. Reich's paper was received by the Congress with indifference; it probably confirmed Jones in his decision not to reinstate him. Reich was definitely an outcast. Some of his former students even delivered papers that were indebted to his ideas, but conveniently neglected to mention his name. Reich left the Congress with a heavy heart.

With Elsa Lindenberg, he took a short vacation, driving through Switzerland before returning to Copenhagen to collect his books and papers. The Swedish authorities at first declined to allow him to cross their country to Norway, but finally relented. In Oslo, in October 1934, Reich once again prepared to make a fresh start.

In *The Life and Work of Wilhelm Reich,* the Belgian critic Michel Cattier ends a chapter on the Swedish period with the words: "He spent five years in Oslo sinking into madness." It is Cattier's contention that all Reich's work after the "psychoanalytic period" is worthless: that he made crude biological experiments that led him to totally false conclusions, and that the "discovery of the orgone" was an elaborate piece of self-delusion. "As the scientists ignored him," says Cattier, "he began to abuse them and suspect them of having hatched a plot to suppress his discoveries." The result, he thinks, was full-blown paranoia.

There can be no doubt that Reich *did* become paranoid towards the end of his Norwegian period, when articles deriding his work appeared in the press almost daily. But the most impressive thing about his work during the period is the logic of its development. At no stage was there any sudden leap into unproven theory or imaginative speculation. Unlike Reich's political ideas, his scientific work shows a commendable pragmatism and caution.

When Reich arrived in Oslo, his aim was simple: to discover whether "sexual electricity" really existed. In 1926, he had reviewed a book by the Berlin physiologist Friedrich Kraus which dealt with the electric currents of the body. Kraus went so far as to say that all life processes can be explained in terms of these currents, and that all illness can be explained in terms of their malfunctions. Absorbed in creating his orgasm theory, Reich had paid little attention at the time; now it struck him that Kraus could have been talking about the "libido."

The idea was logical. If, as Reich believed, the loins flood with a kind of vital electricity at the moment of orgasm, it ought to be possible to measure it with a voltmeter. This was the idea he had put to Sir Almroth Wright in London in the previous year. It was altogether too startling a conception for Wright, whose revolutionary days were far behind him (in 1906, Wright had served as a model for the hero of Shaw's *Doctor's Dilemma*), but it struck Reich as logical, and he proposed to test it. All that was required, he reasoned, was some device that would amplify the natural currents of the skin. Accordingly, he used the proceeds of a series of lectures that Schjelderup had organized at the University of Oslo to pay for an apparatus that would register the electric charge of the skin on an oscillograph. The experiments, which occupied the next two years, fully justified Reich's assumptions. He discovered that the skin has an electrical charge of between ten and forty thousandths of a volt, while the erogenous zones (genitals, nipples, ear lobes, lips, and so on) have a far more irregular electrical potential that could soar as high as two hundred millivolts. Pleasure increases this charge; pain, anxiety, and fright decrease it. He also made the interesting discovery that to breathe in deeply decreases the electrical tension of the abdomen, while breathing out increases it. This confirms an observation that anyone can make at any time: that taking a deep breath produces tension, while breathing out—sighing with relief—decreases it. The pleasure of the release produces electric current.

Cattier is unfair when he suggests that Reich thought he had discovered the libido with his electrical machines; Reich was not naïve enough to imagine that the force of life could be measured in millivolts. Cattier is closer to the point when he says that Reich's attempts to measure the libido are "exactly as if someone wanted to *bottle* thirst or hunger." This *is* the disturbing element about Reich's later philosophy. He often seems so obsessed with the physiological side of health and sickness that he forgets that psychology is about the *mind*. Mental health is basically a sense of *inner breathing space,* a kind of freedom; neurosis is a kind of mental claustrophobia, a lack of inner freedom, a sense of being *tied down.* And what one is tied down to is *the body*. We feel ourselves stranded, trapped in a world of matter, of mere physical reality. On the other hand, health is a feeling of freedom from the limitations of the body, of the physical world. The mind feels powerful and detached; it can do handstands and turn double-somersaults. It is true that mental health is accompanied by a feeling of vital energy, but this energy is basically a function of the will. Whenever human beings have something to *look forward to,* they experience a kind of lifting of the heart, which is followed by a surge of energy. The same energy is summoned by a sense of purpose. It is dependent upon our *attitude* towards the future—as

Frankl realized in Dachau. We might borrow a term from brain physiology and describe this vital energy as "readiness potential." Readiness potential is the energy that surges into the muscles before some voluntary act; it would be compared to the compression of a spring. And our minds also have their store of readiness potential. Lazy, dull people keep a low stock; determined and purposive individuals keep a large reserve store. The basic aim of psychiatry is to persuade people whose readiness potential has been depleted by "discouragement" to increase their store.

What Reich was measuring in the skin was basically "readiness potential." To do him justice, he never, as Cattier asserts, equated this skin-reaction with the libido, but he was, undoubtedly, inclined to look upon this mysterious energy as the *source* of mental and physical health, as if it were a kind of vitamin. His Freudian training led him to look for mechanical models of sickness, and in his later work these tended to be transformed into equally mechanical models of health.

This curious tendency to ignore the purely psychological component can be seen in the section of *The Function of the Orgasm* in which he explains his "break-through into the biological realm." He begins by explaining the new "social" theory of neurosis that he has developed as a result of the years in Berlin. As a social animal, man's chief cravings are "position, fame and authority." These fill him with drives and ambitions that run counter to his biological needs, particularly the need for sex. This simplistic theory enabled Reich to throw the full emphasis on man's need to satisfy his natural demands.

The real nature of the problem, says Reich, began to appear when he turned to the question of masochism. In 1928 he had treated a man of strongly masochistic inclinations, and found that the man's constant demands to be beaten made serious progress impossible. One day, Reich asked the patient what he would say if Reich actually consented to beat him, and the man beamed with delight; whereupon Reich took a ruler and gave him two vigorous whacks on the buttocks. The man gave a loud yell that contained no kind of suppressed enjoyment, and from then on, never again asked to be beaten. This, says Reich, convinced him that it is untrue that masochists derive pleasure from being beaten. And then came a "truly fantastic idea": that masochism is actually a disguised desire to burst or explode, and that the masochist believes that torture will bring this about. That is to say, the masochist is full of desires that he dare not express, and they have the effect of making him, figuratively speaking, blow up like a balloon. But in the case of human beings, the balloon cannot burst, because the person has developed a kind of "armor" to hold it in, like a child struggling to hold back his tears. Thus an intolerable tension is created, an inner pressure that cannot find release. Being beaten, says Reich, is an attempt to find such release, a desire to be struck until the balloon bursts. The alternative would be to find, with the help of Reichian therapy, an "orgastic discharge." But what *is* it that is discharged in such a moment? An orgasm without pleasure does not reduce tension, so some form of *biological* energy, the energy Reich was seeking to measure with his electrical machines, must be released.

This reasoning sounds convincing until it is examined more closely. To begin with, can we really accept that neurosis is due to the clash between biological and social demands (fame, ambition, etc.)? It is easy to see that many young men would enjoy making love to every pretty woman they meet, and that social taboos make this impossible. But is it really society that is to blame? Surely, the women themselves would have some objection? And their objection is just as "biological" as the young men's desires. Neurosis *can* be caused by the conflict between social and sexual desires; but it is not *always* so. A few years later, Abraham Maslow produced a more balanced theory in the concept of the "hierarchy of needs"—that the most basic need of all living creatures is for food and security; after that, sex (and love); after that, success and fame (self-esteem). A man or woman could be satisfied on the sexual level, and still become neurotic out of unfulfilled self-esteem.

Reich's theory of masochism is open to a more basic criticism: He seems to prefer to ignore the sexual component. Magnus Hirschfeld has a chapter on masochism that makes it clear that in the majority of cases, masochism is sexual in nature. A schoolboy enjoys being beaten because his mistress—an attractive young woman—removes his pants before bending him over her knee; she often allows her other hand to stray to his genitals as she spanks him. A young man enjoys lying on the floor, while his pretty cousin stands on him in high-heeled shoes, allowing him to look up her dress to her underwear; as a climax of the "game," she presses her foot on his penis, and he has an orgasm. A girl has a fantasy in which she is bound and naked on a butcher's slab; the butcher prods her all over, as if trying to decide on the best cuts, then inserts a finger in her vagina—which causes an orgasm.[2] In none of these cases can we see any evidence of Reich's "desire to burst." There is simply an *association* of pain with sexual pleasure, so that pain ends by evoking sexual pleasure, as the ringing of a bell caused Pavlov's dogs to salivate when it became associated with food. Because Reich willfully ignores this psychological component, he fails to see why his patient did not enjoy being struck with a ruler. For the masochist, the person who is beating him is an object of sexual desire, the real cause of the excitement. A grim-faced psychiatrist wielding a ruler bursts the soap-bubble of illusion. The actress Florence Farr used to practice the same technique on love-sick swains; she would lean forward, grab them by the head and make them kiss her, and then say: "Now let's have a reasonable conversation." The treatment was intended to extinguish romantic desire, and seems to have succeeded.

So although Michel Cattier is wrong when he claims that Reich became insane during the Oslo period, the suggestion is not entirely without foundation. Reich did become increasingly paranoid in Norway, and—what is more important from our point of view—increasingly simplistic. The paradox is that his simplistic approach enabled him to make some important discoveries.

From the point of view of his psychoanalytic colleagues in Oslo, Reich's work had never been so exciting. This was not on account of the researches into "bio-electricity"—which many of them felt to be a waste of time—but because of the new analytic techniques he was now developing in the field of character analysis. In Copenhagen, Reich had treated a case of a man whose neck muscles were rigid and tense. After what Reich described as an "energetic attack" upon the patient's resistance, it suddenly broke; his stiff neck vanished, but this relief gave way to skin eruptions, pains in the head and neck, diarrhea, and increased heart beat. The problem, apparently, was that the man was basically a passive homosexual, and that he resisted this recognition with an attitude of tense masculinity, which expressed itself in his neck muscles.

If release of psychological tensions could cause relaxation of the muscular armor, then surely the reverse would also be true? If the muscular armor can somehow be destroyed, would the tensions also vanish? In effect, Reich wanted to prick the balloon.

The method he developed can best be illustrated by quoting a passage from Orson Bean's book *Me and the Orgone*. Bean is an American actor who, many years later, went to Reich's follower Elsworth Baker for treatment.

The doctor was feeling the muscles around my jaw and neck. He found a tight cord in my neck, pressed it hard, and kept on pressing it. It hurt like hell but Little Lord Jesus no crying he makes. "Did that hurt?" asked Dr Baker.

"Well, a little," I said, not wanting to be any trouble.

"Only a little?" he said.

"Well, it hurt a lot," I said. "It hurt like hell."

"Why didn't you cry?"

"I'm a grown-up."

He began pinching the muscles in the soft part of my shoulders. I wanted to smash him in his sadistic face, put on my clothes and get the hell out of there. Instead I said "Ow." Then I said "That hurts."

"It doesn't sound as if it hurts," he said.

"Well, it does," I said, and managed an "Ooo, ooo."

. . . I thought of Franchot Tone in the torture scene from *Lives of a Bengal Lancer*. I managed to let out a few pitiful cries which I hoped would break Baker's heart. He began to jab at my stomach, prodding here and there to find a tight little knotted muscle . . .

"Turn over," said Baker. I did, and he started at my neck and worked downward with an unerring instinct for every tight, sore muscle. He pressed and kneaded and jabbed and if I were Franchot Tone I would have sold out the entire Thirty-first Lancers. "Turn back over again," said Dr Baker . . . "I want you to breathe in and out as deeply as you can and at the same time roll your eyes around without moving your head. Try to look at all four walls, one at a time, and move your eyeballs as far from side to side as possible." I began to roll my eyes, feeling rather foolish but grateful that he was no longer tormenting my body. On and on my eyes rolled. "Keep breathing," said Baker. I began to feel a strange pleasurable feeling in my eyes like the sweet fuzziness that happens when you smoke a good stick of pot. The fuzziness began to spread through my face and head and then down into my body. "All right," said Baker. "Now I want you to continue breathing and do a bicycle kick on the bed with your legs." I began to raise my legs and bring them down rhythmically, striking the bed with my calves. My thighs began to ache and I wondered when he would say that I had done it long enough, but he didn't. On and on I went, until my legs were ready to drop off. Then gradually it didn't hurt anymore, and that same sweet fuzzy sensation of pleasure began to spread through my whole body, only much stronger. I now felt as if a rhythm had taken over my kicking which had nothing to do with any effort on my part. I felt transported and in the grip of something larger than me. I was breathing more deeply than I ever had before, and I felt the sensation of each breath all the way down past my lungs and into my pelvis. Gradually, I felt myself lifted right out of Baker's milk chocolate room and into the spheres. I was beating to an astral rhythm . . .

On the way home, Bean describes how "the sky over the East River . . . was a deeper blue than any I had seen in my life, and there seemed to be little flickering pinpoints of light in it. I looked at the trees. They were a richer green than I had ever seen. It seemed as though all my senses were heightened. I was perceiving everything with greater clarity. I walked home feeling exhilarated and bursting with energy."

Clearly, a half-hour of Reich's muscular therapy had produced a more dramatic effect than six months of normal psychoanalysis.

The basic principle of Reich's "muscular therapy" is that the body has a series of seven muscular rings or segments: ocular, oral, cervical, thoracic, diaphragmatic, abdominal, and pelvic. Any or all of these rings can become "armored" by negative emotions—fear, rage, spite, inhibition. The ocular segment, which includes the top of the head, is most frequently "armored" by anxiety, the oral segment by self-pity and the desire to cry, the cervical segment (neck and back) by rage and hysteria, and so on. Asthma —due to chest armoring—can be caused by repressed anxiety *and* rage. (Reich believed that all asthmatics have a hidden fantasy of a penis in the throat.) In the case of Orson Bean, Baker worked his way steadily down through the segments—for example, making him jam his finger down his throat and "gag," without ceasing to breathe; this had the effect of causing Bean to sob violently for five minutes, suddenly recalling his mother.

Baker explains the basic principle of armoring in his book *Man in the Trap*. An amoeba, Baker says, pulsates with life and energy, reaching out pseudopodia for food. If a pin is stuck in it, it contracts, and takes a few moments before expanding again. After several attacks it becomes cautious and takes a long time to reach out. If it is jabbed often enough, it remains contracted; it is now "armored." In human beings, a sudden violent shock can cause such "armoring" the first time. Baker describes the case of a woman patient with fantasies of being strangled, during which she would choke. After therapy, she began to have dim memories of a man and a woman, and of her hatred for the woman. One day when she came to see Baker she was close to death, and her breathing almost ceased. She seemed to revert to childhood and was unable to speak. Baker managed to restore her breathing by massage, and the crisis passed. Eventually, she seemed to recall a man bending over her cot and choking her, and her mother hitting her with a frying pan. She asked her mother, who admitted that she was illegitimate, and that after her birth, her mother had asked her lover to choke her—he had left her for dead. The episode of the frying pan also turned out to be an accurate memory. Baker's muscular therapy had released these early memories that had become bound up with her musculature in the form of permanent inhibitions.

What Reich had discovered was what has since become known as "abreaction therapy." It is based on the fact that when we are severely shocked, or placed under emotional strain, we often react by trying to "ignore" the pain, pretending it is not there. A child sometimes reacts in the same way when he cuts or crushes a finger and is afraid to look at it, *in case it is far worse than he thinks*. But then, human beings have extremely powerful and efficient mechanisms for digesting and assimilating experience; this is why we can eventually adjust to almost any shock. When an experience is "ignored" or repressed, it remains undigested, and so retains its power to cause misery and neurosis. The therapist's problem is to persuade the patient to face up to the experience, and if possible, to actually *relive* it. There are many ways of bringing this about—

for example, the British psychiatrist William Sargant prefers to use drugs. In his book *The Mind Possessed,* he describes his treatment of a shellshocked soldier who had become partly paralyzed; Sargant placed the soldier in a semitrance with ether, then induced him to relive the whole experience of the bombardment; the man went into a kind of emotional orgasm of terror, collapsed, and woke up feeling fine. It is clear that Baker was using a basically similar technique with the woman patient. The problem is to allow the patient's system to "face up" to the undigested chunk of experience. The system will do the rest.

Reich's new technique was revolutionary, as well as highly controversial. In psychoanalysis, it was regarded as strictly forbidden to touch the patient; now Reich was going to the opposite extreme. But it worked spectacularly. Understandably, his Oslo students—Nic (Hoel) Waal, Ola Raknes, Tage Philipson, Harald Schjelderup—were full of enthusiasm, and were inclined to regard Reich with an emotion akin to idolatry. He occupied in Oslo the same kind of position that Freud occupied in Vienna. For the first time in years, Reich had no need to be defensive. He relaxed and expanded in this glow of admiration. In *Wilhelm Reich,* David Boadella quotes Raknes, who met Reich in 1934, and who emphasized Reich's natural warmth. "Although at that time I often felt awkward and embarrassed in the presence of remarkable persons, there was something warm and friendly about Reich that made it easy to speak to him." His students and colleagues knew him as "Willy." Raknes also emphasizes Reich's brilliance as a therapist. ". . . he was naturally and absolutely concentrated on the patient. His acuity to detect the slightest movement, the lightest inflection of the voice, a passing shadow of a change in the expression, was without parallel . . . And with that came a high degree of patience, or should I call it tenacity, in bringing home to the patient what he had discovered, and to make the patient experience and express what had not been discovered. Day after day, week after week, he would call the patient's attention to an attitude, a tension, or a facial expression until the patient could sense it and feel what it implies." That is to say that, like Gurdjieff, Reich was training his patients in *self-observation;* and this undoubtedly played as important a part in the cure as the uncovering of sexual repressions.

And now, it seemed, Reich was finally in the position he had always wanted; he had become the Freud of Oslo, surrounded by admiring coworkers. The Norwegian government apparently had no objection to his political views; and, in any case, Reich had now abandoned active politics. He had a laboratory at his disposal, and his admirers provided the funds for expensive apparatus. In spite of the clashes with the Psychoanalytic Association, his reputation was expanding steadily. The days of conflict and frustration seemed to be behind him, but there remained one major obstacle to his peace of mind, his own dominant and aggressive temperament. Reich was impatient, and capable of uncontrollable bursts of temper which alienated colleagues who might otherwise have remained devoted admirers. Otto Fenichel, who demonstrated his loyalty and friendship for Reich by moving to Oslo with him was a case in point. Fenichel was a gentle, intellectual man of great personal charm; Nic Waal says "he represented Austrian softness and humour in a peaceful way." But then, he and Reich had always been colleagues and equals; now Reich's explosions, and air of confident superiority, began to get on Fenichel's nerves. It was true that Reich was now the central figure in the Norwegian psychoanalytic movement; but was it so necessary to *show* his awareness of it? Within a few months of moving to Oslo, Fenichel had been thoroughly alienated; he moved to Prague in 1935, then went to America. Ilse Reich is convinced that he was the chief source of the rumors in America that Reich had gone insane.

There was another reason for the increasing strain between Reich and some of his Norwegian colleagues. Many of them regarded his electrical experiments and his new biodynamic theories as a waste of time. A. S. Neill, who met Reich in 1937 in Oslo, was one of these, although he expressed his feelings more politely, merely claiming that he was "unable to understand" the orgone theory. Reich was apparently able to accept Neill's scepticism—perhaps because Neill was a distinguished man in his own field of education—but he was unable to show the same patience and constraint towards less gifted colleagues. So within the first months of his sojourn in Oslo, Reich had already begun to undermine his own position by alienating some of his warmest admirers.

In Reich's defense, it should be added that he was not a man to

nurse grudges. Nic Waal says: "Although Reich sometimes exploded and was very aggressive, at times terrifying in temperament, he forgot about it quickly. His mind and creative searching
did not give him time to rest upon old matters." And during his
first years in Oslo, Reich had enough new ideas and "creative
searching" to keep him permanently occupied. In February 1936,
he formed the Institute for Sex-Economic Life-Investigation, and
the name meant precisely what it said, that is, Reich wanted to investigate why and how the life-force, the libido, creates living organisms. And within a few months he had made—or believed he
had made—a discovery so staggering that it eclipsed everything he
had done so far. In a word, Reich believed that he had solved the
age-old problem about the origin of life.

It should be explained that there are basically two theories
about the origin of life on earth. The first is that it came from
outer space in the form of drifting spores; the second that the action of sunlight on various inorganic chemicals suspended in water
caused them to build into more complex molecules, until finally
the amino acids, the basic building blocks of life, were formed. In
the nineteenth century, there was a third view, known as "spontaneous generation," which stated that when certain substances
decay, they spontaneously create new life forms: decaying cheese
creates maggots; decaying apples create grubs. It was even
believed that tadpoles and newts are created by decaying vegetable
matter in ponds, and blowflies by putrid meat. Pasteur disproved
this by showing that if a sterilized yeast solution is placed in a
sealed and sterilized flask, no living organisms develop. The fer-
mentation of yeast and alcohol is caused by tiny living animals
that fall in from the air. Pasteur also placed sterilized hay and
other refuse in sealed vessels, and showed that they would remain
sterile—free of life—for many years; in fact, indefinitely.

Now Reich repeated this experiment. He placed dry sterile hay
in sterilized water, and allowed it to soak for a day or two. When
he looked at it through his microscope, he saw that it was swarm-
ing with living organisms—some of them were even visible to the
eye.

Further experiments showed him that when the hay had been in
the water for a short time, the cells at the edge disintegrated into
tiny bladders, or vesicles, which began to float in the water. These

bladders, said Reich, behaved very like living organisms; they joined together into larger groups, and sometimes split into smaller groups, which in turn would attract more vesicles around them; it looked very much like the process of birth. He became convinced that these tiny balloons *were* a kind of living organism, the basic energy-units of life. He decided to call them "bions," which he said were formed not only from organic substances like grass and egg-white, but from inorganic substances like earth and coke.

What he was asserting, basically, is that life pervades the air we breathe and the space that surrounds our Earth, and that it can "take over" these simple cells, turning them into living matter. He was reasserting the truth of the spontaneous generation theory.

Michel Cattier takes a derisive view of Reich's experiments. "[Reich] bought meat, vegetables, eggs, and milk, put them all in a saucepan, and boiled up the mixture for half an hour. Then he took a drop of this soup and placed it under the microscope. What he saw on the slide took his breath away—a myriad of globules moving in every direction. He immediately came to the conclusion that these globules were full of biological energy and that he had found what he was looking for. (In fact he had simply observed an emulsion, and the vesicles were fat particles in suspension; their agitation was due to Brownian movement [the motion of small particles of matter suspended in liquid, due to the impact of molecules].)"

Even a completely uncommitted reader cannot help feeling that this sounds unlikely. Reich may have been an inexpert biologist, but he was not so stupid as to be unable to tell the difference between globules of fat and living organisms, or between the jerky billiard-ball motions of Brownian movement and the swimming of living organisms.

The natural response of most scientists was that Reich had failed to keep his "soup" sterile, and had allowed microorganisms to get in from the air. Reich answered this by setting up another experiment in which he deliberately contaminated his cultures with dirt taken from a vaccum cleaner. He insisted that the results bore no resemblance to the living cells in his "bion solutions." He convinced himself still further with another experiment; he heated coke until it was red hot, then immersed it in sterile water (or potassium chloride solution, which seemed to produce even better results). The bions formed almost immediately, and there was not time enough for microorganisms to get in from the air.

Reich discovered that the vesicles had an electrical charge, and would move either to the anode or cathode of his electrical apparatus. He further demonstrated that the "bions" could be cultured like other minute living organisms; after heating them to 160° centigrade, to "sterilize" them, he transferred a drop of the solution into a test tube containing bouillon which had been sterilized. Within twenty-four hours, the vesicles were swimming busily in the meat solution.

Dr. Louis Lapique, of the Physiological Laboratory at the Sorbonne, examined Reich's bion solutions, and admitted that the bions seemed to be alive; moreover, they were still "alive" a year later. But he was strongly inclined to believe that he was witnessing Brownian movement. Another researcher, Professor Roger du Teil, also studied Reich's bion solutions, and had no doubt that they contained organisms that behaved as if they were alive. Reich himself came to adopt a view that was not entirely at variance with Lapique's chemical theory. Bions, he decided, were a transitional form between living and nonliving matter. They are the elemental units into which all living matter disintegrates if it is made to swell (by being immersed in liquid). The bion is basically a simple energy unit, containing a "quantum" of "bioelectricity."

Early in 1937, Reich's experiments took another interesting step forward. In his coke bion cultures, he observed tiny black organisms, smaller than ordinary bions, with a rodlike shape. (Under greater magnification they were seen to be oval.) Unlike the bions, they could not be dyed with Gram's stain, a characteristic they shared with typhoid bacilli. The bions in these cultures also seemed to have changed their nature, looking more like amoebas, and there was a definite antagonism between these amoeboid bions and the black rods, which could kill or immobilize the bions. What had happened, Reich concluded, was that the original simple bions had broken down into these two new forms. He called the amoeboid bions "PA bions," and the black rods "T-bacilli." The "T" stood for *tod* (death) for Reich soon discovered that the T-bacilli had the property of killing mice. Moreover, a large proportion of mice injected with T-bacilli developed cancer.

But when mice were first injected with the PA bions, they built up a resistance to the T-bacilli, and usually recovered. Reich became convinced that T-bacilli are always associated with cancer, and were probably its cause. They could also be cultured from the blood of cancer patients, an observation that Reich was later to develop into a method of testing for cancer.

The two years, 1936 and 1937, during which Reich worked on his bion research, were probably the happiest of his adult life. He felt that he was making discoveries that would revolutionize science; and, moreover, that he had finally laid a true and secure foundation for psychology. Kammerer was dead—driven to suicide by his scientific opponents—but Reich had vindicated Kammerer's belief in a "specific life energy," a creative energy that plays its part in the formation of crystals as well as living organisms. This bioelectricity is the energy that fuels our emotions, said Reich, and is therefore the key to psychology as well as biology.

At this period, Reich had another reason for finding life pleasant. In 1936, Elsa Lindenberg had been invited to Dartington Hall, the experimental school in Devon, England, to teach ballet during the summer session; Reich, always interested in educational experiments, went with her. The school had been founded in 1925 by Leonard and Dorothy Elmhirst as an "experiment in rural industry"; by 1936 it was one of the liveliest cultural centers in Europe, full of poets, musicians, dancers, and every type of craftsman. The latter included an attractive young Norwegian textile designer named Gerd Bergersen, who was in charge of the Dartington textile mill.

Gerd Bergersen had, understandably, never heard of Reich, but she was told that the newcomers lived in Oslo and spoke some Norwegian; so one lunchtime in the canteen, she went and spoke to Reich in Norwegian. The smallish, gray-haired man looked friendly and harmless, but his instant reaction startled her. Staring directly at her, he said: "You interest me. I want to know you." Her own reaction was less enthusiastic. "He puzzled me, and somehow I sensed danger."[3]

At twenty-five, Gerd Bergersen was a young woman of independent ideas. Her upbringing had been in the usual tradition of Norwegian middle-class respectability, but an engagement to a fellow student had ended in disillusion and some bitterness. The resultant emotional problems were severe. She revolted instinctively against her fiancé's attempt to treat her as a chattel, an obedient and self-effacing little *hausfrau*. By the time she arrived at Dartington, she had come to recognize that the answer lay in her own individuality and creativity. Her experience of the opposite sex had made her cautious; at Dartington she did her best to steer clear of males and concentrate on her work. She was not wholly successful. One married man with whom she worked tried hard to persuade her to have an affair. Another colleague, a homosexual, was in love with the married man. She found it all emotionally exhausting, and looked forward to returning to Norway, where she had secured a job in a textile mill.

So Reich's obvious interest in her was unwelcome. She had no intention of being seduced, especially by a man who already had a mistress. But lack of encouragement made no difference to Reich. "He took it upon himself to find out more about me, visited me at the studio workshop, and told me: 'I've plenty of time. You're soon leaving Dartington Hall and returning to Norway.'" She pointed out that she would be taking up an important job, and would be busy. "You interest me greatly and I am sure I will manage to find you—I will promise you that."

Back in Norway, difficulties arose; work in a large textile mill outside Oslo was strenuous and demanding. She was soon at cross-purposes with the director, who did his best to force her to leave by being unpleasant. She began to develop ulcers, but her native stubbornness made her fight on. She decided that a change of scene might be beneficial—she had been living next to the mill— and took a flat in Oslo. Soon after she moved in there was a knock on her door; Wilhelm Reich stood there. "I told you I'd find you. I would like to find out more about you."

It soon became clear that Reich's motive in seeking her out was not, primarily at least, sexual. He was genuinely attracted by her independent spirit and her obvious need for creative self-expression. This attractive blonde was a latter-day Norah Helmer, determined to stay out of the doll's house and achieve some kind of individual self-fulfillment; and there was too much of the teacher in Reich to be able to resist the opportunity for guidance. But Reich himself also needed someone like Gerd Bergersen, someone completely unconnected with his laboratory work or his left-wing activities, to whom he could talk frankly about his hopes and fears. With her he could be completely natural.

For Gerd, the relationship was perhaps the most fruitful of her life. Here was an intelligent and famous man, a doctor, who enjoyed spending hours talking to her, opening her mind to new ideas. He introduced her to left-wing intellectuals, and she took part in discussions and debates where her sturdy common sense made a considerable impression. He made her aware of larger issues. He took her to see a performance of a play about the Reichstag Fire trial, where right-wingers booed and threw tomatoes at the actors (she saw her own young cousin among them). They discussed Marx and Freud, and Reich was unoffended when she told him that she rejected Freud's view that sex was the most basic of all human drives; he enjoyed encouraging her to think for herself.[4] "He accepted me as a rational human being." Sometimes their disagreements became warm; Reich frequently told her "You are a very good quarreller."

Understandably, Elsa Lindenberg became alarmed at this renewed intimacy between Reich and the girl from Dartington. One day, she called on Gerd and begged her to give Reich up. She said that she, Elsa, needed Reich more than Gerd did, because she was now alone and in exile; Gerd, she said, was a stronger person than she was, and could stand on her own two feet. (This was true enough; she was now making a success of her job as a textile designer and seemed completely independent.) The Norwegian girl found this unreasonable; the sexual element in her relationship with Reich was far less important than the intellectual companionship, and the new world of ideas she was discovering through him. She told Elsa firmly that it was not for her to renounce Reich; it was for Elsa to hold his interest and respect. (In Gerd Bergersen's view, Elsa was not a sufficiently strong personality to hold Reich's interest.) In fact, Gerd had no intention of "taking" Reich. She regarded herself as his "safety valve," as someone with whom he could relax after a hard day's work. And Reich, whose dominant temper was bringing him into conflict with his co-workers, obviously found it a relief to spend his evenings in the flat of a woman who had no part in his political or scientific activities.

Reich's temper outbursts during this period were basically those of an energetic man who objects to being crossed. In an amusing passage, Ilse Reich explains that "some of the Germans, especially those who worked in the publishing house, ran into some difficulties with Reich. Since it was *his* effort and *his* organization on which things ran, he had to have the prerogative to make final decisions. But some of these young socialists insisted on a political way of running the publishing house with equal rights for everyone. When Reich, in his rather forceful way, insisted on his rights, he was called a dictator . . ." For all his socialist views, Reich felt that a man who knows his own mind has a right to give the orders.

But all Reich's Norwegian acquaintances seem to agree that he was unusually relaxed, good-humored and friendly—a mood for which Gerd Bergersen was largely responsible. He enjoyed Norwegian café life, and was often to be found in the Theatre Café, opposite the National Theatre, with friends like Sigurd Hoel, Arnulf Oeverland (Norway's poet laureate), and the painter Edvard Munch. He was as busy as ever, giving lectures to students, talks to workers' groups, even writing verses for the "Red Revue," for which Elsa was doing the choreography. (Ilse Reich comments that his verses were as banal as his music.) There were also social gatherings at various homes, and camping and skiing trips in the mountains. Reich was fond of Ravel's *Bolero,* and one morning told his friends August and Lizzi Lange about a dream in which he had been riding into Berlin on a white horse, while the band played the *Bolero*. Clearly, he was feeling basically optimistic. In March 1937, his fortieth birthday was celebrated with an enormous party that went on for more than twenty-four hours.

And then, once again, Reich made the same mistake he had made in Copenhagen: he published his revolutionary sexual ideas for public consumption. In 1937, he expanded an article called "The Orgasm Reflex" into a book called *Orgasm Reflex, Muscular Posture and Bodily Expression.* Norway was still basically as puritanical as Sweden; it had not changed greatly since the days portrayed in Ibsen's plays, and to publish a book with "orgasm" in its title was a public offense. The Norwegian press, which had so far paid little attention to the Viennese exile, became aware of his presence after a public discussion of Reich's sex economy theories at the Psychiatric Institute, when Professor Ragnar Vogt accused Reich of distorting Malinowski's views for his own purposes.

(Malinowski himself came to Reich's defense in March of the following year.) Other academics joined in the attack, this time on Reich's biological experiments; three professors from Oslo University announced to the press that Reich's claims about bions were preposterous. Professor Thjotta of the Oslo Bacteriological Institute examined some of Reich's bion preparations and took the opportunity to announce to the press that he had found only two well-known microbes. These attacks were enough to make the Norwegian press scent a victim, a balloon that deserved puncturing. Non-Reichian psychoanalysts joined in the attack, and one of them published an article called "Psychoanalytic Quackery" in January 1938. One article by a hostile psychiatrist made the extraordinary statement that one of Reich's bion experiments involved sexual intercourse between two psychopaths.

The Norwegian public, starved of scandal, was thrilled and horrified to read these insinuations. As far as they could make out, Reich's therapeutic methods were an excuse for a nonstop sexual orgy, while his new technique of "vegetotherapy" (a name Reich had invented for his physiological-psychology) was based on masturbation. The publication in 1938 of Reich's book *The Bion* was the signal for a campaign of derision and calumny. One attack was headed: "God Reich Creates Life." By the middle of 1938, articles of this kind were appearing daily; and altogether, more than a hundred attacks on Reich appeared in the Norwegian press.

From the point of view of Reich's coworkers, it was the worst thing that could have happened. Reich made no reply to the attacks, except on two occasions to appeal for fairness, but he brooded grimly.

Gerd Bergersen now became aware of a new side of Reich. The attacks on him shocked and puzzled her; she knew he was not the monster, or madman, the papers made out. Again, Reich used her as a safety valve. He would call her when some particularly bitter attack had appeared, and go to her apartment with the newspaper under his arm to talk until the early hours of the morning. She became aware of him purely as a human being, hunted and tormented. Reich puzzled and worried her by talking—sometimes for hours at a time—about the coming Nazi holocaust. (No one in Norway believed for a moment that the Nazis would at-

tempt to conquer Europe; everyone was too convinced that war
was out of the question for civilized people . . .) Oddly enough,
she was unaware that he was Jewish, and so failed to grasp the
reason for his alarm. It was during this period that Reich began
proposing to her. He said that they would find a remote cabin in
the mountains, and hide there to escape the holocaust. But although she was deeply committed to Reich, even in love with him,
she was unable to take the idea of marriage seriously. It was not
simply that she knew he had already been married (Reich made
no secret about his first wife, and his love for his children), it was
that she felt an instinctive desire for a husband who would be the
father of her children. And "if I married Wilhelm Reich, there
would be no question of children. He would need all the concentration on himself." As Reich's "safety valve," she was the person
he could turn to when he felt miserable and persecuted. And that,
she felt—perhaps wrongly (in view of his later marriage to Ilse
Ollendorff)—ruled out the possibility of children. Besides, unlike
Elsa Lindenberg, she was independent. She was achieving success,
and creative satisfaction, in her profession as a designer. Marrying
Reich would have meant subjugating her career to his.[5]

She is frank enough to mention another reason. Her first love
affair had left her with a distrust of men and of natural sexuality.
She often expressed strong disagreement when Reich talked to her
about Freud, and about his own belief in the fundamental importance of the force of sexuality. Yet in spite of her disagreement,
she was startled by the awakening of her own physical responses.
"The passion of the body was taking charge, and there was something frightening about this. It was destructive." To someone of her
natural independence, it must have seemed a kind of bewitchment.

So she refused, and her rejection must have struck Reich as another betrayal. His "safety valve" had failed him, and he had his
back to the wall, surrounded by enemies. All the old paranoia
came flooding back, and in this case, his bitterness is understandable. He was convinced that he had made some of the most
important discoveries in the history of science, and unqualified
fools were screaming their contempt. In Vienna and Berlin and
Copenhagen, Reich's troubles had been partly his own fault; but
in Norway he had minded his own business and stuck to his work.
He had not even taken part in any political activities, except for

the occasional lecture. And now, suddenly, the whole country was shouting abuse. Reich was not objective enough to see that small countries like Norway develop a positive craving for scandal; it is doubtful if he had ever read Ibsen's *Enemy of the People*. He took it all personally. It was during this period that he overheard someone at a party describe Krishnamurti as Christ-like, and asked: "If he's Christ-like, why hasn't he been murdered?" The old persecution complex was taking a new form. Now it was not merely *he* who was being vilified and slandered; it was *all* men of genius and good will. Such a negative state of mind is hardly conducive to mental health.

Once again, it was clear that it was time to move on, and, once again, one of his supporters was able to suggest a refuge. Dr. Theodore P. Wolfe, of Columbia University, came to Oslo to study with Reich in the midst of the newspaper scandal. Wolfe ran into difficulties with the Norwegian authorities when it was known that he was there to study with Reich. Now he procured Reich a position as associate professor of Medical Psychology at the New School for Social Research in New York, so that Reich was able to obtain an entry visa. When the rumor of his emigration reached the newspapers, the campaign against him died down. But the damage had been done. Reich had turned against many old friends and supporters, including Elsa Lindenberg. She had become independent of Reich, working again as a ballet teacher, and Reich turned his bitterness against her. His outbreaks of temper cowed some colleagues and enraged others, including Nic Waal. He became sullen and suspicious, believing that his colleagues were all waiting to steal his ideas. Philipson, who had been responsible for bringing Reich to Norway, now accused him of being a dictator who could not bear to allow others to go their own way. (Philipson was one of those who regarded Reich's bion research as irrelevant.) Others, like Sigurd Hoel, felt that he was running away and abandoning them as soon as things became difficult. When Reich finally sailed for America in August 1939, he left little but bitterness and resentment behind him.

Yet although he was full of frustration and anger, it would be a mistake to assume, as Cattier does, that he was insane, or even hovering close to it. He was full of rancor towards his opponents, yet still capable of self-control. Before leaving Oslo, he wrote a long and sarcastic letter to his chief enemy, Johann Scharfenberg—the doctor who had accused him of experimenting on sexual psychopaths—in which he thanked Scharfenberg for advancing his work by giving it so much publicity. "A British scholar recently remarked that 'the whole scientific world was now talking about bions,'" he tells Scharfenberg, then goes on to denounce him as a Fascist. Yet after giving full rein to his bitterness and desire to hit back, Reich decided not to send the letter after all. "Leave the idiot be," he scrawled on it, adding: "But the idiots govern the world."

Reich had an invisible ally against despair: his certainty that he had made a great scientific discovery. In this field, at least, he felt his luck was enviable. Even in the final days before he sailed for New York, the discoveries continued. In January 1939, one of his assistants was showing a visitor the bion experiment. Instead of heating earth in a Bunsen flame, she took the wrong container and used sea-sand. Left to "disintegrate" in a solution of potassium chloride and bouillon, this soon produced a bion culture of unusual purity, groups of bions glowing an intense blue color. It proved to be deadly to cancer cells, causing them to spin around as if shot before dying. Reich called them SAPA (sand packet) bions. After examining them for long periods through a microscope, one's eye began to swell. It seemed that the SAPA bions were giving off some powerful radiation. Placed on the skin, the culture would produce an anemic spot. The effect was more powerful on healthy people than on those of low vitality. In a dark room, the sand glowed with blue light. It affected photographic plates and magnetized metal objects. Placed near a wart on Reich's cheek, it caused it to vanish. A pair of rubber gloves became highly charged and caused a strong deflection in an electroscope. There could be no doubt, according to Reich, of the existence of an energy of extreme biological activity.

By the time Reich sailed for America, he was convinced that his twenty-year quest was at an end. He had finally succeeded in isolating the libido, the fundamental energy of life, in the laboratory. Because it was identical with the energy of the sexual orgasm, he decided to call it "orgone energy."

CHAPTER SEVEN

Reich's first year in America was crowded, eventful and, as usual when he found himself in a new environment, triumphantly successful. Those who are interested in astrology will note that Reich was an Aries, a sign associated with the pioneer and explorer. He had the ability to make himself at home, to draw people around him, and to make his environment seethe with activity. Within days of arriving, he had begun to teach at the New School for Social Research in New York, where his course on biological aspects of character formation was so successful that a group of his students, mostly professional people, began to meet at his home for regular seminars. The house was in Forest Hills, Queens, and as soon as the equipment arrived from Oslo, Reich turned his residence into a laboratory and clinic. All he needed now was a female companion. His first wife Annie (whom he had divorced in 1933) was in New York, but through his assistant Gertrude Gaasland he met Ilse Ollendorff at the beginning of October, noted that she was bored in her office job, and married her on Christmas Day, 1939. Within a week she was working as his laboratory assistant, and taking a course in laboratory techniques at the same time.

Reich continued to see Annie, and he and Ilse took the children for Sunday drives and to local beaches, but relations with his first wife had soured; two years later, he would be convinced that it was she who caused him so much trouble with the immigration authorities. With the exception of Malinowski—who was also at the New School—he avoided colleagues from Europe; he even refused to go to chamber music concerts in case he bumped into acquaintances like Rado. He seems to have been determined to make a completely new start.

Reich had reason for optimism about the future; he was convinced that his orgone radiation was a cure for cancer—in which case, it should only be a matter of time before he achieved the kind of world recognition that he felt was his due. He had held a tube containing sea-sand bions against a wart on his cheek; the wart had disappeared. A growth on the left side of his tongue contained T-bacilli; the bions killed the bacilli and made the growth vanish. A woman suffering from pus discharges from the vagina was cured by the insertion of a test tube containing SAPA bions. Orgone energy seemed to be as efficient as radium in destroying cancer, and a great deal safer, since it apparently had no destructive effects on other tissues.

A basic problem remained: how to get the radiation to the site of an internal cancer? In New York that fall, Reich tried injecting cancerous mice with his sea-sand culture. The tumors softened and grew smaller; then grew again. More puzzling still, healthy mice also developed cancers when injected periodically with bions. The explanation was probably that healthy PA bions could break down into T-bacilli, in which case, injection was no answer.

In January 1940, Reich stumbled upon the solution—and failed to recognize it. He had constructed a kind of isolation chamber for his sea-sand culture, to try to stop its energy from dissipating. It was a box with a layer of metal enclosed in a layer of wood, with a lens in the door for observing the bion culture inside. One day when the box was empty and the room was in darkness, Reich observed a dim luminescence through the glass. Assuming that his chamber had been absorbing radiation from the sea-sand, Reich took it to pieces and cleaned it thoroughly. Still the dim glow was visible. He had another box made; still the radiation seemed to be present. In *The Cancer Biopathy,* Reich admits that it was unintelligent of him not to realize what was happening; he explains that the Norwegian smear campaign had eroded his self-confidence.

In July 1940, Reich and Ilse went on a camping trip through New England, using the equipment he had brought from Europe. A spell of wet weather led them to rent a bare log cabin by the side of Mooselookmeguntic Lake in Maine. It was here that Reich made what he later considered the greatest discovery of his life.

One clear, warm night, he was looking at the stars above the lake when he noticed that the stars directly overhead seemed to twinkle less than those on the eastern horizon, near the rising moon. The phenomenon intrigued him. The twinkling of the stars is supposed to be due to the Earth's atmosphere (in the same way, you would expect objects to twinkle, or shimmer, if seen through clear water). But surely, Reich reflected, the twinkling should be the same all over? He directed a wooden tube at the sky, and realized that it was not only the stars that were shimmering; the blue sky in between seemed to be alive. It also seemed to be crossed with threads and points of light. He inserted a magnifying glass in the tube, and it became clearer still. The explanation dawned on him: it was the same flickering flashing that he had observed so frequently in the orgone box. He was looking at orgone energy, free orgone energy in the atmosphere. And this, he felt, explained why the stars on the horizon twinkled more than those overhead; they had more atmosphere—and therefore more orgone energy—to pierce, so to speak. It is true that the same explanation would apply if the twinkling was due to the atmosphere, especially after a hot day; but this would still not explain the flashes of light. No, the answer had to be orgone energy, a free-streaming energy that penetrates all space. This would also explain the meaning of the luminescence in the wood and metal box; it was somehow acting as a greenhouse to capture this atmospheric orgone energy.

But if one layer of wood and metal could trap the energy, would not several layers work even better, just as a greenhouse made of several layers of glass would be hotter than an ordinary greenhouse? And so the orgone accumulator was born, the device that would eventually cost Reich his freedom.

Those who are inclined to dismiss Reich's discovery as self-delusion should at least do him the justice to read the relevant sections in *The Cancer Biopathy*. For this makes it clear that, delusion or not, Reich approached the problem with the objectivity of a true scientist. The first question he asked was whether the flickering was inside his own eye rather than in the atmosphere. When he put the magnifying eyepiece into his tube, it made the phenomenon more distinct; he could make out individual dots and flashes. This suggested that what he was observing was outside his own eye, since the eyepiece would hardly magnify a subjective impression. But how did he know that he was observing biological energy? Could it not be some ordinary electrical phenomenon, since we know that the air is full of static electricity? But if the phenomenon *was* biological, then it should be intensified in the area of living things. And this was just what he observed; there was a greater concentration of the energy around trees and bushes than in the "empty" air. It was stronger over earth than over asphalt. In another attempt to determine whether the energy could be electrical, he built an "accumulator" around a Faraday Cage (a cage of copper mesh that cannot be penetrated by any form of electrical radiation). After sitting for half an hour inside this cage, Reich's eyes adjusted so that he was able to see the blue orgone radiation. It seemed that the cage provided no obstacle to orgone energy.

But was the orgone accumulator the answer to the problem of how to administer the energy to his patients? Reich tried the experiment of placing the cancerous mice inside a small accumulator. The results were spectacular: the fur of the mice became smooth and sleek, the general appearance of illness vanished, and the tumors either stopped growing or began to shrink. But they failed to disappear entirely. The mice's life span was increased, but they still died. Nevertheless, in December 1940, Reich built his first full-size accumulator for human beings, and he quickly observed a result that proved conclusively that *something* was happening. Within a few minutes of being in an accumulator, the temperature of a human being would rise by as much as a whole degree centigrade (1.8 degrees Fahrenheit). This could only mean that something proceeded to happen in the body of the patient, some chemical reaction, so to speak. Reich concluded that the orgone energy was exciting the body's cells, and causing an increase in its rate of metabolism. This in itself was exciting and promising, for an increase in metabolism is the opposite of "energy stasis." The orgone energy was apparently "unfreezing" the body's vital energies, which suggested that it might be a cure for psychological as well as physical illness.

In fact, experiments with cancer patients over the next few months showed remarkable results. Reich treated fifteen cases, all in advanced stages of cancer. Every one showed immediate improvement: pains decreased, general health improved. One patient who had already had a breast removed developed cancers in both legs; within two months, these cancers had vanished, and the patient was still alive and well two years later. A patient suffering from an inoperable cancer of the esophagus, who was unable to swallow, was soon able to eat soft food, and lived for another two years. None of the patients was permanently and totally cured, but all showed undoubted improvement; Reich was convinced that his orgone box would be capable of curing cancer if the disease could be caught at a sufficiently early stage.

Many of the cases confirmed Reich's belief that the basic problems are usually sexual. One female patient began to experience a certain genital excitement in the orgone box, and this was followed by sexual stasis (i.e., loss of feeling in the genitals). Reich concluded that the vital energies were flooding through her system, arousing sexual excitement, and that her natural response was one of fear and repression.

In fact, the greatest problem with the orgone treatment could be compared to what happens when ice melts in spring. The "thaw" could overwhelm the patient. On the physical level, the waste matter from the dissolving cancer could overwhelm the body's waste-disposal system. The psychological problems could be almost as bad. A male patient developed pains in the pelvis that were different from his earlier pains (due to a bladder tumor). For the previous fifteen years the patient had had no sexual outlet—an abstention which Reich was convinced had caused the cancer. Now the orgone energy was dissolving the cancer, and the sexual needs reappeared as pain. Reich advised the patient to masturbate; when he did this, the pain vanished. (Reich found it incomprehensible when a medical journal, commenting on the case, took him to task for encouraging masturbation.) The woman who had developed sexual stasis died before Reich could recommend the masturbation treatment; Reich wrote that it seemed obvious that she died because her "instinct for life" had never functioned normally—that is, her illness was caused by a lack of vital enjoyment.

Reich's account of these months of experiment and discovery hint at some of the immense excitement felt by everyone in the laboratory. After all, if he was correct, and he had no reason to doubt it, then he had made the greatest medical discovery of modern times, a feat of scientific detection that should place him on a level with Einstein. Yet ironically, the professional people who surrounded him were incapable of grasping its significance; they were interested in psychotherapy, and Reich had gone off at a tangent into the realms of biology and physics. Ilse writes: "I think that he felt desperately alone . . . He needed to talk and I was there to listen, but I did not understand the implications of what he talked about, and neither did anyone else around him."

This last sentence may cause some puzzlement. What was so incomprehensible about Reich's discovery of a cancer cure? Why should intelligent psychologists fail to see its significance, even if they *were* more interested in psychotherapy? But the point, of course, is that Reich did not consider his discovery in isolation. As far as he was concerned, it was simply a logical extension of his work with Freud. Libido-blockage caused neurosis, and he had shown that it was a specific sexual energy that was blocked. Now he was convinced that he had isolated this energy in the laboratory, and that its blockage was responsible for cancer as well as neurosis. Freud had already recognized that neurosis can cause many physical illnesses; now Reich was moving towards a new, holistic conception of medicine in which there was no clear dividing line between mental and physical illness. *This* is obviously what his colleagues found hard to take.

It also helps to explain what seems otherwise incomprehensible: why the medical world remained determinedly deaf to Reich's discoveries. It was because Reich wanted to sell his cancer cure as part of a package that involved the whole "genital theory." This almost certainly explains the curious "Einstein episode" that took place at this period. In December 1940, at the time he was constructing his first full-size accumulator, Reich wrote to Enistein to ask for a meeting to explain his new findings. Ronald Clark's biography of Einstein contains a brief and uncharitable account of what happened. "This eccentric, distraught figure

[Reich] seems already to have slipped down the slope towards charlatanry or madness by the time he asked Einstein to investigate his discovery of a specific biologically effective energy which behaves in many respects differently to all that is known about electromagnetic theory." Reich first wrote to Einstein on December 30, 1940, informing him that he had been Freud's assistant at the Polyclinic in Vienna from 1922 until 1930, and was now teaching "experimental and clinical biopsychology" in New York. Anyone other than Einstein would have been warned by the letter, which continued with the admission that he had not reported his discovery to the Academy of Physics because of an "extremely bad experience." But Reich added that it might possibly be used in "the fight against the Fascist pestilence." "Einstein . . . was the last man to resist such a bait . . ."

Reich called on Einstein at his home on Mercer Street, Princeton, on January 13, 1941, and launched into a five-hour explanation of his ideas. The meeting was cordial. Einstein sat in the dark for twenty minutes, and agreed that he could then see the flickering of orgone energy in the atmosphere through the magnifying tube. When Reich told Einstein about the temperature difference caused by an accumulator within ten minutes or so, Einstein was interested, and replied that if this could be confirmed, it would certainly be a bombshell for physics. Reich finally left, promising to send Einstein an accumulator. He did this soon after, and Einstein confirmed that a thermometer inside the box registered 4 degrees centigrade when a thermometer suspended in the room outside only registered 3 degrees. But then, the air above the table top (on which the accumulator was standing) proved to be warmer than that below it, because cool air from the floor cooled the air below the table, while warm air from the ceiling warmed the air above it. Reich replied with a long letter, pointing out that he had obtained the same temperature differences in the open air, so Einstein's explanation could not be the correct one. To this Einstein failed to reply, as he failed to reply to subsequent letters. Three years later, Einstein *did* finally excuse himself, explaining that he had been too busy to give Reich's twenty-five-page letter the attention it required. Reich subsequently wrote a short book about it called *The Einstein Affair,* published by Reich's own press in 1953. By that time, Reich had reached the conclusion that

Einstein's change of heart had been due to a Communist conspiracy against him, a notion that Ilse Reich admits to be almost pure imagination.

The truth is that the Einstein episode encapsulates the problems that were to dog Reich for the rest of his life (which we have already highlighted in the Introduction). It is worth trying to pinpoint their precise nature. According to Reich's version, it is a case of one great scientist failing to acknowledge another, first out of laziness and indifference, then as a result of a sinister plot. This is the view accepted, for example, by David Boadella in his important study of Reich. There is a certain amount to be said for it since, as we have seen, Reich was not a crank or a madman; he had good reason for believing that his orgone energy really existed. Clark's statement that Reich had already "slipped down the slope towards charlatanry or madness" is palpably unfair.

But if we look at the matter from Einstein's point of view, it takes on a different aspect. Einstein was a world-famous scientist—*the* most famous in the world—and as an exile from Nazism, he was the target of daily requests of all kinds from other exiles. Clark writes: "During these wartime years, Einstein was to many scientists the ultimate court of appeal, and this fact drew him, the most amiable of men, into some cantankerous disputes." He goes on to describe one with Felix Ehrenhaft, an old acquaintance who had been forced to leave behind in Vienna a great electromagnet to which he had devoted years of his life. Ehrenhaft became increasingly irritable and assertive, "a capable experimenter who had gradually developed into a kind of swindler," according to Einstein, and "a strongly paranoiac creature." When Einstein disputed some of Ehrenhaft's claims about magnetism, it brought a request to "repair the great injustice done to Felix Ehrenhaft by your attitude towards him and through the unfounded and defamatory reports about his discoveries which you spread . . . ," etc. Einstein was forced to ignore him.

When Einstein received Reich's letter—talking about "bad experiences"—he must have groaned, "Here comes another." But, being a polite and helpful person, he agreed to see Reich. Ilse Reich describes how Reich came home towards midnight, bubbling with excitement. He said that the five-hour conversation with Einstein had been friendly and cordial, and that Einstein had agreed that if Reich was correct about the temperature difference, it would be a "bomb." Reich was already daydreaming of working with Einstein at Princeton; as far as he could see, the battle was almost won.

We know nothing of Einstein's inner reactions, but they are not difficult to infer. He was an overworked man who really cared for nothing but science; he wanted to be left alone to think out his ideas. His own experience with relativity had proved to him that a man with valid ideas will usually be recognized by fellow scientists —even if he has no academic qualifications—provided he goes about it in the right way. Scientists who became paranoid about opposition, and went around demanding apologies and reparation, were probably bad scientists anyway. Emotional self-discipline should be an essential part of the scientist's equipment.

For all his genius, Reich was not a man who possessed much self-discipline or self-criticism. He was, quite simply, a man who liked his own way, and who created havoc when he didn't get it. Ilse tells how, at about this time, Reich and his long-time assistant Gertrude Gaasland began to argue about "work democracy" as they were driving back from the New School. The dispute was prolonged and became acrimonious; Gertrude Gaasland left the next day and went back to Norway. Ilse adds that because of Reich's unforgiving attitude, she was not allowed to keep in touch with her. Reich could behave with the vindictiveness of a thoroughly spoiled child. Einstein could have accepted that assistants are allowed to have their own point of view; but for Reich, to contradict him was a sign of a kind of criminal wrong-headedness. Again, Ilse tells how she accompanied the children, and Eva's husband, on a climb up a mountain; they came back later than expected, and Reich's fury completely spoiled what had been a delightful day. When Reich experienced an emotion, he had no interest in what other people might be feeling; they had to share his point of view.

When a man feels and behaves like this habitually, it begins to show in his face and general demeanor; no amount of charm and enthusiasm can wholly conceal it. It can be seen very plainly in most of the later photographs of Reich, and in some of the early ones, as well: the look of a man too involved in his own subjectivity, in his self-esteem and his need to have his own way. If this was not plain to Einstein within the first half-hour of their conversation, it must have become apparent over the remainder of the afternoon. If Reich had been sensible he would have explained his ideas in half an hour, left a small orgone box for Einstein to try out, and gone away; instead, he talked for five hours. (From what we know of Reich, it is doubtful whether Einstein said much.) The eagerness with which Einstein plunged on the temperature difference phenomenon suggests the relief of a man who is at last able to perceive something he can grasp in a sea of bewildering generalities. Being asked to sit in the dark and peer through a tube at some "flickering" in the air must also have struck him as an unnecessary trial of his patience. At one point, he seems to have shown a flicker of humor when Reich told him that he was a psychologist as well as a physicist, and Einstein asked, "What else do you do?" His emotion when Reich finally took his leave must have been one of immense relief. And Reich, who had never been given to paying attention to other people's feelings—in spite of his training in "character analysis"—left in a state of effervescent optimism, which was basically as exaggerated and unreal as his more normal state of suspicion.

So, in fact, Clark has a grain of truth when he talks about Reich's slide into charlatanry and madness; at least, this is undoubtedly the way it struck Einstein. We are able to take a more balanced view because we can see that Reich's orgone experiments were not the delusions of a madman; even if we are sceptical about orgone energy, we can at least agree that it deserved thorough investigation. Yet there is no point in allowing this recognition to push us too far in the other direction. Reich *was* a misunderstood genius, but he was not a persecuted genius. If he was persecuted at all, it was not because of his genius, but because of a determined refusal to acquire any self-discipline or self-knowledge.

But what of the *objective* content of his ideas? Should this not have entitled him to recognition, or at least, to an unprejudiced examination of his claims? Even here, the answer cannot be an unqualified affirmative; and the reason takes us to the very heart of the "Reich problem." In his scientific work, Reich revealed the same peculiar blind spots as in his personal life. That is to say, when he became convinced by an idea, it became a matter of personal loyalty, or prejudice; his emotional commitment to it made

him incapable of looking at it objectively and, if necessary, modi-
fying it. In a letter to Hitschmann in 1942, Reich talks about his
loyalty to "Freud's good old doctrines," as if he and Hitschmann
were members of a students' guild, or political party, toasting one
another with steins of beer.

We have already seen how Freud himself virtually came to
abandon the sexual theory in its most dogmatic form in *Civilization and Its Discontents*; he did so because Reich's theory that
all neurosis is genital in origin made him aware of its absurdity.
Now, as Reich's orgone research brought new insights, Reich himself was coming close to the point where he must have recognized
that "Freud's good old doctrines" were an intellectual straitjacket.
Yet he was incapable of the admission that perhaps his "genital
theory" was a little *too* rigid, a little too wholesale.

The problem becomes clear if we look at Reich's development
since the Freudian days. He began by believing that the "libido,"
the life force, would one day be as well understood as electricity.
This already smacks of reductionism—like the belief of Mary Shelley's Dr. Frankenstein that he could animate his monster with
some electrical machine. Reich was inclined to treat consciousness, and its corollary, free will, as a by-product of this energy.

His first step towards pinning down the life energy involved a
machine to measure skin resistance; when he discovered "bions"
in 1936, he was convinced that these were the basic units of this
"bioelectricity." In due course, he went on to develop the orgone
accumulator, which enabled him to capture this energy in its free
form.

But he was still convinced that neurosis was caused by a blockage of orgasm-energy, and that a person without such a blockage
is, ipso facto, psychologically healthy. Now he had his energy on
tap, so to speak, what could he *do* with it? Open a vein and pour
it in through a funnel? Develop an orgone cream that could be
rubbed on the genitals? Obviously not: Reich's answer sounds anticlimactic; people can sit in the accumulator to improve their general health.

Now, at last, he is face-to-face with something he had avoided
all his life: the recognition that psychological illness is basically
psychic in nature, that its root lies in the mind, not in blocked sex-

ual energies (which, by definition, belong to the region of the genitals). He noted, for example, that patients with low vitality took longer to respond to the orgone energy, as if they needed to be "charged up" before they were capable of response. That, of course, could be interpreted mechanistically, but then, the more "vital" patients were also able to cope better with the "thaw" effect produced by the orgone accumulator. If orgone energy *was* vital energy, there should be no such distinction; an increase in orgone energy should mean an increase in vitality. The same point emerges from Reich's comment on the patient who died after experiencing sexual stasis—that her instinct for life had never functioned correctly, and that her vital system "gave up for want of joy in life." Reich has recognized that there *is* another factor here: what he calls "joy in life." This joy, it seems, is quite independent of the orgone energy absorbed from the accumulator; it resides in the patient's *attitude to life*. And "attitude" must be defined entirely in mental terms; it is what Husserl called an "intention."

Thus Reich has come very close to Frankl's recognition that the vital factor in psychological health is *purpose*. It would be easy to write: "the patient died because her 'instinct for life' had never functioned correctly, and her vital system gave up for want of purpose in life." But Reich's hand would have declined to write the word. "Joy in life" can be used as a loose synonym for sexual release, "genital potency"; but the word "purpose" remains stubbornly unreducible. To recognize the element of purpose would have been an admission that sexual blockage *is an effect, not a cause*. And for Reich, sex had to be the cause, the prime mover. Therefore he found another explanation for the anomaly; some patients, he explains, arrive with a pronounced *libido deficiency*—a convenient synonym for "joy in life." This explains the difference between vital and nonvital patients. He fails to see that his explanation is circular. The libido *is* orgone energy, and this is precisely what the accumulator provides. So it should make no difference whether the patient suffers from "pronounced libido deficiency."

A Reichian might object that, even if this were so, it would make no difference to the importance of Reich's discovery of orgone energy, but this is not true. Reich's attitude effectively blocked any further development, and left him trapped in this peculiarly illogical vicious circle. Neurosis is due to blocked orgone energy. But can the accumulator cure neurosis? No, because it also exists on a characterological level, in the form of repressions. And the nature of these repressions? Sexual, always and invariably. So the "good old Freudian doctrine" remained to serve as a straitjacket for the new discoveries about orgone energy. In the *International Journal of Sex-Economy and Orgone Research,* published in the 1940s, the body of Reichian philosophy remains as rigid and doctrinaire as ever; there is an implication that if you accept one part, you must accept the lot. Reich's ideas form a single corpus, like those of Karl Marx. Anyone who might feel inclined to accept the idea of muscular therapy—which worked so spectacularly for Orson Bean—is rebuked for "wrong attitudes." ". . . the vegetative energies are released from their anchoring in the musculature not by work on the muscular tensions, in any mechanical way, but by the systematic analysis of the character attitudes which express themselves in—or rather, are identical with —muscular attitudes which, in their totality, form the muscular armour."[1] But in the case of Orson Bean, we have seen that "vegetotherapy" *did* amount to "work" on the muscles, not to character analysis. For Reich, it had become an article of dogma that psychological problems always express themselves in muscular armor, just as it was essential to Freud to believe that neurosis is always due to childhood sexual traumas. In the same way, it was esssential to believe that mental health was closely connected with the sexual orgasm. When an unmarried nursery school teacher explained that she had never masturbated, although she regards herself as a happy and normal person, the standard Reichian answer came back like a packet of cigarettes from a slot machine: she must be frigid, due to repressed memories of infantile masturbation; any normal individual has the desire to masturbate if normal sexual expression is denied. If she regards herself as happy, she must be mistaken . . . Reich found it impossible to accept that the sense of purpose could express itself on any level but the sexual one.

All this makes it clear why Reich continued to encounter so many difficulties in getting others to take his discoveries seriously. Many psychiatrists might have found his muscular therapy useful; many cancer specialists might have been interested in the orgone accumulator; many biologists might have been intrigued by his "bions"; but anyone who wanted to learn more about these subjects and opened a copy of the *Orgone Journal* would find them inextricably bound up with Reich's belief in the genital theory, muscular armor, emotional plague, and Communist conspiracies. Reich was like a religious prophet who insists that every one of his "revelations" is of equal value. Again and again, he challenges scientists to examine his findings without prejudice; but the whole tone of the *International Journal of Sex-Economy* seems calculated to arouse prejudice; at times it sounds like the magazine of an odd religious organization, directed specifically at the faithful. It was not necessary to be suffering from emotional plague to find the whole thing rather distasteful.

Reich repeated the mistake by setting up his own Orgone Institute Press, instead of trying to persuade some respectable commercial publisher to bring out *The Function of the Orgasm* or *Character Analysis*. After his death in 1939, Freud had almost been canonized in America; as a Freud disciple, Reich would have had no difficulty in publishing his more "orthodox" works through the usual channels. Instead, his own press brought out *The Function of the Orgasm* under the title *The Discovery of the Orgone, Volume One*—the kind of miscalculation that becomes so frequent in his later life that it begins to look like a disguised suicidal urge.

Reich's obsessive character made him increasingly difficult to deal with—the desertion of Gertrude Gaasland was only one symptom of the problem. Ilse writes: "Reich was a hard taskmaster . . . At times I had the feeling that our whole life was ruled by the stop watch." The neighbors objected to the rats in Reich's basement; so they were forced to change houses. When war broke out in December 1941, Reich was arrested as an enemy alien and taken to Ellis Island; the reason was almost certainly his Communist past. He was released just over three weeks later, after threatening a hunger strike. In a letter to Malinowski—who had since moved to Yale—he accuses his first wife of being behind the arrest, forgetting that his own political past was sufficient explanation. It was shortly after this, in the spring of 1941, that Reich declined the advice of his old Vienna colleague, Dr. Walter Briehl, to take the New York State medical licensing examination, which would have enabled him to practice medicine; it might have saved Reich a great deal of trouble later. Ilse Reich records that Briehl broke

with Reich because of his "disappointment in not finding in Reich
the same person he had known in Vienna." This seems to be an
admission of the deterioration which she denies elsewhere in the
biography. She admits that Reich had become much more formal
than in his Scandinavian days—female assistants were always
addressed as "Miss So-and-so," by their maiden names, and the
males were called by their surnames. It was Reich's own way of
armoring himself against a world that he felt increasingly hostile.

Yet in many ways, life was easier than it had ever been before.
Reich might be ignored by the medical establishment, but he had
plenty of pupils eager to learn about vegetotherapy, and even
about the use of orgone accumulators. He was well paid, and the
money was used to purchase a cabin on Mooselookmeguntic Lake
in the summer of 1941, and then, in the following year, an abandoned farm on Dodge Pond (in the same area near Rangely,
Maine) which was to become his new laboratory; he called it Orgonon. Prices were reasonable; Ilse Reich mentions that they
bought 280 acres of land for about $2,000. In spite of his convic-
tion that the world sets out to destroy its great men, Reich was
becoming prosperous and successful.

Advances in his orgone research were slow but encouraging. In
December 1943, an experiment with a photographic plate convinced Reich that orgone energy could be "photographed." The
plate was kept close to a bion sample for several days, then briefly
exposed to light before being developed; a black patch was visible
in its center. It seemed that orgone energy repelled light. Reich
tried taking an x-ray photograph of his two hands, held a few
inches apart, and it showed a foggy patch between the two palms.
Reich was convinced that he could actually feel the orgone energy
flowing between the hands when they were moved gently towards
one another. In effect, he was rediscovering the odic force of von
Reichenbach and Kilner's "human aura," but the thought would
certainly not have given him any pleasure—he would probably
have associated both of them with "occultism."

Yet his own conclusions were steadily taking him further away
from orthodox science. The most startling of these was the result
of an accidental discovery in December 1944. An earth-water solution (made by boiling earth, then filtering off the water) was left
outside for three weeks in freezing weather. When it thawed,

Reich noticed that it contained a number of brown flakes. He was about to throw the sample away, assuming it had been contaminated, when he decided it might be worthwhile to examine it under a microscope. What he saw excited him. The flakes were undoubtedly some form of matter which contained clusters of bions. Reich came to the breathtaking conclusion that the bions in the earth-water had been made to "cluster" by freezing, and in so doing had created solid matter. In short, bions had been created in the earth-water solution through the inter-reaction of its molecules with orgone energy, and then these bions had coagulated under the freezing process to form solid matter. He states his conclusion—in the book *Ether, God and Devil*—that "primary matter originated in the cosmos, and the process of matter formation apparently continues uninterruptedly." Understandably, he regarded this experiment—which he called Experiment XX—as the most crucial he ever performed. In his book on Reich, David Boadella describes how he and A. McDonald repeated the whole experiment, freezing sterile earth-water in tubes, then allowing them to thaw slowly; they also observed the "smooth, plasmatic and well defined forms," and the clusters of bions with a blue glimmer. Boadella also mentions that the experiment was repeated by the well-known biologist Bernard Grad, who not only observed the flakes, but photographed them. If there is some fundamental error, either in Reich's postulates or in his experimental method, it is difficult to see what it is.

Ilse Reich's account of life at Orgonon makes it sound idyllic. In April 1944, their son Peter was born; Reich suddenly became fascinated by the problems of child upbringing. In the month after Peter's birth he wrote to Neill: "I assure you that after twenty-five years of intensive and extensive psychiatric work, I am discovering for the first time . . . the real nature of the newborn baby . . . I would never have guessed how little we know about newborn babies . . ." Reich believed that a child should be brought up with the maximum of love, freedom, and self-determination. His ideas have since become so much a part of our culture—through the writings of child psychologists and the authors of popular books on child care—that few people are aware that Reich deserves the credit for formulating these attitudes. This was an area where the influence of Freud's ideas was wholly beneficial. If neuroses can be traced back to childhood traumas, then the best way to prevent neuroses is to prevent the traumas. Since there is a flow of orgone energy between mother and child, body contact is of prime importance in the "prophylaxis" of traumas. The idea now sounds so obvious that it seems hardly worth stating; most mothers feel instinctively that there is a flow of energy between themselves and the baby. But even as recently as 1944, Victorian ideas of child rearing were still prevalent: babies should be allowed to cry if there is nothing obviously wrong with them, that they should be replaced in the cot or stroller as soon as feeding is over; they should receive toilet training and other forms of discipline from the earliest possible age. Reich's ideas, developed by his students and coworkers (like Lucy Bellamy Dennison) created a quiet revolution in the field of baby care and upbringing. His work in this field may one day be regarded as his most solid and undeniable achievement.

With the end of the war in 1945, there were again contacts with the international community—particularly with old friends from Scandinavia. Reich was now forty-eight years old, and his reputation was spreading slowly but steadily. It was necessary to build a new laboratory at Orgonon to house the increasing body of students. A group had been formed in England to study Reich's work with orgone energy, and in the summer of 1946 they sent a student to work with Reich. A seminar on newborn children in the fall of 1945 was attended by educators, social workers, and pediatricians. Reich had every reason to feel pleased with the course of his life and the progress of his ideas. Yet it was in 1945 that he wrote the bad-tempered and (at times) querulous book called *Listen, Little Man!*, a tirade against the "small men" of the world, with the clear implication that Reich was one of the great. "After thus having driven the great man into loneliness, you forgot what you did to him. All you did was to utter other nonsense, to commit another little meanness, to administer another deep hurt. You forget. But it is of the nature of the great men not to forget, but also not to take revenge, but instead to try to UNDERSTAND WHY YOU ACT SO SHABBILY . . ." And so on, for over a hundred pages. It is true that when Reich wrote the book, he had no thought of publication; but this is hardly relevant.[2] What is so surprising is

198 The Quest for Wilhelm Reich

that a man who had apparently achieved so much success and security in his newly adopted country should feel the need to pour out so much bile. What is even more disturbing is that the book is so fundamentally aimless. Swift and Voltaire felt the same contempt for human stupidity and cruelty, but their books were deliberately *aimed,* like arrows, at their target. Swift wrote *Gulliver's Travels* as a story because he wanted to lure his readers into accepting it as a harmless fable; the same is true of Voltaire's short novels like *Zadig* and *Candide.* But Reich could hardly hope for readers who would acknowledge that they were "little men" and buy the book to see what he said about them. There are moments when Reich becomes conscious of this appalling negativity, and attempts to disguise it: "Stop a minute, Little Man. I do not want to belittle you, I only want to show you why . . . you have not been able to get freedom or hold it." But the tone soon switches back to choleric denunciation: "But you are a little, cowardly thief. You are clever but, being psychically constipated, you are unable to create . . ."

In Reich's favor, it should be acknowledged that there is a great deal of sense in the book. "Your Napoleon, this little man with the gold braid . . . is displayed in your bookshops in large golden letters, but my Kepler, who foresaw your cosmic origin, cannot be found in any bookstore. That's why you don't get out of the morass, Little Man." But such comments only emphasize the overall tone of negativeness. When Reich tells the Little Man passionately that "only you yourself can be your liberator," it is suddenly very clear that he, Reich, is quite incapable of being *his* own liberator. This is not a free man. It is a man who has become the victim of all that is worst about himself: bile, envy, hatred, self-righteousness, self-pity, self-aggrandizement, all adding up to self-destructiveness.

To read *Listen, Little Man!* after the earlier books is to realize that it was a turning point in Reich's life. As long ago as 1941, he had invented the term "emotional plague" to describe the negative, aggressive side of human nature that tries to conceal itself under various respectable disguises. At that stage, it was basically a synonym for mass hysteria, and he insisted that it had no more "defamatory connotation" than any other form of mental illness. As time went by, it became increasingly a term of abuse, a blanket explanation of any opposition his work aroused. And although the term does not appear in *Listen, Little Man!*, it is clear that the change from the descriptive to the pejorative has taken place in Reich's mind, and that the book is really a denunciation of emotional plague. It is as if, where his mental balance was concerned, Reich had passed a point of no return. The "yang" side of the equation—the purely personal—had finally overbalanced the "yin," the element that Keats called negative capability. When he tells the Little Man: "Your life will be good and secure . . . when the mood of Beethoven or Bach will be the mood of your existence," he makes us aware that *this* is what has gone wrong with his own existence: it will never again be dominated by the mood of Beethoven or Bach, only by a rankling sense of injustice and persecution. Reich himself has fallen victim to the emotional plague.

In the fall of 1946, Ola Raknes visited Reich, and spent the month of September working at Orgonon; then he took a house close to Reich's Forest Hills laboratory in Queens, where he lived for another three months. Apart from Neill (who was to visit Reich in the following year), Raknes was one of the few men Reich trusted and accepted without reservation. If Raknes found Reich changed since the Oslo days, he is too loyal to say so in the chapter on "Reich as I knew him" in his book *Wilhelm Reich and Orgonomy*. What he *does* say is that Reich "liked to trust the people he liked and, on the other [hand], was too prone to distrust them as soon as they disappointed him in any way. That is certainly one reason why so many of his pupils and even friends came to desert him . . ."

It was undoubtedly Reich's increasing tendency to react with distrust and suspicion that triggered the "persecution" that was finally to bring about his downfall.

What happened was that, sometime in the fall of 1946, a woman telephoned Reich at his Queens house, and told him that she was calling him at the request of a West Coast friend. Reich invited her out to Queens. She was a forty-year-old writer and journalist named Mildred Edie Brady, the wife of a professor of Economics at the University of California. It was while working as an industrial analyst, studying the beer industry, that Mrs. Brady became interested in the subject of alcoholism, and read various books on psychoanalysis, including some of Reich's. A colleague who was suffering from terminal cancer renewed her interest in Reich's cancer therapy (which she regarded as "crack-pot nonsense"), and she decided to get an interview with Reich.

Once in his office, she mentioned that she was a writer who was interested in his ideas, and said that she would like to write an article about him. Reich's reaction to this expression of sympathetic interest was to tell her that he made a practice of refusing interviews to writers, and that he would prefer it if she wrote nothing. Mrs. Brady was understandably irritated by this high-handed attitude; she went ahead and wrote two articles anyway. Their tone was thoroughly hostile.

Reich was later to take the view that it was his own courtesy and restraint that were to blame for the attacks; he should have thrown her out the moment she admitted to being a writer. This view has been echoed by dedicated Reichians like Jerome Greenfield (in his book *Wilhelm Reich Vs. the U.S.A.*), yet it is plainly nonsensical. The two articles were not based on the "interview" (which Reich refused to give) but on Reich's published work, available in abundance from the Orgone Institute Press. There is no reason to disbelieve Mildred Brady's assurance to Reich that she felt his work to be significant, and that this was why she wanted to write about him. It is true that she had described his cancer therapy as "crack-pot," but she was probably ready to be enlightened and convinced. Whether Mildred Brady would have become a convinced Reichian is open to question, but at worst her criticism might have been tempered with some friendly regard, and the admission that Reich was a sincere and dedicated scientist. As it was, Reich's snub turned her against him, determined to get back at him. The article that appeared in the April 1947 issue of *Harper's* was entitled "The New Cult of Sex and Anarchy," and it was followed by an equally astringent piece in *The New Republic* called "The Strange Case of Wilhelm Reich." Reich's typical, and indignant, reaction was that "she turned her normal, natural desire into mud, which she then throws into my decent face." He preferred to believe that it was her genital frustration, rather than his own rudeness, that provoked the hostility.

Having decided that Reich was a man who deserved taking

down a peg or two, it was not difficult for Mrs. Brady to work up
an effective case against him. To a woman of her background and
training, the whole notion of sexual freedom and orgastic potency
would arouse a certain innate resistance. Even if, like many Americans, she regarded Freud as a great medical innovator, she might
still feel that Reich was carrying his theories to absurd extremes—
as Freud himself had felt. Consequently, Reich was a sitting target
for an attack that linked his theories of sexual freedom with the
new postwar bohemianism of the San Francisco Bay area—the first
stirring of the Beat Generation. Jerome Greenfield admits that this
article is in many ways perceptive.

The second article did damage. Basically an accurate account of
Reich's career and his theory of character armor, it contained the
statement that Reich believed that his accumulator could produce
orgastic potency in people who used it. In retrospect, this distor-
tion also sounds trivial enough. Reich *did* believe that the accumulator could charge the blood with vital energy; so it probably
would increase most people's orgastic potency, assuming that
there were no deep-seated inhibitions and repressions. But the
distinction is important. Reich was not trying to hawk his orgone
accumulators as a cure-all for cancer and impotence. At most, he
was claiming a tonic effect.

The avalanche that followed these first two well-aimed boulders
was, admittedly, a tragedy for Reich and his ideas, but it can
hardly be represented as an expression of "emotional plague."
The Norwegian débâcle will bear this explanation because Oslo
was basically an overgrown provincial town, whose ideas had
hardly changed since the nineteenth century. But the America of
1947 could hardly be accused of nineteenth-century puritanism.
The problem here was that Reich looked a little too much like
that well-known American phenomenon, the false messiah or
prophet, and his sexual ideas bore a remarkable resemblance to
those of John Humphrey Noyes, founder of the Oneida Community. Reich had set himself up on his own estate in Maine—
Mildred Brady stated, inaccurately, that he had named a town Organon—and published his books and the *Orgone Journal* on his
own private press. He was surrounded by disciples who believed
that his ideas would be the salvation of modern civilization. He

had announced his discovery of an unknown cosmic energy, which could be captured in boxes. His sexual ideas sounded as if they were an excuse for orgies. He was an authoritarian who was intensely, neurotically, touchy about criticism. He lacked medical qualifications to practice in America, yet he was firmly convinced that his own heterodox ideas were right, and that the rest of the medical profession was hopelessly misguided. He *sounded* like a crank and a false messiah, and it was partly his own fault for setting up an organization that looked like a crank religious movement. In short, it is unnecessary to call upon the concept of emotional plague to explain why Reich now found himself the object of widespread ridicule and hostility.

On August 27, 1947, the Food and Drug Administration sent an investigator named Charles Wood to interview Reich at Orgonon. This time, Reich was co-operative and fairly cordial; he did his best to explain his concept of orgone energy, and how the accumulator worked. Wood seemed friendly and open-minded. He went on to the nearby workshop at Oquossoc, where the accumulators were built by a woman named Clista Templeton. Reich had treated her father—a woodsman and carpenter—for cancer of the prostate in 1941, and had prolonged his life for more than two years beyond the medical prognosis. He had encouraged Templeton to build himself an accumulator which he used in his own home; the results were so satisfactory that Reich decided that this home use of accumulators should be extended. By August 1947, there were about 170 large accumulators in existence, and Reich was renting them for $10 a month, bringing in something in excess of $20,000 a year. The accumulators were sold for $225, a reasonable sum considering the cost of manufacture. In view of the running cost of the two laboratories at Forest Hills and Orgonon, $20,000 a year could not be regarded as an excessive profit.

For various reasons, Clista Templeton herself had ceased to be happy with the Reich organization—probably, like so many co-workers, she found Reich's despotic temper a strain. She and the FDA agent fell in love, and she married him three months later. The result was that the FDA gained access to a great deal of information about Orgonon and the accumulators, but none of this in any way compromised Reich, since none of his activities could be considered fraudulent or criminal.

In fact, Reich had very little to worry about. There was no way in which the FDA could stop his work with accumulators. They could not even prevent him from renting them or selling them provided he made no false claims about them. All they *could* do, if the accumulators were judged to be worthless, was to prevent him from shipping them across state lines. But again, there was nothing to prevent Reich from having them built in individual states and sold there. What *could* be said, even at this early stage, was that unless Reich could succeed in proving the existence of orgone energy—or the efficacy of the accumulators—he would probably have to stop sending them across state lines, but since most of the users were in one state, New York, this should not raise any insoluble problems.

Mildred Brady's first article had aroused the suspicion that Reich was operating some kind of a sexual racket—perhaps even a vice ring—but the FDA's attempts to follow up this lead soon came to nothing. A female patient who was supposed to have been masturbated at Orgonon told the investigators that she had never been there, and the medical practitioner who had reported the story had to admit that it was only hearsay. There were plenty of psychiatrists who were willing to state their opinion that Reich's latest ideas were worthless, and that Reich himself was psychotic, but their testimony could not influence the practical course of the investigation. Nevertheless, the side effects were unpleasant. Two doctors who practiced Reichian techniques were dismissed without reason from the New Jersey State Hospital, and the townspeople of Rangeley became distinctly hostile to Reich and Orgonon. All this was reprehensible, but understandable. Reich claimed to be a scientist who had made an epoch-making discovery. Then why had he not done what scientists have always done: published it to the world, and allowed other scientists a chance to judge it, instead of setting up a private institute to exploit it? Reich addresses himself to this question towards the end of *The Cancer Biopathy*—written at the time the investigation was beginning—and gives an illogical and unconvincing answer: that no "social institution" had offered to finance orgone research, while in Scandinavia he had had to cope with the irrationality of petty officials. But then, Reich could hardly be expected to give the true reason: that he was suspicious to the point of paranoia, and unable to trust anyone.

In spite of the cloud hanging over Orgonon, its activities continued normally. The number of students continued to increase, and the foundations of an observatory were laid—Reich's interest in cosmology was increasing. He purchased a Geiger counter, and discovered that it was sensitive to orgone energy, although it had to be "saturated" for some months before it would work. In the summer of 1948, an "orgonomic convention" was held at Orgonon, attended by thirty-five doctors and educators, including Neill and Raknes. When Dr. Hoppe of Israel was detained by the Immigration and Naturalization Service for five days, Reich reacted with fury, sending cables protesting "persecution" to various authorities. To a young assistant he kept repeating: "This is research. He cures their cancers and they throw him in jail." And, predictably, Reich addressed the conference on the subject of emotional plague. He also decided to publish *Listen, Little Man!* Significantly, he was encouraged by various followers to whom he showed it. No one seems to have had the honesty, or the sense, to advise him to put it on the shelf. In due course, it was quoted with telling effect in Martin Gardner's attack on Reich in *Fads and Fallacies*.

Ilse Reich mentions that, in spite of the crowds at Orgonon that summer, Reich was withdrawn, taking part in few social activities. He also forbade her to go with the others to the weekly square dances in the village, claiming that too much familiarity with trainees would lead to contempt. The true reason was probably his violent and irrational jealousy—she mentions that when she came back from a trip to Europe in the previous year, Reich had subjected her to a third degree to make sure she had remained faithful, although he had had an affair in her absence.

To counter the increasing attacks from the American Psychiatric Association, a group of twenty-three Reichian doctors formed the American Association for Medical Orgonomy. In a letter to Neill, Ilse reported that Reich's books continued to sell well, and that an increasing number of young psychiatrists were attending his lectures. The attacks were depressing, yet it seemed clear that the enemy was failing to destroy Reich's influence and reputation. In fact, the attacks were having the opposite effect, and arousing the interest of people in search of new ideas.

With a little common sense and patience, Reich could have been certain of ultimate victory. Unfortunately, these were qualities that he had long ceased to possess.

CHAPTER
EIGHT

It says a great deal for Reich's incredible capacity to spawn ideas that the last phase of his life is as fascinating and controversial as anything that had gone before.

Where Reich was concerned, the most interesting event of 1947 was not the beginning of the campaign against his work, but the discovery that a Geiger counter—a machine for detecting radiation or cosmic rays—would respond to orgone energy. This suggested that orgone energy could exert *force,* like atomic energy. But unlike atomic energy, this was a living force, the force that is responsible for the locomotion of living organisms.

In 1947, the entire civilized world was much preoccupied with the problem of atomic energy. The destruction of Hiroshima and Nagasaki had made its murderous qualities apparent, but could it also be used in the service of civilization? In 1946, the Americans proposed the creation of an international authority for the development of atomic energy, but flatly declined to destroy their own nuclear stockpile. In fact, America started an extensive testing program of atomic weapons at Bikini Atoll in the Pacific. The Cold War began in earnest; in 1948, the Russians blockaded West

Berlin; in 1949, they announced their own first successful test of
an atom bomb. A few months later, in January 1950, Klaus
Fuchs revealed that he had been betraying American atomic secrets to the Russians since 1945.

Most intellectuals were pessimistic about the future of atomic
energy; Reich's theory of emotional plague made him more so
than most. Inevitably, he found himself wondering whether, in the
event of a nuclear war, orgone energy could be used to counteract
radiation sickness. This is why, in mid-December 1950, he applied
to the Atomic Energy Commission at Oak Ridge, Tennessee, for a
small quantity of radioactive Phosphorus-32. When this failed to
arrive, he ordered two milligrams of radium from a private laboratory; this arrived on January 5, 1951, in two small lead con-
tainers. One of these was placed in a garage on the other side of
the hill, to act as a check; the other was placed in an orgone accumulator in a room that was itself an accumulator.

Reich was hoping that the orgone energy would neutralize the
atomic radiation. The reverse happened. The Geiger counter
began to register such high levels that the mechanism jammed. Yet
the radium itself was not giving off more energy, for when it was
tested outside its count became normal.

The laboratory workers, including Elsworth Baker, and Ilse and
Eva Reich, quickly began to feel the unpleasant effects. There was
a salty feeling on the tongue, nausea, and dizziness; some experienced hot and cold shivers. When the radium was taken out of the
room, the room itself continued to register high levels of radiation.

Nevertheless, the experiment continued. Reich wanted to ex-
pose mice to the radiation, then see if they could be cured by orgone energy. The radium was placed in the orgone room for an
hour every day—although no longer in its accumulator—and the
mice were exposed to it. On January 11, Ilse Reich found that
most of the mice were dead. Dissection revealed that they were
suffering from radiation sickness. Reich should have been warned;
but he wanted to continue the tests. The following day, the radium
was once again placed in the room, this time inside the accumulator. The effect was immediate. Through the windows of the room,
bluish clouds could be seen; while the people outside experienced
the dizziness and nausea even at a distance of ninety yards. After
only half an hour, the radium was removed; but the damage had

been done. Everyone was ill. Peter Reich had to be sent away. Some female assistants felt too ill and depressed to remain at Orgonon. Eva Reich made the mistake of placing her head inside an accumulator which had been in the orgone room, and went into a semicomatose state in which her breathing became labored and her pulse became faint. For two hours it looked as if she might die; then she began to recover. She also had to leave.

The Oranur (Orgone antinuclear) experiment also produced long-term emotional depression. Since the FDA was at this time intensifying its pressure on Reich, the atmosphere at Orgonon became unbearable. Ilse became so ill at the end of March that she collapsed and had to have an operation. She blames the Oranur experiment and its effect on Reich's moods for her final break with Reich, which was to occur in 1954. Reich himself, who had been suffering from hypertension for the past few years, had a heart attack the following October, and was in bed for six weeks.

What, then, had happened? It seemed clear that the orgone accumulator had not increased the atomic radiation, a scientific impossibility, since radium decays at a fixed rate. Then how could Eva Reich have contracted severe radiation sickness? The logical inference was that the atomic radiation had somehow caused the orgone energy to change its nature, and become negative and dangerous, as healthy bions can deteriorate into T-bacilli. Reich labeled this negative energy DOR, "deadly orgone radiation." It was to lead him increasingly to take the view that there is a negative principle in the universe, the equivalent of the Devil in the Christian religion. This has provided sceptics with some effective ammunition, since it seems to show that Reich was all along a cryptoreligious crank, yet, on the basis of the Oranur experiment, it is difficult to see how Reich could have reached any other conclusion. Neither is it possible to agree with Martin Gardner that the Oranur experiment was a "comic opera"—with the implication that all that went wrong was due to incompetence in handling radioactive material. A half-milligram of radium (i.e., a two-thousandth part of a gram) cannot, under normal circumstances, cause radiation sickness at a distance of ninety yards. Even allowing that Reich and his assistants may have been as incompetent as Gilbert and Sullivan's Sorcerer, there can still be no possible explanation of what happened in the Oranur experiment unless we accept Reich's premise that the normal effect was somehow *amplified* beyond normal possibility.

Reich's assumption that he had caused some kind of chain reaction seems to be supported by an item in *The New York Times* of February 3, 1951, three weeks after the experiment; it reported that there was an unusually high level of radiation in an area with a 300- to 600-mile radius, *with its center in Rangeley*. The explanation offered is that atomic tests had taken place in Nevada in the previous week. But since these took place more than two thousand miles away from Rangeley, this seems unlikely.

Reich also observed, in the months following the experiment, that the atmosphere in the area became dull and heavy. There were immobile black clouds in the sky; the vegetation became limp; human beings and animals lost their vitality and felt tired and depressed. What had happened, Reich decided, was that the "deadly orgone radiation" had affected the normal atmospheric orgone, producing a kind of spreading rot, like bacteria. The implications were alarming, suggesting that nuclear radiation may be far more dangerous than was generally realized—the danger lying not so much in the radiation itself as on the effect it produces on orgone energy. In effect, according to Reich, the interaction produces a kind of poisonous gas. This is as true of "the peaceful use of atomic energy" as of atom bomb tests. It can also be produced by television sets, fluorescent lights, and even luminous watches.

As usual, Reich succeeded in using these negative results as the basis for further discovery. The problem was to deactivate the polluted atmosphere. His solution was the "cloudbuster," his most controversial and bizarre invention.

In 1942, Reich had observed that when hollow metal tubes—presumably those used to manufacture "orgonoscopes"—were pointed at the surface of Mooselookmeguntic Lake, they seemed to influence the motion of the waves. He stored the observation for future reference. After the Oranur experiment, he returned to the problem, and although, as far as I know, there is no record of his reasoning, it seems to have gone something like this. What could have caused the water to ripple when he pointed a hollow metal tube at it? Probably orgone energy. Why? Because, presumably, the metal absorbed energy from the atmosphere (the greenhouse effect) and built up a kind of "orgone pressure" in the tube.

And since the tube was open at the end, the energy could stream out again. The fact that it caused ripples on water suggests that water attracted it (a notion that seems to be confirmed by an observation made by another Reichian, T. R. Constable, that when an orgone accumulator is suspended over running water, its underside develops warmth).

Reich applied these principles in constructing the "cloudbuster." It consisted of a whole bank of metal tubes, with one end "earthed" to water by a steel cable. (A well at Orgonon was used for this purpose.) The tubes were mounted on a swivel and a turntable, so they could be pointed in any direction. Reich tried pointing this device at a low black cloud; within minutes it had dispersed. The inference seemed to be that the tubes set up a kind of convection current of orgone energy, flowing from the atmosphere into the water. And since, according to Reich, "DOR" consists of stagnant energy, the orgone current acts like a breeze and disperses it. The principle, he explains, is similar to that of a lightning conductor, except that the energy is drawn piecemeal, in small amounts.

Conversely, Reich discovered, a cloud, any cloud, could be increased by pointing the cloudbuster into the clear sky somewhere near it. In this case, the orgone "breeze" causes the cloud to attract more energy, and therefore more water vapor.

In 1953, Reich had an opportunity to prove the practical value of his invention. By early July, New England was parched after seven weeks without rain. Reich's son-in-law, Bill Moise, told a worried farmer that he knew a scientist who might be able to help. Reich was hired to produce rain on a basis of "payment by result." The story, as told by a reporter of the *Bangor Daily News* of July 24, 1953, is that Reich and his assistants set up the cloudbuster near the Bangor hydroelectric dam at 10:30 A.M. on July 6—this, presumably, was so that the lake could be used as the "earth." By Monday evening it was drizzling, and by midnight a steady rain, which continued through the next morning, had occurred. By the time the report appeared in the newspaper, Reich had already turned his attention to ending the drought over New York State. This took longer, but after four attempts, the drought ended with a freak rainstorm.

One witness of the Bangor experiment reported that the cloud-

buster was able to change the wind direction. In the following
year, Reich conducted his most spectacular experiment in weather
control when he made an attempt to divert Hurricane Edna, which
was expected to pass over the center of New York, and then over
Boston. On the evening of September 9, 1954, the radio reported
that "only a miracle could prevent the hurricane from hitting New
York." The next day, "New York got its miracle," and the hurricane passed fifty miles to the east.

Again, it is impossible not to feel regret that Reich's attitude to
the scientific establishment prevented him from making any attempt to publicize his invention, or to have it subjected to independent testing. There are numerous accounts by Reich and his
coworkers of "weather control" by means of the "cloudbuster,"
and of the dispersal of "DOR" clouds. They sound so circumstantial that the hypothesis of self-deception becomes untenable.
Moreover, David Boadella has described two sets of experiments
conducted by scientists Dr. Charles Kelley and Dr. Richard Blasband; both reported unequivocal success. (Kelley, who was a
weather researcher for the US Air Force, was so impressed that he
wrote a book entitled *A New Method of Weather Control*.) But
these took place after Reich's death. If the cloudbuster was as obviously effective as Reich claims, it should have been possible to
gather together a few sceptical, or even hostile, scientists to witness a demonstration. But Reich had turned his back on the "establishment," and continued to work alone, with the predictable
result that any scientists who came to hear about his results
dismissed them as the delusions of a crank.

From the point of view of the biographer, the element of tragic
paradox becomes steadily more pronounced in Reich's later years.
It is impossible to blame the scientists for regarding him as a madman; that is clearly Reich's own fault. Yet at no point is it possible to feel that Reich simply abandoned scientific logic and allowed himself to be controlled by imagination—or wishful
thinking. A book like *Ether, God and Devil* (1951) looks, at first,
like a total break with his earlier psychological pragmatism. What,
asks Reich, does he mean when he talks about the "devil" as opposed to "God," and answers that he means precisely what a
Christian means when he talks of evil. But in the next sentence he

changes his stand; the problem, he says, is a deep anxiety in the organism and it is obvious that he is still a long way from being a religious convert. In fact, *Ether, God and Devil* is basically Reich's first open repudiation of Freud. Freud had dismissed the "oceanic feeling" of poets and mystics as some kind of "sublimation" of the sexual instincts; Reich argues that the "oceanic feeling" is the mystic's intuition of the great ocean of orgone energy streaming through the universe. Reich's concept of God was basically a sense of mysterious underlying laws governing orgone energy. Christ had become Reich's favorite symbol of a completely "unblocked" human being, the ideal non-neurotic who responds directly to the life impulses. Evil, at this stage, is not an independent force, but merely man's capacity to repress his own vital "streamings," and to try to impose his neuroses and repressions on other people, particularly children. *Cosmic Superimposition* (1951), written at the same time, is Reich's first and only attempt at a scientific cosmology based on his orgone research; its most controversial assertion is that matter can be created "out of nothing," or rather, out of orgone energy: again, a conclusion that Reich felt to be amply justified by "Experiment XX." To anyone who has followed Reich as far as *The Cancer Biopathy* of three years earlier, these books seem eminently logical and reasonable.

The Murder of Christ (1953), subtitled "Volume One of The Emotional Plague of Mankind," is a rather more special case. This is the volume that Neill described as the most important book he had ever read; Reichians are inclined to regard it as Reich's "Great Testament." Non-Reichians, like myself, will see it simply as an extension of Reich's paranoia. Reich identifies himself with Christ and preaches a sermon on the various stratagems of the forces of emotional plague, with chapters on Judas Iscariot, St. Paul (the man who turned Christianity into a life-hating morality), and Mocigeno, the man who betrayed Giordano Bruno to the Inquisition. This chapter, entitled "The Murder of Christ in Giordano Bruno," is a typical example of Reich's tendency to see everything in his own crudely oversimplified terms. The historical truth is that Bruno was another "Right Man," a bitter, violent egoist—the *Encyclopaedia Britannica* speaks of his "disdainful, boasting nature"—who taught a sinister, anti-Christian form of magic.[1] The death sentence was, even so, not inevitable; Bruno only had to recant—like Galileo—and he would have received a prison sentence; he refused to recant, and had to receive the mandatory death sentence for unrepentant heretics. Reich's picture of Bruno as a life-force mystic who was destroyed by the emotional plague has no relation to historical fact.

As to Mocigeno, there is little to be said in his favor, but he was certainly not the kind of person Reich represents: the "nonentity" who goes around "habitually breeding evil." According to Reich, Mocigeno is a pestilent killer who commits murder because he cannot stand the sight of greatness of soul in men like Bruno and Christ, and, by implication, in Reich. Mocigeno had two reasons for handing Bruno over to the Inquisition; he was a conservative who disliked Bruno's liberalism, and he had come to hate Bruno's bullying temper. Bruno's biographer Frances Yates says that he was "subject to pathological accesses of rage in which he said terrible things which frightened people" (i.e., made them fear his magical powers—he was at this stage practicing black magic), and adds that Bruno "seems to have given way to some of his more alarming outbursts while in Mocigeno's house." This seems to suggest that Mocigeno's reason for betraying Bruno was not entirely a wicked man's hatred for a saint.

But Reich was not concerned with historical accuracy. Mocigeno was a convenient symbol for emotional plague; in due course, his name was combined with Stalin's (Djugashvili) to represent the essence of petty-minded malice—Modju.

Still, allowing for the fact that Reich identified himself with Christ, and his enemies with Modju, *The Murder of Christ* is not the product of a mind that has lost its sense of reality. What Reich is saying is what he has been repeating since *The Function of the Orgasm*: that most human evil is the result of repression. It may be an oversimplification, but it contains a nugget of truth. Reich may have more than a touch of paranoia, but he is a long way from being insane.

And this is the irony, and the tragedy, of the postwar years: that while, from his own point of view, Reich's development seemed totally rational and logical, the detached, and necessarily superficial, observer could only see increasing evidence of extravagance and disintegration. Close and faithful supporters—like Ilse Reich and Myron Sharaf—left him because they found his demands too great. The books seemed to reflect increasing delusions of grandeur. His "scientific" discoveries became ever more preposterous—the orgone accumulator, the cloudbuster, even a motor that was supposed to work off orgone energy. (Many Reichians claim to have seen the motor operating; the driving force was an orgone accumulator, excited by a half-volt battery; it drove a twenty-five-volt motor.)

And then, in what seemed like an irrevocable step into sheer insanity, Reich suddenly decided that the human race, and himself in particular, were being observed by beings from outer space in flying saucers.

Reich's UFO phase began in November 1953, when someone sent him two books on Unidentified Flying Objects. Flying saucers had been in the news since June 24, 1947, when a businessman named Kenneth Arnold, flying his private airplane near Mount Rainier in Washington State, reported seeing nine shining disks traveling against the background of the mountain. After this reports became so frequent that in September of that year, the US Air Force inaugurated an official project for the study of Unidentified Flying Objects—Project Blue Book, under the direction of Edward J. Ruppelt. Ruppelt's team dismissed almost seventy-five percent of the sightings as hoaxes, exaggerations, or mistakes; that still left more than twenty-five percent of sightings that were too well-authenticated to be dismissed or explained away. On July 4, 1947, the crew of an airliner watched nine "flying saucers" for several minutes; in Portland, Oregon, on the same day, hundreds of people watched a dozen flying disks move across the sky; on January 7, 1948, three F-51 pursuit planes from the US Air Force base at Fort Knox chased a vast UFO that had flown above the town. As Captain Thomas F. Mantell reported over the radio that he was going to try to get closer to the object—which he described as "metallic and of tremendous size"—his plane disintegrated. In spite of this, a Commission of Enquiry concluded, in December 1949, that UFOs could be dismissed as hallucinations or misinterpretations of natural phenomena. Another Commission reported in 1953, somewhat more ambiguously, that the phenomena were not a threat to national security, but that the continual reporting of UFOs "does . . . result in a threat to the orderly functioning of the channels of the body politic"—a suggestion that the situation needed to be "cooled."

Reich had paid no attention to all the publicity about flying saucers, even when, in 1952, some visitors to Orgonon reported seeing shining objects in the sky. In the spring of 1952, he observed a black substance forming on rocks around Orgonon; it caused headaches and nausea, and when scraped off the rocks produced an unpleasant burning sensation and high blood pressure; Reich assumed it to be some kind of aftereffect of the Oranur experiment. But after reading Major Donald Keyhoe's *Flying Saucers Are Real,* Reich remembered the visitors who had reported shining objects the previous year. He himself had heard something flash past at a great speed as he sat on the steps outside the house one night. What intrigued him was that Keyhoe said that UFOs were often surrounded by a bluish light, and moved noiselessly. To Reich, this immediately suggested orgone energy. He began examining the stars, wondering how it would be possible to tell if some of them were actually UFOs. The answer was obviously time-lapse photography. Reich tried it, and was excited when he discovered that some of the stars did *not* produce the white lines due to the earth's motion; they simply vanished. He needed no more persuading that Orgonon was under observation from UFOs, and that they were responsible for the "melanor" that was giving everybody headaches.

No doubt this conclusion *was* due in part to Reich's paranoia, but it is also necessary to admit that even if he had been completely balanced and unsuspicious, he might still have arrived at the same conclusion. For Reich's basic philosophy, his belief that the whole universe is permeated with life energy, implied that there must be other inhabited worlds in space. Reich would have had every reason for accepting the existence of UFOs even without the very considerable body of evidence that existed in 1953. There is still a widely held theory among "ufologists" that it was the atomic explosions of the mid-forties that drew the attention of the UFOs to earth. There was therefore nothing illogical in Reich's belief that the Oranur experiment, with its massive pollution of the Maine area, had drawn the attention of the UFOs to his own activities. When Reich's own observation, which all his coworkers agreed to be exceptionally keen, confirmed that there *was* evidence of UFO activity above Orgonon, it was natural that he should assume that he was the subject of their special attention. On May 12, 1954, Reich tried pointing the cloudbuster at a hovering point of blue light in the sky above Orgonon. It faded, then gradually reappeared. Reich pointed it at another point of blue light hovering nearby; the same thing occurred. Reich was startled and shocked. This was the first genuine evidence for the existence of UFOs. His next feeling was of alarm. What he had done was the equivalent of poking a tiger with a stick. Reich decided that, for the time being, at any rate, he would make no further move against the UFOs.

He had, in any case, plenty of other problems to occupy his mind. On February 10, 1954, after seven years of investigation, the Food and Drug Administration finally served Reich with a twenty-seven-page Complaint, containing a proposed injunction against the interstate shipment of accumulators. The essence of the Complaint was that the orgone accumulator did not work, *could* not work, since orgone energy did not exist. It cited various publications by Reich to show that he believed the accumulator could cure cancer, but made no mention of the various qualifying clauses Reich himself had added in *The Cancer Biopathy*.

Dr. Charles Kelley, in an article entitled "The Life and Death of Wilhelm Reich," has described the Complaint as "so vicious, so false, so twisted and sick, that it was difficult to believe it could ever be taken seriously in court." But a study of the actual Complaint (reprinted in full in Jerome Greenfield's *Wilhelm Reich Vs. the U.S.A.*) hardly justifies that description. Taking into account the basic attitude of the FDA, that Reich was a crank, it is, on the whole, a fair and balanced document. Moreover, if the FDA believed that there was no such thing as orgone energy, and that therefore the accumulators were worthless, they had no alternative than to try to prevent their use; for patients who relied on them rather than on proper medical attention were placing their lives at risk.

Reich should have been rational enough to see this, and to concede that in future the accumulators would not be shipped across state lines. Instead, he made his most appalling mistake so far, possibly the greatest single mistake of his life. Instead of appearing in court to try to explain his position, he wrote the court a rambling, four-page "Response," quibbling about whether the FDA was the "US Government," quoting Abraham Lincoln on freedom, and talking about "conspirators whose aim is to destroy human happiness and self government." Reich's main argument was that the court was trying to interfere with the course of scientific investigation; therefore, he said, he did not intend to appear.

Reich was missing the point. The FDA was not trying to interfere with his research; only with the sale of what they considered to be a quack remedy *across state lines* to finance that research. But the whole tone of the Response was bound to irritate even the most open-minded judge. Its last sentence: ". . . I submit that the case against orgonomy be taken out of court completely," sounded like a challenge. The judge took the view that the Response was a "crank letter," and the FDA seized the opportunity that Reich had offered on a plate by demanding a default injunction against him, which Judge Clifford promptly granted.

In retrospect, it is almost impossible to understand what made Reich play into the hands of his opponents, for this was not simply a question of being forbidden to ship accumulators across state lines. The sting of the Complaint was contained in its penultimate paragraph: a plea that Reich be forbidden to do "any act whether oral, written or otherwise" to promote the sale of the accumulators. The Complaint lists a dozen or so of Reich's publications which could be regarded as "promotion material," including *The Function of the Orgasm, The Cancer Biopathy,* and most of the later books, including *The Murder of Christ.* In effect, the FDA was asking that all these works should not be sold outside the state of Maine. And here Reich was on very firm ground indeed. The most incompetent lawyer in America would have pointed out that this was a violation of the right of freedom of speech, and that the suppression of books (except on grounds of obscenity) ran counter to the whole spirit of the US Constitution. No court would have granted such an injunction under normal circumstances, and the FDA probably took it for granted that the judge would refuse to ban Reich's books. By writing the court a defiant "crank letter," Reich took the only possible step that could have led to the suppression of some of his most important works.

The question of Reich's motives will probably never be clear.

The most obvious explanation is that his persecution mania had reached a point where he believed that the banning of his books was as likely as the banning of the accumulator. But surely any lawyer, or for that matter, any intelligent US citizen, could have told him he had a powerful case? Here the answer could be that Reich's followers were deserting him in droves, and that those who were left accepted whatever Reich said or did without question.

There remains one other hypothesis that seems to me plausible. As long ago as 1920, Reich had identified himself with Peer Gynt, the individual who falls out of step with the rest of humanity, who is misunderstood, derided when weak, and attacked when strong. Reich had written his own scenario, and the thread of "outsiderism" runs throughout his life. He almost gives the impression of being determined to be misunderstood and rejected; to be understood and accepted would embarrass him. And the later identification with Christ suggests that, unconsciously at least, he *wants* to be crucified. The root of the urge could lie in his sense of guilt about being responsible for his mother's suicide; but this "Freudian" explanation could be too glib. It seems just as simple to say that his belief in his own genius was linked with a romantic conviction, based on self-pity, that greatness invites martyrdom. For what would Reich have done with success and world acclaim? It is impossible to imagine that haunted, suspicious face relaxing into a smile of reconciliation. If Reich had been given the Nobel Prize, his acceptance speech would have been a torrent of reproach and scorn. His unconscious mind was geared to the idea of persecution and martyrdom.

This view is supported by Reich's line of argument in the Response, his insistence that what is at issue is his right to conduct scientific research. He gives the impression of someone who is determined to stoke up a sense of injury and injustice. The underlying message seems to be "Very well, ban my books. Make me a martyr. You are only proving what I've said all along . . ."

When Judge Clifford granted the default injunction on March 19, 1953, he was unaware that Reich had cast him in the role of Pontius Pilate.

Reich heard about the injunction three days later, when his caretaker told him about local gossip; later that day, a US marshal came to Orgonon to deliver a copy of the injunction. Reich's instant reaction was rage, and the formation of a plan called OROP-EP (Orgone Operation Emotional Plague)—Reich's tendency to make use of these grotesque abbreviations is one of his most irritating characteristics. OROP-EP was basically a plan to prove the existence of orgone energy, and confound his enemies, by using the cloudbuster to flood the eastern states. Later that afternoon, Reich dispatched a telegram to this effect to the US Weather Bureau in Washington declaring that his cloudbuster was drawing east to west from Hancock, Maine, and Rangeley, to cause storms to prove that Orgone energy actually exists. The consequences of this action, he says, are the responsibility of Federal Judge Clifford. He also declared that he would be flooding the East as the weather bureau was drying out the Southwest. This expressed Reich's conviction that it was the nuclear tests in the Nevada desert that were creating DOR, which was in turn creating more desert; but it is not clear why he thought the US Weather Bureau was responsible. Jerome Greenfield remarks that in these accusations "there is a hint of the merging of two issues that until then had been separate: [the FDA case and] Reich's fight against the 'planetary DOR emergency.' This merging will become more marked in *Contact with Space* where descriptions of scientific work are often interspersed with comments on trouble with the FDA, as if there were some actual inner connection between the two." That is to say, Reich's persecution mania was finally beginning to reflect an element of certifiable delusion. David Boadella is inclined to agree. "Now it is one thing to indulge far-reaching hypotheses about certain relationships, as Reich had done in *Cosmic Superimposition,* it is quite another to state as a matter of irrefutable fact that one's speculations have been proved correct . . . This kind of breakdown in reasoning indicates that something in Reich's mind had 'tumbled beyond retrieve . . .'" He is speaking of Reich's conviction that the black substance on rocks— melanor—"stems from the Core men and their space ships."

Yet Reich's conviction that he could control the weather seems to have been no delusion. He began pointing the cloudbuster at the sky immediately after sending the telegram to the weather bureau. A few hours later the weather bureau forecast fair to good weather for the following day. But at seven the next morning, there was an acknowledgment: "Yesterday's forecast an error," and a prediction of light snow. Fair, sunny weather with higher temperatures was predicted for the morrow, but by four that afternoon, snow was falling in Rangeley. Reich sent off a triumphant telegram: "Snowstorm in Rangeley region as predicted" to the weather bureau, with copies to President Eisenhower and J. Edgar Hoover, as well as various newspapers. Three days later, the *Bangor Daily News* was commenting gloomily: "U.S. Weather Bureau forecasts fair and warmer for today, but you couldn't tell it from the snow that was pelting Bangor streets last night." But Reich's "demonstration" must be regarded as a failure. He had hoped to "flood the East"; but a few local snowstorms in March convinced nobody.

Reich's failure to answer the Complaint had more serious consequences than anyone had expected. The Injunction not only forbade "interstate commerce" involving orgone accumulators and "promotion material," but also ordered the return of all accumulators "shipped in interstate commerce," and their destruction under the supervision of the FDA. Yet even this was not necessarily as disastrous as it sounded. The wording of the injunction meant that accumulators in Maine should have been exempted. Moreover, if the accumulators "shipped in interstate commerce" were destroyed, then the various books and other material would automatically cease to be promotion material or "labeling." It is hardly possible to advertise something that does not exist, since advertising is an attempt to influence prospective purchasers.

Even at this stage, then, there was room for maneuver. The most sensible course would have been to recall the "interstate" accumulators, and to destroy these under the supervision of the FDA, then to point out that the books and magazines could no longer be considered as "labeling." Reich would then have been free to manufacture and sell accumulators in New York. It seems clear that the court had no real intention of trying to prevent Reich from selling his books; in October 1954, his son-in-law Bill Moise wrote a letter to the court stating that Reich had every intention of continuing to sell his books, and asking them to state if they had any objection; no reply was received.

But Reich seemed to be in the grip of some fatal laziness or indifference. When he received the original Complaint, he refused to allow a panel of Reichian doctors led by Elsworth Baker to "intervene" in the case. ("Intervention" means that other people concerned may, in effect, insist on standing beside the defendant.) If Baker and the others had intervened and appeared at the original hearing, they might well have prevented the injunction. Instead, they attempted to intervene after the injunction, which was too late; the judge denied their right. (Jerome Greenfield states: "the timeliness of the application is a factor.") And even after the injunction, Reich made no attempt to carry out its instructions. A letter was prepared to advise renters that they would have to return the accumulators, but it was never sent out. All Reich did was to stop further rental of accumulators. He seems to have had no suspicion that he was placing his head on the chopping block.

Reich felt he had more important matters in hand. His experience with the cloudbuster in May 1953, when he "extinguished" two UFOs, convinced him that the human race has another enemy besides the emotional plague. He was also convinced, by this time, that the government of the United States was taking an active and benevolent interest in his researches. He had written to the government to describe the Oranur experiment and its aftermath; when airplanes flew low over Orgonon, Reich took this to indicate that the President was aware of the importance of his work, but was not at liberty to offer open support. The persecution of the FDA was therefore of less importance than the continuation of his research into the activities of the spacemen—particularly their use of Deadly Orgone Radiation to create deserts. On Reich's instructions, Bill Moise wrote to the Air Technical Intelligence Center in Dayton, Ohio—the site of Project Blue Book—to inform the Air Force about the "space gun" and its effectiveness against UFOs. Moise later saw a Colonel Wertenbaker at the base, and was convinced that he had made a powerful impression. But Wertenbaker's report refers to Moise as "this person," and says that the Air Force "will do well to avoid any entanglements . . ." He clearly felt that Moise was just another UFO nut.

On October 18, 1954, Reich set out to drive from Maine to Arizona to undertake his most ambitious weather project so far: to prove that his cloudbuster could cause rain in a desert area. The project was called OROP Desert, another of Reich's cryptic abbreviations, meaning Orgone Energy Operation in the Desert. Bill

Moise drove ahead with Peter Reich; Wilhelm Reich came behind in a second car with his daughter Eva. Reich's assistant Bob McCullough also moved to Arizona with his family and the cloud-buster equipment. Ilse stayed behind; by this time she had finally separated from Reich. (She explains that this was basically due to his "irrational accusations about my supposed infidelities," leading to an increasingly bitter relationship.)

The nearly three-thousand-mile trip convinced Reich that America was suffering widespread attacks from DOR; everywhere he seemed to see blackened rocks, decaying vegetation, withered trees. He arrived in Tucson on October 29, 1954; Bob McCullough was already there. They quickly located a fifty-acre property, eight miles north of Tucson, which Reich named "Little Orgonon." They were surrounded by desert; it had not rained in Tucson for five years. On the night they moved in, October 31, Reich observed several flying saucers, which he called Ea (for Energy alpha), hovering in the sky. The cloudbuster was put to work immediately. It proved, predictably, far more difficult to obtain results here than in New England. To begin with, the cloudbuster worked by focusing somewhere near a cloud, which would then become larger as streams of free orgone energy were drawn to it. Here, the nearest large sheet of water was the Pacific Ocean over the mountains. Nevertheless, Reich persevered; in his book *Contact with Space* (published posthumously), he notes that by November 7, the moisture in the atmosphere had increased five-fold, and the clouds had begun to form thickly over Little Orgonon. Then, suddenly, the clouds vanished. What had undone their work? That night, Reich found the answer. A large luminous ball rose slowly and hovered over Mount Catalina for most of the night. It looked as if the flying saucers were actively opposing his attempts at rain-making. "There was no escape from the fact that we were at war with a power unknown to man on Earth." He felt there could now be no doubt that the UFOs had caused all the deserts on Earth, a notion that seems to ignore such factors as natural weather conditions. At the same time, he reached a conclusion that seems altogether more interesting and relevant: that the action of the spacemen was aided by the "emotional desert" created by man. The emphasis Reich laid on this concept in his last years suggests that what he had in mind was not simply the emotional plague, or man's fear of his own vital forces. There is an implication that the *mind* of man has somehow influenced his physical environment, not simply through pollution or destruction of natural resources, but *directly*.

Throughout November and December, Reich's battles with the UFOs continued; he could feel the presence of UFOs when they "drew" upon him—presumably using their own equivalent of space guns to suck Reich's energy. But President Eisenhower's speech about "atoms for peace" on November 22 convinced Reich that Eisenhower was still behind him; Reich himself had used the same phrase in his writing, and believed that Eisenhower had borrowed it from him. When an US Air Force plane circled Mount Catalina after Reich had seen a UFO there, Reich took this to be another attempt to assure him that the government knew all about DOR and Eas, and was behind him. Before dismissing Reich's talk of UFOs as a kind of Don Quixote fantasy, we should bear in mind that everyone else at Orgonon and Little Orgonon witnessed the phenomenon of the "lights" blinking out when Reich pointed the cloudbuster at them—Peter Reich, for example, describes witnessing it in his *Book of Dreams*. Reich may have been suffering from paranoid delusions by this time—even the most staunch Reichians admit as much—but his impressions were not entirely subjective.

Early in December, Bob McCullough had an unpleasant experience of the power of DOR. As he was using a cloudbuster (there were now two) on a DOR cloud, he experienced a crippling sensation in his right leg, followed by paralysis in his right side. When he staggered away from the cloudbuster, his condition improved. But the next day, the 7th, as he was again using the cloudbuster, the paralysis came again, this time so powerfully that he had to drag himself back to his quarters. It took him two months to recover, and even then his right foot was permanently affected.

Reich decided that this "attack" justified a further reinforcement, and asked his assistant, Dr. Michael Silvert, to bring the two "needles" of radium from Orgonon in Maine (he used them in a technique to hasten rain-making). They arrived on the morning of the 14th, towed behind an airplane. Later that day, according to Reich, there was another attack from the East. An immense black and purple cloud rose over Tucson, and the atmos-

phere became so charged with DOR that they all felt sick.
According to Reich, the situation appeared menacing, eerie, and
terrifying. Several Air Force planes flew overhead, but their vapor
trails dispersed quickly, a sure sign of DOR in the atmosphere.
Reich ordered one space gun to sweep the sky overhead, and the
other to point at the cloud over Tucson. This cloud gradually grew
smaller and vanished. Finally, about an hour after the attack
began, four Air Force bombers flew low over Little Orgonon, as if
to congratulate him.

The whole story, recounted in *Contact with Space,* sounds like
paranoid fantasy; again, it is necessary to remind ourselves that it
was witnessed by everyone at Little Orgonon, and that the dispersal of the black cloud really happened. (Since Tucson was still
suffering from a drought, it could not have been a rain cloud.)

Back in Maine, the FDA was still trying to find out if Reich had
complied with the court order, but experienced some difficulty,
since Orgonon seemed almost deserted. On December 30, 1954,
Reich made another of those fateful miscalculations that would
ensure his downfall: when an FDA agent called at Little Orgonon
with a marshal, Reich declined to see him. He had decided that
the FDA was part of a plot against him, and that the injunction
had been engineered by Communists. An FBI agent named Holliday only wanted to find out whether Reich was building accumulators in Texas, and it would have been to Reich's advantage to reassure him on this point. Refusing to see him could only make the
FDA more determined to "get him."

In January 1955, Silvert, now back in Maine, decided to send a
truckload of accumulators and books by Reich to his own address
in New York. This was, of course, a direct violation of the injunction, and was probably the crucial factor in sending Reich to
prison.

Unaware of these ominous developments, Reich continued his
cloudbusting experiments with increasing enthusiasm, convinced
that success was now in sight. He proved to be correct. On January 13, 1955, there was heavy rainfall in Arizona—so heavy in the
Tucson area that the airport was temporarily closed. This could
conceivably have been coincidence, yet it is more difficult to explain why the humidity over the desert had increased steeply since
the beginning of Reich's operations, to such an extent that there

was now a covering of grass in places where many people could
remember nothing but desert. When, in March, Reich drove
west, he found grass extending for fifty miles before the desert became bare again.

On March 7, 1955, Reich resumed his rain-making operations
at Jacumba, California. Again, the results were spectacular; by
March 9, heavy rain was falling; by the 12th, bare mountain
slopes were turning green. Reich was convinced that he had broken the "DOR barrier" caused by atomic explosions and Eas, and
that the life-giving cycle had again been restored to the area.
Satisfied with his six months' work, he returned to Orgonon in
April.

Here another type of cloud was gathering. The FDA had
finally become convinced that Reich had done nothing to carry
out the court order; they now applied for the initiation of proceedings for contempt of court. On March 30, the Attorney General gave instructions for the legal documents to be prepared. But
Reich continued to stonewall attempts to inspect the premises at
Orgonon, and Silvert blocked the FDA's attempts to inspect his
premises in New York, where the books and accumulators had
been delivered. It looked, quite simply, as if Reich was defying the
injunction and continuing his activities as before. On June 16, the
FDA again complained to the Attorney General about the refusal
of Reich and Silvert to permit inspection or to furnish information. Finally, officialdom lost its temper. On the same day, Judge
Clifford issued an order for Reich and Silvert to appear in court to
explain why legal proceedings should not be instituted against
them. Bill Moise wired the judge to ask if he could see him pri-
vately; at the meeting, he asked if Reich could be excused from
appearing in court on the grounds that he always told the truth,
and that he might say something that would be "disastrous nation-
ally." The judge refused; Reich and Silvert were ordered to appear
in court on July 26.

Reich became increasingly paranoid; he was convinced the
FDA was trying to find out his "secrets"; heavy chains were put
up across the entrances, and his followers were armed with rifles.
Several people who strayed innocently onto Reich's land were indignant when they were shown off at gunpoint.

At the hearing on July 26, Reich's lawyers argued that the court had no jurisdiction to order the recall and destruction of accumulators. After this, Reich spoke for half an hour about UFOs, and about the conspiracy against him. He made a thoroughly bad impression, insisting that he was a humble man, then adding that he was one of the greatest scientists alive. When he became too excited and began to shout, his own lawyers had to caution him. Altogether, it was a disastrous day. The judge ordered the defense lawyers to present their case in writing by September 9.

At this later hearing, the FDA argued that whether or not Reich thought it was unjust, the injunction should have been obeyed. They were undoubtedly right. Three days after this hearing, one of Reich's lawyers withdrew from the case after Reich insisted that he wanted to cross-examine witnesses personally. Not long after that, the other lawyer withdrew.

The hearings continued to drag on—October 10, October 18, November 4—and Reich defended himself; he signed his motions as a "representative of the EPPO" (the Emotional Plague Prevention Office). He continued to talk about conspiracy and about the misrepresentation of his ideas. With considerable patience, the judge kept explaining that the present case had nothing to do with either of these matters; it was simply a question of whether Reich had actively disobeyed the injunction. He also pointed out that if Reich had wanted to present these arguments, he should have appeared in court to answer the original Complaint. It was the nearest he came to telling Reich that he had mishandled the whole affair from the beginning.

In late December, Reich decided to move to Washington. In the previous August, at a conference on OROP Desert, Reich had met Aurora Karrer, a biologist who lived in Washington; they formed a relationship that was to last until Reich's death. He rented a suite in the Alban Towers Hotel, and took the pseudonym Walter Roner. Peter Reich, who was now living with his mother, spent the holidays with him there, and an increasing closeness developed between them.

The trial was postponed several times, from December to March, then to April. Reich continued to be difficult, and the trial was delayed because he insisted that the attorney had failed to sign the notice of the trial. Ilse Reich, who was also named in the indictment, checked with a lawyer, and discovered that it was customary for the US Attorney's signature to be typed, so she appeared in court, as ordered, on April 30. Reich was not there. He had also told the judge that he would not appear for trial unless the order had the judge's personal signature. On April 30, Reich was arrested, placed in handcuffs, and taken to Portland, Maine, where he was charged with contempt of court. Silvert and Thomas Mangravite, an associate who rented accumulators in New York, were already there in handcuffs. They spent the night in jail, and were later all fined for contempt.

The trial finally began on May 3, 1956, and lasted three days. It may have been Reich's misfortune that there was a new judge, George C. Sweeney. Judge Clifford, who had shown increasing signs of sympathy towards Reich in the previous hearings, now pleaded overwork. Judge Sweeney was less pliable; but his impatience was directed impartially at Reich, for presenting irrelevant issues, and at the prosecution attorney, Joseph Maguire, for being long-winded. Reich continued to act as his own attorney, and showed a failure to grasp what was at issue—or a determination to introduce testimony he knew to be irrelevant. When a witness testified that he had continued to rent an orgone accumulator after the injunction, Reich asked him whether the accumulator had done him any good. The judge promptly stopped him.

In fact, the prosecution had an airtight case, and all Reich's attempts to throw a wrench in the works could have made no difference. The government could prove that Silvert had shipped accumulators across a state line, and that these accumulators had subsequently been rented in New York, and, of course, that Reich had accepted the money. Reich's only hope might have been to dissociate himself from Silvert's action the moment he found out about it on his return from Arizona. The fact that he had not done so meant that he had condoned the action, even though he was unaware of it at the time.

The offense could have been mitigated if Reich had attempted to show that he started to obey the injunction—by drafting the circular letter to accumulator renters, for example—but had been prevented from going further by the noncooperation of the FDA, who were supposed to supervise the destruction. Reich made no such attempt; instead, he kept arguing that there were weighty reasons for disobeying the injunction. This was, of course, totally irrelevant. The only question at issue was whether he had obeyed, or tried to obey, the injunction. The judge made this clear in his summation to the jury. And, inevitably, the jury came back with a verdict of guilty. Reich looked stunned; he seems to have expected an acquittal.

Judgment was postponed until May 25; then the Wilhelm Reich Foundation was ordered to pay a $10,000 fine, and Reich himself was sentenced to two years in prison. Silvert was sentenced to prison for a year and a day.

Reich decided to appeal. But meanwhile, the orders of the injunction had to be carried out; in June, the FDA supervised the destruction of accumulators and copies of journals and pamphlets at Orgonon; in New York, a truck was loaded with the books and journals from the Orgone Institute stockroom and transported to the Lower Manhattan incinerator. The books included volumes like *Character Analysis* and *The Sexual Revolution* that contained no reference to orgone energy. On March 11, 1957, Reich's appeal was denied. The appeal argued that the original injunction contained false claims; the law ruled that even if this was so, it either had to be contested or obeyed. Reich had done neither.

The following day, Reich and Silvert entered the Danbury Federal Corrective Institution in Connecticut. The prison psychiatrist quickly diagnosed Reich as paranoid, and he was transferred to the Lewisburg Penitentiary, Pennsylvania, which had psychiatric facilities. The psychiatrists there decided against treatment; Reich firmly resisted the idea, and their only alternative would have been to declare him insane. They were unwilling to inflict this humiliation on a man of Reich's standing. Reich was permitted to write— he began a book called *Creation*, a kind of sequel to *Cosmic Superimposition*—and to work in the prison library.

Reich became friendly with the prison doctor, who supplied him with an oil preparation—he was suffering from a skin complaint—and who told Ilse that everyone in his office had been impressed by Reich's knowledge and unquestionable genius. "But they all felt strange when he would look up any time a plane flew overhead and say: 'There they are, watching over me, encouraging me . . .'" Reich was still convinced that Eisenhower knew all about his problems, and would soon intervene; he applied for a presidential pardon, but this was turned down. Meanwhile, however, he was making a surprisingly good adjustment to being in prison. Lewisburg was noted for its relative comfort—Greenfield says it had the reputation of being a country club. The imprisonment may actually have benefited Reich's health, Ilse Reich comments that he had begun to drink very heavily during the last years. He also seems to have derived much comfort from the thought that he was sharing the fate of Socrates, Christ, Bruno, Galileo, Savonarola, Dostoevsky, and Nietzsche.

He also seems to have undergone a kind of religious experience, writing, after he had attended some church services: "I was deeply moved; I felt a new *universal* faith in *Life and Love*."

Reich was allowed three visitors; he chose his daughter Eva, his son Peter, and Aurora Karrer, whom he regarded as his fourth wife. On November 1, 1957, Aurora Karrer spent three hours with Reich; he looked ill, and told her he was experiencing the same symptoms as in October 1951, when he had had a heart attack. He had been unwilling to mention this to the prison authorities in case it delayed the parole hearing due on November 5. Always optimistic, Reich was already making plans for spending Christmas outside prison. But on the following night, November 2, he died quietly in his sleep. The cause was heart failure, a disease Reich believed was caused by heartbreak.

Silvert was released from prison the following December, having served nine months of his sentence. He committed suicide five months afterwards.

Reich was buried at Orgonon, overlooking the lake. The controversies continued, but now mainly in the Reichian camp. "There was already, before the funeral, a takeover by a number of 'pure Reichians' who wanted to exclude others from the funeral because Reich had not approved or completely trusted them," records Ilse Reich, although she does not mention whether she was among those who were mistrusted.

The FDA supervised another session of book burning as late as 1960, when Mary Boyd Higgins, trustee of the Reich estate, wanted to dispose of "banned" material that was occupying storage space and could not be sold under the terms of the injunction. But in 1961, the tide began to turn at last when the respected New York publisher, Farrar, Straus & Giroux reissued *The Function*

of the Orgasm and *Character Analysis* in the "banned" edition.
(This could now be done legally since those named in the injunction had ceased to exist.) By the mid-1960s there were distinct
signs of a Reich revival, both in the U.S. and Britain. Reich had
the treble benefit of being a sexual revolutionary at a time when everyone was discussing the "permissive society," a leftist when the
younger generation was chafing against the "establishment" and
the war in Vietnam, and a believer in UFOs when the market was
being flooded with books on "the occult."

By 1970, Reich had joined J. R. R. Tolkien, Hermann Hesse,
and Che Guevara as one of the heroes and symbolic mentors of
the younger generation. Not least among his qualifications for this
position was the fact that he had died in a federal penitentiary,
hounded by the establishment. The FDA had helped to place
Reich among the ranks of revolutionary martyrs.

It would have given him grim satisfaction to know that he had
had the last word.

POSTSCRIPT

It was the "pure Reichians" who became custodians of the official legend: Reich the visionary and prophet, who was destroyed by pigmies in the grip of the emotional plague. There was no question of insanity, or even of his fate being, to some extent, Reich's own fault. But in a new edition of *Fads and Fallacies,* issued in the year of Reich's death, Martin Gardner continued impenitently to assert the view that, with the possible exception of the early Freudian period, Reich's work was unalloyed nonsense. The same view was supported by Reich's biographer Michael Cattier.

Temperamentally, my sympathies are with Gardner and Cattier—Reich seems to me a thoroughly dislikable human being. Moreover, I agree with the critics that it was not Reich's ideas, but his paranoiac behavior, that landed him in jail. Colleagues in the Vienna group had already noted his paranoid tendencies when he was in his twenties. It was Reich's combination of aggression, ambition, and craving for success that led to most of the rebuffs he received. It seems to me that it was this eagerness for recognition that thwarted the natural expression of his genius. By the mid-1930s, the sense of rejection had turned him into a man with a huge chip on his shoulder, and it was this, rather than his revolutionary ideas, that caused his endless personal problems.

I must also admit to a thoroughgoing dislike of the Communist aspect of Reich's personality. I am not now speaking of his "Communist phase," which he later repudiated so violently, but of that tendency in him that made him seem, for a time, such an admirable recruit to Communism: a kind of intellectual thuggery, an ability to treat complex issues with a crude and unrepentant reductionism. It seems to me to compound the offense that he did it in the name of an idealism, a sympathy for human suffering, that was foreign to his basically self-centered personality.

Then why write a book about someone I find it so hard to like? First, because there is a kind of horrifying fascination in watching a man of Reich's immense vitality make a series of wrong choices that bring him to disaster. But second, and more important, because I find it impossible to agree with critics who feel that he went off the rails after the discovery of the orgone. Anyone who takes the trouble to follow Reich's development in detail quickly realizes that these critics were not in full possession of the facts. There was no sudden insane conversion to the idea of orgone energy; Reich made the discovery slowly and logically, step-by-step, in the most approved scientific manner. He began, as we have seen, with electrical experiments to try to determine whether the orgasm produced any change in skin resistance. (Sir Almroth Wright told him it could not be done, but here Reich's intuition proved correct.) These immensely painstaking experiments continued for two years. They led him to study protozoa, to find out whether his tension-discharge formula could be observed in simple organisms. The standard procedure for obtaining protozoa is to soak dry hay in water; it is generally accepted that the tiny organisms are formed by the interaction of the hay and free spores from the air. While studying this procedure Reich first observed "bions." When he boiled the water, which should have destroyed all atmospheric spores, the bion activity increased. This led Reich to conclude that bions were not spores, but some semiliving organism that was formed "spontaneously" in the hay solution. But how? His answer was logical: that the life energy must exist in a free state, but that it could somehow "take over" and animate "dead" cells. Hundreds of experiments were then performed to make sure that Reich was not making some absurd mistake, and allowing his samples to become contaminated from the air. Reich could have been mistaken about the bions, but it is impossible to maintain that he arrived at his conclusions through dubious, nonscientific methods.

It was Reich's misfortune that his aggressive and paranoid personality seemed to type-cast him as a crank. It must be admitted that he fits perfectly into Martin Gardner's gallery of religious messiahs and flat-earthers. But Reich was undoubtedly justified in feeling indignation when colleagues dismissed him as a crank, for he was a scientist by temperament and training. As it was, the genuine injustice increased the paranoia, and the paranoia had the effect of provoking further injustice. The result is that writers like Martin Gardner and Christopher Evans have no difficulty in "proving" Reich a crank by describing his personality and quoting some of his typical utterances.

In retrospect, Reich's greatest mistake was probably to cut himself off from the scientific community. During the Norwegian period, he at least persuaded other scientists—such as Roger du Teil and Louis Lapique—to check his results. But in America, where this was more essential than ever, if only because the public is more easily impressed by scientists, he practically withdrew into solitude, working with a few chosen disciples. By behaving like the founder of some offbeat religion, he invited the kind of attacks that destroyed him.

This was Reich's tragedy, for within two decades of his death, the scientific attitude towards such matters had changed beyond recognition. In 1973, eminent scientists from twenty countries gathered in Prague for a conference on "psychotronics"—the possibility of direct interaction between mind and inert matter—and one of those present wrote: "Can it be that all forms of energy (from that which moves a muscle to that which propels a rocket . . .) derive from one basic energy, an energy about which we still know almost nothing?"[1] In the same paragraph, Reich is mentioned as a forerunner of the idea. There is still today probably just as little acceptance of orgone energy among the scientific community as in 1957; but the atmosphere has become altogether more open-minded and receptive. It now seems perfectly conceivable that, by the end of the century, Reich will be regarded as the paranoid genius who stumbled on an important discovery, and was ridiculed for his pains. While his own claim to belong among the prophets and visionaries will probably make no headway, it may well be conceded that he belongs in the same company as Semmelweis, Boltzmann, Mendel, and others whose discoveries failed to achieve recognition while they were alive.

The question of Reich and the Eas (or flying saucers) is a slightly different matter. Here again, we have a curious and complex phenomenon, which the sceptics prefer to dismiss by pretending that it does not exist. In the long run, their attitude may prove to be justified, but meanwhile, there is a great deal that needs to be explained. The phenomenon has been witnessed by too many people to be written off as mistaken identification, and by too many sensible and reliable people to be dismissed as hysterical hallucination. It seems clear that *something* is going on. Neither is it true that UFO reports began to pour in only after Kenneth Arnold's original 1947 sighting; there are many others dating from earlier periods. To cite only one: Nicholas Roerich, a Russian painter and archaeologist (who collaborated with Stravinsky on *The Rite of Spring*), was with an expedition which crossed the Himalayas in 1927; on August 5, he describes looking into the sky at an eagle, then seeing something else above it: "We all saw, in a direction from north to south, something big and shiny reflecting the sun, like a huge oval moving at great speed . . . We even had time to take our field glasses and saw quite distinctly an oval form with a shiny surface . . ." The book in which this report appears, *Altai-Himalaya,* was published in 1930.

In spite of these circumstantial reports, Jung has suggested that UFOs may be some kind of "psychological projection,"[2] that is, that in some way, the unconscious mind may not only be capable of creating hallucinations of UFOs, but of somehow projecting them against the sky, where they can be seen by other people; he suggests that they have some religious significance. This intriguing theory has the disadvantage of being no more nor less likely than the notion that UFOs are visitors from outer space.

Yet this notion that there may be a *mental* element involved in such phenomena is worth further study. We have already noted that Freud was alienated by Jung's belief in "exteriorization phenomena" and, more particularly, by the explosions in a bookcase, apparently produced by Jung's unconscious mind. Since the last quarter of the nineteenth century, psychical researchers have been aware that "poltergeist" phenomena seem to be produced by the unconscious minds of human beings, usually disturbed adolescents; yet although this is now widely accepted even among the most sceptical researchers, no one has yet even suggested a plausible theory of how the mind can move physical objects. Split-brain research naturally suggests the possibility that the right rather than the left hemisphere is the source of the mystery, but this takes us no further. It seems that at the present time we lack some essential concept that would provide the key to the whole problem —as scientists before Volta and Faraday lacked the key to understand lightning.

Jung discussed another aspect of the unconscious that looks like a type of "exteriorization phenomenon"—coincidence or "synchronicity." In fact, this had first been systematically described by Paul Kammerer, the biologist whose anti-Darwinian views influenced Reich, who called it "the law of seriality." Kammerer noted the paradox that absurd sequences of coincidence, far outside the laws of probability, nevertheless seem to be everyday occurrences. We hear an unusual name for the first time, then, over the next few hours, come across it repeatedly in completely unrelated contexts.

Peter Fairley, science editor and TV science correspondent, described in a broadcast on the BBC how he became involved in such a series of "coincidences." In 1965, a virus made him blind in both eyes; one day, in a state of fury and frustration, he threw down the dish cloth and said: "I *must* make contact with some blind people . . ." As he said this, the telephone rang, and a total stranger asked if he would be willing to go and talk to an audience of the blind. After his sight had returned, the coincidences continued, many of them, as he emphasizes, completely meaningless and pointless. One day, driving to London, he heard a record request on the car radio by a Mrs. Blakeney. He had just driven through a village called Blakeney. A few minutes later, there was a mention of another Blakeney in a totally different context. At the office, he heard the name again, this time, that of a horse running in the Derby. Although he was not a gambler, he decided that this was too good to miss; he backed the horse and it won. From then on, he says, he was able to pick winners merely by looking down a list of horses; "Somehow the thing would be there, leaping out of the page: *that* horse is going to win . . . But as soon as people started to ask me to do it for deliberate reasons, it just went. I realized that it wasn't going to work to order, that it had to be almost subconscious or unconscious . . ." In the following year, it came back again, and he backed six winners in a row; again he was unnerved, and it went again. All this suggests that the "foresight" was a right-brain activity, promptly suppressed by any "left" interference.

It is not difficult to accept, at least for the sake of argument, that his right brain might have become somehow "attuned" to the future, possibly by the powerful emotion that started the chain of coincidence. But how could it "cause" the coincidence involving Blakeneys? What is the relation between such "synchronicities" and "paranormal" perception? The sensible response is to say "None." The fact remains that we all know certain people who seem to attract some particular kind of disaster over and over again, almost as if the unconscious had steered straight towards it. And people who suddenly become deeply interested in a subject discover references to it all over the place, and meet total strangers in a subway who are equally interested. These kinds of "synchronicity" we take for granted, without even attempting to explain them.

Where Reich is concerned, these speculations provide an interesting alternative to the two theories that have so far held the field: i.e., that he was a sublime genius, and that he was a demented crackpot. For Reich was undoubtedly the type of personality that produces "exteriorization phenomena" and odd synchronicities. He was the kind of man who was always seething with anger, resentment, jealousy; some of the photographs even have that defensive look of a tormented adolescent. Exteriorization phenomena often seem to be related to rage (for example, Jung mentions that when the explosions occurred in the bookcase, he was feeling enraged with Freud; he says the explosions were preceded by a "glowing" feeling in the diaphragm, as if it were becoming red hot). All of which suggests that the kind of extraordinary events that Reich records in *Contact with Space* may not be paranoid delusions—an interpretation rendered unlikely by the other witnesses—but some kind of "exteriorization phenomenon" triggered by Reich's abnormally active unconscious.

The same explanation could apply to some of the experiments with orgone energy and weather control. Reich's coworkers have insisted repeatedly that there was no element of self-delusion in these experiments; they all observed the phenomena. The sceptics reply that in that case, they must all have been infected by Reich's delusions. Is it not also conceivable that Reich's own weirdly active unconscious played its part in producing the phenomena on cue? For example, T. R. Constable states in *The Cosmic Pulse of Life* that clouds can be dissipated by a form of psychokinesis, a claim that has been substantiated to some extent by parapsychological research.[3] Yet it never seems to strike Constable that, in that case, the success of the cloudbuster might be due, to some extent at any rate, to the same powers. I can never read Reich's account of his experiments in spontaneous generation of life without wondering how far his own unconscious mind was aiding and abetting the procedures. His later concept of "the emotional desert," the notion that violent and destructive emotions were partly responsible for the deterioration of our environment, suggests that he also began to suspect that the mind can even exert psychokinetic effects on nature.

All this is not to suggest that Reich's orgone experiments were only some more bizarre and paranormal kind of "wishful thinking"; only that the "discoveries" involved could be more complex and bewildering than anyone has so far realized.

There is, it seems to me, still one major problem that remains unexplained: the nature of that obscure anguish that tormented Reich all his life. Reich behaved like a man with a thorn in his side: a thorn that no one was able to reach. The behavior that led to his downfall was paranoid, insanely defensive and suspicious. But it was also masochistic; he *brought about* his downfall as if he was his own worst enemy. Three times Reich began to be psychoanalyzed; three times he broke it off without explanation. He seems to have been singularly lucky in his relations with women; we receive the impression that he was a "good chooser," and that Annie Pink, Elsa Lindenberg, and Ilse Ollendorff were all gifted with patience, understanding, and the ability to adjust to Reich's unpredictable moods. Yet a point always came when Reich seemed compelled to destroy the relation. When Ilse Reich went to England in 1953—by which time their relationship had already deteriorated badly—he wrote her letters that show that he loved and missed her. Yet he admits to a kind of fear of expressing his love: "But this time I feel somewhat safer, although I still do not quite grasp the change . . ." The moment they were back together again, he felt the compulsion to destroy. The final relationship with Aurora Karrer never reached this stage since they were together for less than two years; yet on Reich's past showing, it seems fairly certain that it would only have been a matter of time. There was an element in Reich that treated happiness with fear and suspicion, as if he felt he had no right to it.

The obvious explanation is that he was obsessed by guilt about his mother's death, and his part in "betraying" her. But if this is the answer, and it seems to be by far the most traumatic event of his childhood, then it is complicated by his relation to his father. Normal boys usually "identify" with their fathers; the father is their first model, he provides the basic "self-image." Because Reich's father was a despot, a Right Man, Reich's attitude to him seems to have been ambivalent. Ilse Reich's description of him makes him sound very like his son. "The father has been described as a rather brutal man, with feudal attitudes towards his fieldhands and family, given to violent temper outbursts, but very much in love with his wife and very jealous . . ." She says that for one of the Reich brothers to tell the other "You behave like Father" was close to being an insult. She adds: "All through his life Reich idolized his mother . . ." But Reich not only caused his mother's suicide; he also caused his father's breakdown. "The father was so devastated by the death of the mother that only the thought of his two sons kept him from taking his own life . . ." But he tried to contract pneumonia by standing in a pond, so that the boys would receive the insurance money. It seems, then, that the tyrant was humanized by his wife's death, and began to show his love for his sons.

From then on, Reich showed a powerful father fixation. He seems to have been the kind of person whose friendships easily soured, who turned on those who had been close to him. Yet throughout his life he showed rigid loyalty towards Freud. After the "Einstein affair," he might have been expected to turn against Einstein and to dismiss him as a time-server, a man who had become part of the establishment and so was afraid to look closely into Reich's heterodox ideas. Again, he showed the same kind of loyalty to Einstein. Finally, when the FDA was persecuting Reich in the name of the US government, Reich declined to believe that the government, and more particularly, President Eisenhower, could be concerned. The Response to Judge Clifford that did all the damage went out of its way to make the point that it was not correct to say that the US government was complaining against Reich, although it made no practical difference whatever.

So although Reich revealed a mistrustful and suspicious nature from his early days, there were certain men whom he would on no account mistrust or accuse of wishing him harm. It was as if these men had become mental landmarks whom he could cling to in his sea of general mistrust. Again and again he became a prey to a despair and mistrust that made him believe that everyone was plotting against him; yet the mental landmarks were never touched by it; he believed to the end that Eisenhower was watching over him through the Air Force.

A Jungian might conclude that these father figures were Reich's "gods," his substitutes for the God whom, as a young agnostic, he had dismissed. Freud would simply have talked about the father substitute. But in this case, since Reich and his father were so much alike, it seems reasonable to speculate that, in some strange way, these men also represented Reich's essential self. To have turned against Freud or Einstein would have been to turn against himself, a kind of suicide. A healthy, mentally pliable man would have denounced Freud as intellectually timid, and called Einstein an old humbug; and although neither accusation would have been true, it would have been a healthy explosion of annoyance. Reich would have been incapable of such an explosion because it would have destroyed something inside himself.

So, if this interpretation is valid, Reich's guilt about his mother was deepened and exacerbated by guilt about his father. In which case, the destruction of his own happy marriages could have been based on a feeling that *he* had no right to a happy marriage when he had destroyed that of his parents. (Conversely, his relationship with his children, particularly with his son, seems to have been powerful and normal, which is as might be expected if Reich "identified" with his father.)

Where the development of his own ideas was concerned, Reich's loyalty to Freud was disastrous, for the heart of Freud's thinking is his doctrine of the unconscious. Reich expressed it in the Peer Gynt chapter of *The Function of the Orgasm*: "You imagine that you can determine your actions by your own free will? Indeed not! Your conscious actions are only a drop on the surface of an ocean of unconscious processes of which you can know nothing, and besides, you would be afraid of knowing them. You pride yourself upon the 'individuality of your personality' and the 'breadth of your mind'? Naïve! Really, you are only the plaything of your instincts, which do with you what *they* want . . ." In short, man is "a little worm in the stream of his own feelings."

Yet having embraced this doctrine, Reich spent the rest of his life trying to escape it, for by temperament, he was an optimist. Freud was willing to spend years on a case like that of the Wolf Man, then admit that the results were minimal. Reich's optimism demanded results. His first major step was to formulate the orgasm theory, according to which, the great "stream of feelings" finds its outlet through the loins. This, said Reich, provides the key not only to the cure of neurosis, but to its general prevention. It is true that the genitally healthy man or woman remains a "worm," but at least he or she is a healthy worm.

Reich took this step only after thoroughly convincing himself that it was in no way a repudiation of Freudian doctrine. On the contrary, it was a rigorously logical development of Freud. The next step, into revolutionary politics, could also be justified as an attempt to "bring Freud to the masses"; in fact, it was another attempt to escape the cul-de-sac created by Freud's denial of the will. But here Reich was on dangerous ground; for if man is a "worm in the stream of his feelings," a plaything of his instincts, how can he attempt to shape his own political destiny?

It is after the "discovery of the orgone" that it becomes possible to see the precise nature of Reich's inner contradictions. Orgone energy is, according to Reich, the basic life energy. But if this is so, then the accumulator should be a universal cure, instantly increasing the vitality of anyone who sits in it. Instead, Reich observed that some patients seemed to respond instantly, while others responded slowly or not at all. This should have suggested to Reich that there is another factor involved: the *mind* of the patient and its attitudes towards its problems: its "joy in life" (or lack of it). In short, mental health is not simply a matter of the patient's bank balance of psychic energy, but of how that energy is spent. That is to say, Reich was ignoring the *organizing principle* that decides what to do with the energy: whether to direct it towards important objectives, or to waste it in some pleasant and mindless activity; whether to use it to write a Ninth Symphony or to commit a murder; whether to fight adversity or surrender.

In short, although Reich spent his life talking about human freedom, he totally failed to grasp its fundamental role in psychology. He might conceivably have grasped the point if he had come across Professor Harold Burr's researches into the "life field" of trees and animals, for in the mid-1930s, Burr not only showed that living things are surrounded and permeated by electrical fields —just as Reich said they were—but that the fields *organize and control* them. Burr described these fields as "nature's jelly molds." According to Burr, the "L-fields" shape matter in much the same way that a magnetic field will cause iron filings to fall into a pattern. And if a lizard loses its tail or a worm is chopped in half, the reason it can grow another half so easily is that the molecules are poured into a pre-existing electric mold.

This is what is lacking in Reich's orgone theory, the notion of organization and control. But then, if this analysis is correct, Reich would have been incapable of developing such a notion. It would have been in total contradiction to his Freudian reductionism. That is, it would have involved a repudiation of Freud, and this would have produced a psychological upheaval that might have destroyed Reich.

As it was, Reich tried to convince himself that orgone energy was the key to all problems of health, both physical and mental. After all, if orgone energy *is* life, the libido, then free will becomes irrelevant. A sick person is suffering either from stagnation, or from a kind of withdrawal of the energy (the "shrinking" that produces cancer.) And the physician's problem is to restore the flow. It was almost a mechanical problem, like servicing a robot. In effect, Reich ceased to be a psychologist after the "discovery of the orgone." He had banished the psyche from psychology.

Thus it was that in the early 1940s Reich found himself in an intellectual cul-de-sac. This was already becoming clear to him by the time he began to write *The Cancer Biopathy*. He says: "Additional practical experiences are needed before any conclusive observations can be made . . . ," but by that time he had been experimenting with the accumulator for more than five years, and it was quite clear that it was not the universal solution he had hoped. In *Character Analysis* (the later edition) he describes the treatment of a schizophrenic woman patient in which he used the accumulator; it went on for more than two years, and although it was finally successful, it would probably have been so if Reich had treated her with the old methods of "character analysis." It seemed that the accumulator could stimulate the vital powers, but could not guarantee a cure. For the cure, particularly in cases of mental illness, depended ultimately on the patient's own attitudes. Where psychotherapy was concerned, Reich was in effect back where he was before the "discovery of the orgone." At this point, he switched his attention conclusively from psychology, and refused to take any more patients. Instead, he turned to cosmic theorizing, and to such down-to-earth matters as weather control. For in fact, he had come to the end of the road.

It is probably a pointless exercise in speculation, but it is tempting to wonder what might have happened if Reich had not handicapped himself with the Freudian ball and chain. If, for example, instead of falling under Freud's exclusive influence, he had encountered the psychology developed by Freud's eminent French contemporary Pierre Janet. Janet's starting point was identical with Freud's—both had received their initial stimulus from the work of Charcot on hysteria—but from that point, their paths diverged considerably.

Pierre Janet was three years Freud's junior; in 1885, when Freud was at the Salpêtrière with Charcot, Janet was a young professor of philosophy in Le Havre whose chief interest was in psychology, and he was considering a thesis on hallucinations. At this point, someone told him of a woman called Léonie who could be hypnotized from a distance. Janet investigated this claim, and found it to be true; Léonie could be put into a trance at a distance, and called from her house to Janet's. What was equally curious was that Léonie possessed two totally distinct personalities. The "everyday" Léonie was a dull peasant woman; under hypnosis she became gay and vital. This "second" Léonie flatly denied that she was the same person as the first, explaining that "Léonie one" was "a good and stupid woman, but not me." Another patient, Lucie, suffered from fits of terror, and also proved to contain a totally distinct secondary personality named Adrienne. A patient named Irène, at the Salpêtrière (where Janet served as director from 1890–98) was also a dual personality; as with Freud's Anna O, the illness began during the lengthy nursing of a dying parent, in this case, her mother; from then on, Irène had been subject to attacks of "somnambulism," in which she was subject to hallucinations. Janet cured her through hypnosis.

Like Freud, Janet realized that these strange manifestations revealed the presence of an "unconscious mind" (although Janet preferred the word "subconscious"—which, in fact, he virtually invented). But how could a piece of consciousness become split off from the rest, and then take on a separate identity? Janet made an interesting observation that supplied part of the answer. If he spoke to a hysterical patient in a low voice, for example, commanding her to raise her arm in the air, she would obey unconsciously. When he asked her, in a normal voice, why she had raised her arm, she would look at it with bewilderment. Her "conscious self" had ignored the order, concentrating on her obsessive anxieties. But beyond this conscious self, a kind of "penumbral" self had responded normally.

We can begin to grasp the implications if we think of the conscious mind of a healthy person as a large, wedge-shaped fragment, rather like a segment cut out of a circular cheese. The rest of the cheese remains in "shadow"; it is unconscious (or subconscious). When a person becomes tense with anxiety, this wedge-shaped segment becomes even narrower; the person's "field of attention" is contracted. Yet on either side of this contracted field of attention, the rest of the wedge continues to exist in a kind of half-light. *This* is what responded to Janet's order to raise the arm. The task of the psychotherapist is to persuade the hysteric to "unwind," to relax back into the "wider personality."

This image also provides an explanation of what happens in those moments of intense happiness, sudden semimystical experiences, when the world becomes self-evidently a richer and more fascinating place than we usually realize. This is the *opposite* of hysteria. Instead of narrowing, the personality widens; consciousness "relaxes" into an area that would normally be subconscious. Yeats once used a similar image in describing what happens in such experiences:

> Something drops from eyes long blind,
> He completes his partial mind.

Ordinary consciousness is "partial," like the moon in its last quarter. Yet the rest of the moon is still there, hidden in darkness. Ordinary consciousness is only a narrow sliver of this complete circle.

This is far from being a complete explanation of the phenomenon of multiple personality, but it is a step in the right direction. Janet regarded multiple personality as a special form of hysteria; it is as if the "penumbral" part of the mind is tired of being denied its proper ration of consciousness, and has seized its own share by a kind of coup d'état. Again, such cases can best be understood if we think of the "total mind" as a complete circle, and the "everyday self" as a mere segment. In which case, there are presumably dozens, perhaps hundreds of other "selves" waiting their turn to emerge, or to be integrated smoothly into consciousness through "widening."

There is an important corollary to all this. The hysteric also experiences a *limitation of vital powers*. (We are all familiar with the nervous person who says: "No, I *can't* do it"—then relaxes and discovers that he can.) "Narrowness" not only brings a sense of separation from the outside world (schizophrenia) but also a sense of impotence. "Widening" brings a sense of the richness of the universe, and also of increased powers. In such a state, nothing seems impossible.

How is this widening brought about? By what Janet called "psychological tension." The mind has the power to contract, to concentrate. When this power is used negatively, in mere anxiety, the field of consciousness contracts, and the result is hysteria. When it is used positively, to grasp "something interesting," the result is a widening, an expansion.

It is important to grasp the distinction between "psychological tension" and mere force. A man wheeling a barrowload of stones needs force, but very little tension. A jeweler repairing a Swiss watch needs a great deal of tension, but very little force. Tension is *organized* force.

It is this vital concept of "creative tension" that is missing from the psychology of Freud and Reich, with the inevitable result that they overlook the mind's primary function: the act of choice. In "creative tension," the mind's scattered energies are drawn together and organized, and such "concentration" is as much a function of the conscious will as breathing is of the lungs. (Unfortunately, it is not an automatic function, like breathing, so human beings can cease to exercise "psychological tension" and experience a kind of mental suffocation: neurosis.)

This basic function of the will could be expressed by an image of billiard balls on a tabletop. When I am tired and bored, they lie in a random pattern all over the table. The moment something captures my interest, I "summon" my energies, and the balls move together. (In fact, I use the phrase "pulling myself together.") When I become deeply absorbed, the balls draw together into a tight mass. At this point, I may begin to experience the "feedback" effect of creative excitement, and the tension pulling the balls together may become so great that some of them move on top of others, to form a second tier. In "inspiration," they may even build up into a pyramid. If I become tired, or lose my concentration, the tension vanishes, and the balls again move apart.

Weak personalities have very little power of inducing psychological tension; their minds are almost permanently in a scattered state, at the mercy of every passing impression. (We even speak of "scatterbrains.") When threatened by serious problems, their response tends to be purely defensive, a negative tension. This is the hysterical "narrowing" of personality we have been discussing. The opposite response is the most fundamental expression of human freedom: to "pull ourselves together," to fight back. Yet this may still have no obvious advantage; the problems may still be overwhelming. The point at which "fighting back" becomes self-evidently the right decision is when psychological tension becomes *creative,* that is, when it begins to reveal new vistas of meaning which, in turn, reinforce the tension: the "feedback effect." This is the point at which a man who has been struggling with some difficult task suddenly begins to feel equal to it, then actually to enjoy the struggle. His "personality" has widened, giving him access to more energy.

It can be seen that this picture of the mind throws the emphasis on decision, on "intentionality." It also brings a new meaning to the concept of the unconscious. This ceases to be a vast, impersonal ocean, in which man is a floating worm. The "worm" (the ego) is now seen to be a segment of self-awareness—the segment I call "me." But it now becomes clear that this is my mistake. This "identity" can be contracted by anxiety or expanded by pleasant anticipation or creative excitement. The "true me" is the *full* moon. The "unconscious" is an invisible extension of my conscious identity, a kind of immense Lebensraum into which the "I" is free to expand—provided it has the courage and the intelligence to make the effort.

All this enables us to state precisely what is wrong with Reich's psychology. Because his concept of the mind is basically mechanical, he leaves out the most important factor: freedom. So his concept of a healthy being is, like Freud's, limited and static.

Now in any science but psychology, this would hardly matter. When a physicist talks about horsepower, it makes no difference whether he means a living horse or a machine; all that matters is how many foot-pounds per minute are involved. A materialist who regards the human body as a machine makes as good a doctor as a Plymouth Brother who regards it as the temple of the Holy Spirit. But effective psychotherapy depends basically upon the will of the patient—upon a certain determination and optimism. The psychotherapist's most important task is to persuade the patient to start *fighting back*. If courage could be bought in bottles, psychotherapists would be unnecessary.

Even on the physical level, we are all aware of the importance of optimism. We all know, for example, that it is possible to stop feeling sick by making a certain kind of mental effort. It involves, first of all, thinking about something else, not brooding on the feeling of nausea; then a further effort can somehow summon vitality, and lift us beyond the sickness. The same principle applies to neurosis, even if the problem is more complex. This means that anyone who can grasp the basic principle of Janet or Frankl or Maslow—that the "unconscious" regions of the mind contain enormous reserves of power—is in an admirable position for fighting off the invisible bacilli of neurosis. Conversely, anyone who accepts the major premise of Freud and Reich—that the unconscious is nothing more than a repository of dangerous repressions—has been robbed of his most powerful weapon against discouragement and defeat. For man is ultimately an evolutionary animal; that is, the only animal who seems to remain permanently unsatisfied. He struggles for security, for love, for respect and recognition, and even if he is fortunate enough to achieve them all, he is still unsatisfied. He seems to come closest to fulfillment in *problem-solving,* but his nature is such that he never remains satisfied with the solution of any particular problem; if he runs out of problems he will invent them. It is as if his deepest sense of purpose is geared to problem-solving, that is, to creativity. He is the only creature on earth who wants to know how the universe got here, and what man is doing in it. And this, in turn, seems to be closely connected with what goes on in his own mind. One of the main reasons he is so obsessed by problem-solving is that when he has successfully overcome some difficult challenge, he receives a strange glimpse of unsuspected powers inside himself. This glimpse also seems to reveal the world around him in a new light, as in some way *unknown,* as if his mind normally imposed a completely false familiarity on it. It is not even necessary to overcome problems to obtain the same tantalizing insight; it can happen on any spring morning or fall afternoon.

The familiarity through which our minds force us to see things is undoubtedly necessary; it provides us with a basic stability. But our deepest hunger is for the strangeness that lies on the other side of this familiarity. If we remain fundamentally optimistic and curious and *expectant,* we can keep tugging aside the curtain of familiarity and glimpsing the strangeness. Thinkers and artists who deaden this sense of curiosity by insisting that human life *is* as limited as it seems, are performing the worst kind of disservice to humanity.

Now as a human being, Reich possessed this curiosity and expectancy in abundance. This is the reason that "Reichians" hold him in such high esteem. The "elephant's child" never lost his "satiable curtiosity." Where sex was concerned, he was a liberator in the tradition of Blake, Whitman, and Lawrence. By instinct and conviction, he was what Shaw called a "world betterer." In *Cos-*

mic Superimposition he even emerges as a kind of mystic. Yet this liberator and visionary tied himself into a straitjacket of old-fashioned nineteenth-century materialism that prevented him developing his instinctive insights. And since, with German thoroughness, he connected all his ideas together into a "system," it is difficult to take what is valuable and reject the rest.

The effort is nevertheless worth making. Although Reich's thinking was limited by his Freudian premises, his intuitions can leap out like flashes of lightning. This can be seen, for example, in the remarkable concluding pages of *Cosmic Superimposition,* where he drops the role of the scientist and takes on that of the visionary. Like Blake, he is attempting to explain just what went wrong with human beings, searching for an explanation of the "Fall."

> Before there was any life, there was the streaming of cosmic orgone energy. When climatic conditions were sufficiently developed on the planet, life began to appear, most likely in the form of primitive plasmatic flakes . . . From these flakes, single-cell organisms developed over the eons. Now cosmic energy was flowing not only in the vast galactic spaces but also in tiny bits of membranous matter . . .

And so life on Earth began its long, slow struggle. Finally, man developed, and little by little, "man slowly began to reason *beyond* his strong orgonotic contact and harmony with nature . . ." But then man turned reason in upon himself; he became self-conscious, and so the Fall occurred. ". . . *in attempting to understand himself and the streaming of his own energy, man interfered with it, and in doing so, began to armour, and thus to deviate from nature.* The first split into a mystical alienation from himself, his core, and a mechanical order of existence instead of the organic, involuntary, bio-energetic self-regulation, followed with compulsive force."

And now follows a passage which reveals Reich plumbing new depths of insight:

> The fright that still overcomes man in our time when he thinks about himself; the general reluctance to think at all; the whole function of repression of emotional functions of the self; the pow-

erful force with which man resists knowledge about himself; the
fact that for millennia he investigated the stars but not his own
emotions; the panic that grips the witness of orgonomic investigations at the core of man's existence; the fervent ardour with
which every religion defends the unreachability and unknow-
ability of God, which clearly represents nature *within* man—all
these and many other facts speak a clear language regarding the
terror that is connected with the deep experience of the self.

Here, suddenly, Reich has formulated a new concept of evolutionary purpose: not merely to get "back to nature," but to explore the depths of his own being. Already, some men have learned
to do this. "The few who, far from being frightened, enjoy sub-
merging in their innermost selves are the great artists, poets, scientists and philosophers who create from the depths of their free-
flowing contact with nature inside and outside themselves; in
higher, abstract mathematics no less than in poetry or music." Are
these few men, these "outsiders"—Reich asks—the exception to the
rule? Or are they the norm from which the rest of the human race
has deviated? If, in fact, the majority is "the exception," then "it
would become possible, by the most strenuous effort ever made in
the history of man, to adjust the majority to the flow of natural
processes."

This, Reich firmly believes, will come about as the human race
gradually absorbs the discovery of "cosmic orgone energy." The
"armored" majority will fight against it bitterly; but then, fighting
is in itself a method of acknowledgment, and slowly, "the hardest,
toughest and cruellest character structure will be forced to make
contact with the basic fact of the existence of a life energy . . ."
And so the conclusion will not be a simple "return to nature," but
a man who possesses both "naturalness" *and* self-awareness.

When this happens, says Reich, the politicians will realize that
man is far more than a political animal; religion will revise its
foundations and recognize that the godlike lies *within* man.

"In this manner, the blocking of natural contact with the self
and the surrounding world will slowly, possibly over several cen-
turies, diminish, and finally . . . will completely vanish from the
surface of the earth."

The last sentence of the book is almost unrecognizable as com-

ing from the man who once proclaimed that human beings have
no free will:

> This is no prophecy. Man, and not fate, is burdened with the full
> responsibility for the outcome of this process.

Reich may have been responsible for his own misfortunes, but
in passages like this, he reveals a remarkable power to transcend
them. He may have had many faults, but these did not include
lack of courage.

NOTES

CHAPTER ONE

1 *The Sexual Offender*, selected by Robert Ollendorff, London, 1967.
2 Ernest Jones, *Sigmund Freud: Life and Work*, Basic Books, New York, 1953, Vol. 1, p. 415 *et seq.*
3 Paul Roazen, *Freud and His Followers*, Alfred A. Knopf, 1975, p. 224.
4 Paul Roazen, *Freud and His Followers*, p. 73 *et seq.*

CHAPTER TWO

1 Ed. E. J. Dingwall, *Abnormal Hypnotic Phenomena, A Survey of 19th-Century Cases*, 4 vols., 1967; particularly Vol. 1, p. 158 *et seq.* See also Brian Inglis, *Natural and Supernatural*, Chapter 19.
2 Axel Munthe, *The Story of San Michele*, Chapter 19.
3 Adam Smith, *Powers of Mind*, New York, 1975, p. 49.
4 Ed. Muriel Gardner, *The Wolf Man and Sigmund Freud*, Hogarth Press, London, 1972.

5 A full account of the relations between Freud and Kraus can be found in *Karl Kraus and the Soul-Doctors* by Thomas Szasz, Louisiana State University Press, Baton Rouge, La., 1976.

6 Paul Roazen, *Brother Animal: The Story of Tausk and Freud,* Alfred A. Knopf, New York, 1969.

CHAPTER THREE

1 Ernest Jones, *Free Associations: Memories of a Psychoanalyst,* London, 1959, p. 169.

2 Republished in America in 1971 as *Hidden Symbols of Alchemy* (Dover).

3 Unpublished.

4 When I wrote *The Outsider* in 1955, I was unaware that Reich had already used this term in the sense of rebel or outcast; I borrowed it from Shaw, who uses it in this sense in the preface to *Immaturity*.

5 Quoted in *Reich Speaks of Freud,* p. 148. It was never sent.

6 This first version of the book—published in 1927—has little in common with the more autobiographical work published in 1942 as Vol. 1 of *The Discovery of the Orgone*. It is this later version that has been quoted in these pages so far. The earlier version is a more strictly clinical work, with analyses of case histories.

7 C. G. Jung, *Memories, Dreams, Reflections,* Random House, New York, 1963, p. 147.

CHAPTER FOUR

1 "The Logic of Tacit Inference," in *Knowing and Being,* University of Chicago Press, Chicago, 1969.

2   See *The Nature of Human Consciousness, A Book of Readings,* ed. Robert Ornstein, p. 72.
3   William James, *Varieties of Religious Experience,* Modern Library edition, Random House, N.Y., Chapter 9, p. 203. He is quoting Starbuck.

CHAPTER FIVE

1   Reich, *Reich Speaks of Freud,* Farrar, Straus, & Giroux, New York, 1967, p. 45.
2   Reich, *Selected Sex-Pol Essays, 1934–1937,* Reich and Teschnitz, Socialist Reproduction, London, 1972.
3   In a letter to me dated October 1, 1978, Dr. Eva Reich wrote: "We were sent to a Marxist house for children in Fronau, a suburb of Berlin, to live, also to their summer camp on the Baltic Sea. But I also went to regular school there. It was HORRIBLE!—neglected, dirty, no protein—I remember eating salted boiled potatoes and bread and lard —no sheets on straw sacks at Baltic . . . (the little children had sheets). I remember little as it was so unpleasant."

CHAPTER SIX

1   *Reich Speaks of Freud,* Part 2.
2   Ed. Arthur Koestler, Magnus Hirschfeld, *The Sexual Anomalies,* Emerson Books, Buchanan, N.Y., 1948.
3   This account is taken from letters and cassettes sent to me by Gerd Bergersen (now Hay-Edie). In the fall of 1978, Gerd Hay-Edie heard me broadcasting on the BBC's *Desert Island Discs* program when, in answer to one of Roy Plomley's questions, I mentioned that I was working on a book on Reich. She wrote to me; and as a result I learned of this fascinating, and so far unrecorded, episode in Reich's life.

4   After her separation from Reich she discovered the writ-
    ings of Jung, and became a convinced Jungian. Jung's
    view of the psyche seemed to her altogether closer to the
    truth.
5   She later married, as she admits, "on the rebound from
    Reich, someone completely different: a safe English gen-
    tleman—only to learn there is no such thing as a safe
    partner."

CHAPTER SEVEN

1   Theodore P. Wolfe, "A Sex-Economist Answers," *Interna-
    tional Journal of Sex-Economy and Orgone Research*,
    Vol. 3, No. 1, March 1944.
2   In fact it was published by the Orgone Institute Press in
    1948.

CHAPTER EIGHT

1   Frances Yates, *Giordano Bruno and the Hermetic Tradi-
    tion* and *The Art of Memory*, Random House, New York,
    1968. Also Colin Wilson, *Mysteries*, G. P. Putnam's, New
    York, 1978, Part 2, Chapter 1.

POSTSCRIPT

1   Thelma Moss, *The Probability of the Impossible*, New
    American Library, New York, 1975.
2   C. G. Jung, *Flying Saucers: A Modern Myth of Things
    Seen in the Skies*, 1959.
3   See, for example, Rolf Alexander's *The Power of the
    Mind*, which contains newspaper photographs of an ap-
    parently successful experiment in "cloud dissipation."

BIBLIOGRAPHY

WORKS BY WILHELM REICH

The Function of the Orgasm, 1927. Simon & Schuster, New York, 1974. (Later edition published as *The Discovery of the Orgone,* vol. 1), 1942. New American Library, New York, 1974.

Sex-Pol Essays, 1929–1934, edited by Lee Baxandall: "Dialectical Materialism and Psychoanalysis," "The Imposition of Sexual Morality," "What Is Class Consciousness?" Vintage Books, New York, 1972.

The Invasion of Compulsory Sex-Morality, 1932. Farrar, Straus & Giroux, New York, 1971.

Character Analysis, 1933. Farrar, Straus & Giroux, New York, 1972.

The Mass Psychology of Fascism, 1933. Farrar, Straus & Giroux, New York, 1970.

Selected Sex-Pol Essays, 1934–1937. Socialist Reproduction, London, 1972.

The Sexual Revolution, 1945. Farrar, Straus & Giroux, New York, 1974.

The Cancer Biopathy, vol. 2 of *The Discovery of the Orgone*, 1936. Farrar, Straus & Giroux, New York, 1973.

Listen, Little Man!, 1948. Farrar, Straus & Giroux, New York, 1973.

Ether, God and Devil, Cosmic Superimposition, 1951. Farrar, Straus & Giroux, New York, 1973.

Selected Writings, An Introduction to Orgonomy, 1951. Farrar, Straus & Giroux, New York, 1973.

People in Trouble, 1953 (vol. 2 of *The Emotional Plague of Mankind*). Farrar, Straus & Giroux, New York, 1976.

The Murder of Christ, 1953 (vol. 1 of *The Emotional Plague of Mankind*). Farrar, Straus & Giroux, New York, 1966.

JOURNALS

International Journal of Life Energy: vol. 1: *Reich's Life and Work: Some Interrelations* by Myron R. Sharaf, Ph.D. vol. 2: *Reich, The Man and Thinker* by Ted Mann & Ed Hoffman. vol. 3: *Reich, Radix, and the Enhancement of Sexuality* by Charles R. Kelley, Ph.D. (All three journals dated 1979.) Published by: Life Energy Action Research Network, Canada.

International Journal of Sex-Economy and Orgone-Research. Editor: Theodore P. Wolfe, M.D. vol. 3, no. 1, March 1944. Orgone Institute Press, New York.

Annals of the Orgone Institute. Editor: Theodore P. Wolfe, M.D. Orgone Institute Press, New York, 1947.

WORKS ON WILHELM REICH

Baker, Elsworth F., M.D. *Man in the Trap.* Avon Books, New York, 1967.

Bean, Orson. *Me and the Orgone*. Fawcett Crest, New York, 1971.

Boadella, David. *Wilhelm Reich—The Evolution of His Work*. Contemporary Books, Chicago, 1974.

———. *In the Wake of Reich*. Ashey Books, Port Washington, New York, 1978.

Cattier, Michel. *The Life and Work of Wilhelm Reich*. Avon Books, New York, 1971.

Chesser, Eustace. *Reich and Sexual Freedom*. Vision Press Ltd., London, 1972.

Eden, Jerome. *Orgone Energy—The Answer to Atomic Suicide*. Exposition Press, New York, 1972.

———. *Planet in Trouble—The UFO Assault on Earth*. Exposition Press, New York, 1973.

Eissler, Kurt R. *Reich Speaks of Freud*. Farrar, Straus & Giroux, New York, 1967.

Greenfield, Jerome. *Wilhelm Reich Vs. the U.S.A.* W. W. Norton, New York, 1973.

Mann, W. Edward. *Orgone, Reich and Eros*. Simon and Schuster, New York, 1973.

Raknes, Ola. *Wilhelm Reich and Orgonomy*. Penguin Books Inc., New York, 1970.

Reich, Ilse Ollendorff. *Wilhelm Reich—A Personal Biography*. Elek Books Ltd., London, 1969.

Reich, Peter. *A Book of Dreams*. Harper & Row, 1973.

Rycroft, Charles. *Wilhelm Reich*. Viking Press, New York, 1972.

Teschitz, Karl (with Wilhelm Reich). *Selected Sex-Pol Essays 1934–1937*.

Wyckoff, James. *Wilhelm Reich: Life Force Explorer*. Fawcett Publications Inc., New York, 1973.

INDEX

Abnegation of will, 130
Abortion, 120, 156
Abraham, Karl, 71, 133
Abreaction therapy, 166–67
Academy of Physics, 187
Actual neuroses theory, 81
Adler, Alfred, 5, 31, 36, 57, 63, 69, 70, 71, 73, 90, 116, 121, 151
Air Technical Intelligence Center, 222
Alchemy, 72
Alcoholism, 199
Alexander, Franz, 133
Alienation, 103
Allen, Hervey, 18
Almanach of Psychoanalysis, 122
Alpha waves, 108
Altai-Himalaya (Roerich), 236
American Association for Medical Orgonomy, 204
American Men of Science, 19
American Psychiatric Association, 204
Andreas-Salomé, Lou, 66
Animal magnetism, 40
Anna Karenina (Tolstoy), 30
Anna O, *see* Pappenheim, Bertha
Anthroposophy, 35
Anti-Semitism, 25, 26

Anxiety, 77–78, 93, 101, 127, 160, 165, 245, 248; neurosis and, 101–2, 119; unconscious and, 132
Aquinas, St. Thomas, 115–16
Arbeiterhilfe (medical group), 117
Armoring, principle of, 166
Arnold, Kenneth, 215, 236
Art of Emily Brontë, The (Wilson), vi
Astrology, 181
Atomic energy, 207–8
Atomic Energy Commission, 208
"Atoms for peace" speech (Eisenhower), 224
Auschwitz (concentration camp), 51
Austro-Hungarian Empire, 23–25
Ayer, A. J., 3

Bach, Johann Sebastian, 199
Badeni, Count Casimir, 24, 25
Badeni Language Ordinances, 24
Baker, Elsworth, 164, 165–66, 167, 208, 222
Bangor Daily News, 211, 221
Bangor hydroelectric dam (Maine), 211
Bean, Orson, 164, 193
Beard, George M., 39–40
Beat Generation, 201

Beethoven, Ludwig van, 17–18, 124, 199

Bergersen, Gerd, 172–75, 176–77

Bergson, Henri, 3, 35, 115

Berlin Association of Socialist Physicians, 134

Berlin Psychoanalytic Institute, 133

Bernfeld, Siegfried, 133, 134, 148

Bernheim, Hyppolite, 41, 42, 43, 48, 57

Beyond the Pleasure Principle (Freud), 85

Bikini Atoll, atomic weapon testing, 207

Biodynamic theories, 168

Bio-electricity, 163

Bioenergy, 123

Biographia Literaria (Coleridge), 51–52

Biological energy, 162, 170

Bion, The (Reich), 176

Bion cultures, 10

Bion research, 170–72, 176, 178–79, 182, 191, 194, 195–96, 234–35

Birth control, 156

Bischoff, 136, 140–41

Blake, William, 249, 250

Blakeney, Mrs., 237, 238

Blasband, Dr. Richard, 212

Bloch, Ivan, 31, 32

Boadella, David, 16, 122, 167, 188, 196, 212, 220

Bohr, Niels, 154

Bolero (Ravel), 175

Boltzmann, Ludwig, 236

Book of Dreams (Reich), 224

Brady, Mildred Edie, 199–201, 203

Braid, James, 41

Brain, neuroses and, 104–12

Breathing, 160; to reduce tension, 12

Breuer, Josef, 20, 44–45, 46, 47, 54–55, 57, 64, 100; break with Freud, 56

Briehl, Dr. Walter, 194–95

Brill, A. A., 57

British Broadcasting Corporation (BBC), 237

British Medico-Psychological Association, 32

Brontë, Emily, vi

Brownian movement, 170

Bruno, Giordano, 6, 213, 214, 230

Buddhism, 35

Burford, Mrs. Suzanne, 12

Burr, Dr. Harold, 8, 243

California Institute of Technology, 104

Cancer, 182, 185, 200, 202; Reich's basic idea about, 3; Shaw's theory of, 3–4; T-bacilli and, 4, 171–72, 182, 209

Cancer Biopathy, The (Reich), 1, 3, 4, 5, 182–83, 184, 203, 213, 217, 218, 244

Candide (Voltaire), 198

Carstens, Eric, 153, 154

Catatonia, 88

Cattier, Michel, 159, 160, 161, 163, 170, 178, 233

Character Analysis (Reich), 128, 130, 148, 194, 229, 231, 244

Charcot, Jean Martin, 20, 41–43, 45, 46, 48, 54, 56, 75, 244

Charlatanism, 40, 41, 188

Christianity, 213

Christian Science, 2

Christian Socialists (Austria), 122

Chuang Tzu, 19

Civilization and Its Discontents (Freud), 84, 123–24, 191

Clare, John, 84

Clark, Ronald, 186–87, 188, 190

Clemmenson, Dr., 153

Clifford, Judge, 218, 219, 220, 228, 241

"Cloudbuster" experiments, 210–12, 220–21, 222, 224–26, 239

Cold War, 207

Coleridge, Samuel Taylor, 51–52

Columbia University, 178

Comintern (Third International Organization of Communist Parties), 155

Commedia (Dante), 124

Communism, 1, 7, 10, 115–18, 120–22, 125, 133–37, 149, 155, 188, 194, 233–34; expulsion of Reich, 122

Communist Academy (Moscow), 122

Communist Party (Denmark), 153

Communist Party (France), 141
Communist Party (Germany), 125,
   134–37, 140, 141, 144, 151–52,
   155, 156; cell meetings, 134–35
Consciousness, 51, 104, 110, 245,
   246
Constable, T. R., 211, 239
Contact with Space (Reich), 220,
   223, 225, 238
Cosmic Pulse of Life, The (Con-
   stable), 239
Cosmic Superimposition (Reich),
   213, 220, 229, 249–50
Crawshaw, Andrew, 9
Creation (Reich), 229
Creative tension, concept of, 247

Dachau (concentration camp), 51
Danbury Federal Corrective Institu-
   tion (Connecticut), 229
Danish Psychoanalytic Association,
   154
Dante, 17, 124
Dartington Hall (school), 172, 173,
   174
Darwin, Charles, 101
Da Vinci, Leonardo, 20, 65–66, 110
Davos Sanitarium (Switzerland), 91–
   92, 94, 95, 113
Death-instinct theory, 53, 85, 121,
   150, 154; Reich's criticism of, 148
Death-urge, concept of, 20
Dennison, Lucy Bellamy, 197
Deutsch, Helene, 57, 67, 91
Deutsche Volkszeitung, 139
Dialectical materialism, 115–16
*Dialectical Materialism and Psycho-
   analysis* (Reich), 116, 119, 120
Discovery of the Orgone, The
   (Reich), 4, 5, 194
Discovery of the Unconscious, The
   (Ellenberger), 39
Doctor's Dilemma (Shaw), 159
Dogmatism, 7
Dollfuss, Engelbert, 114
DOR barrier, 226
DOR (Deadly Orgone Radiation),
   209, 211, 212, 220, 222–24, 225
Dostoevsky, Fedor, 20, 60, 66, 230
Dragons of Eden, The (Sagan), 106
Driesch, Hans, 3, 35, 115

Drugs and alcohol, 110
Du Teil, Roger, 171, 235
Dynamism, 40, 112

Ea (Energy alpha), 223, 236
Eddy, Mary Baker, 2
Edna (hurricane), 212
Eeden, Frederik van, 52
Ego, 85, 97, 99, 106, 131
Ehrenhaft, Felix, 188
Einstein, Albert, 4, 17, 19, 154,
   186–90
Einstein Affair, The (Reich), 187
Eisenhower, Dwight D., 221, 229,
   241
Eissler, Emmy, 152
Eissler, Dr. Kurt, 36–37, 69, 73, 82,
   88, 90, 93, 94, 123, 125, 133, 149,
   152
Eitington, Max, 149, 158
Ejaculation, premature, 81–82
Elephant's Child (Kipling), 82
El Greco, 142
Ellenberger, Henri, 39
Elliotson, John, 41
Ellis, Havelock, 31, 32
Elmhirst, Leonard and Dorothy, 172
Emotional plague, 2, 3, 198–99, 201,
   204, 208, 213, 222
Emotional Plague Prevention Office
   (EPPO), 227
Encyclopaedia Britannica, 213
Enemy of the People (Ibsen), 178
Engels, Friedrich, 115, 117, 141
Engrams, 127
Entelechy, 35
Equilibrium, 112
Erwartung (Schönberg), 82
Esdaile, James, 41
Ether, God and Devil (Reich), 196,
   212, 213
Eureka (Poe), 18
Evans, Christopher, 235
Experiment XX, 196, 213
Exteriorization phenomena, 53, 236–
   37, 238

Fackel, Die (magazine), 65
"Fackel Neurosis, The" (Wittels), 66
Faculty X, 111–12

Fads and Fallacies in the Name of Science (Gardner), 1, 4, 204, 233
Fairley, Peter, 237
Faraday, Michael, 237
Faraday Cage, 184
Farr, Florence, 163
Farrar, Straus & Giroux, 230
Fascism, 141–42, 156, 179
Faust (Goethe), 124
Federal Bureau of Investigation (FBI), 225
Federn, Paul, 70, 76–77, 88, 90, 91, 93–94, 95, 122, 148, 151, 158
Fenichel, Otto, 133, 134, 168
Ferenczi, Sandor, 71, 77
Fichte, Johann Gottlieb, 119
Fliess, 56
Flying Saucers Are Real (Keyhoe), 216
Food and Drug Administration (FDA), 2, 4, 6, 13, 202–3, 217–18, 220, 221, 225–27, 230, 231, 241; Complaint against Reich, 217, 221–22, 227
Forel, August, 31, 34–35
Fort Knox, 215
Frankl, Viktor, 51, 101, 129, 161, 192, 248
Franz Ferdinand, Archduke, 25
Franz Joseph, Emperor, 23–24
Freedom, 40, 148, 151, 160, 196, 201, 218; loss of, 53–54
Free will, 54, 74, 80
French Academy of Sciences, 41, 42
Freud, Anna, 62, 73, 158
Freud, Julius, 58
Freud, Sigmund, 1, 4, 6, 9, 19, 20, 29, 31, 115, 116, 120–21, 123–25, 132–33, 134, 137, 149–50, 151, 154, 167, 168, 174, 186, 187, 191, 193, 197, 201, 213, 241, 242, 244, 247, 248, 249; break with Breuer, 56; distinction between Reich and, 102–3; failure to grasp the "tennis mechanism," 46, 48, 97; fundamental concept of, 20; hostility toward Reich, 147; International Psychoanalytic Congress (1922), 85; and Jung, 52–53, 63–64, 93; last visit with Reich, 133; on orgasm theory, 88; politics of,

122–23; reaction to Tausk's suicide, 68; rejection of Silberer, 72–73; relationship with Reich, 36–37, 68, 69–70, 72, 73–74, 87–95, 147–48, 242; relations with leading followers, 64–68, 70; Tausk's relation with, 66–67; view of the Hippocratic oath, 94; *See also* names of theories
Freud and His Followers (Roazen), 71, 73, 122
Freudianism, 5, 21, 33, 54, 61, 62, 150, 151, 161, 193, 219, 244; Reich's conversion to, 34
Freud Journal, 66
Frink, H. W., 57
Fromm, Erich, 133, 134
"From the History of an Infantile Neurosis" (Freud), 61
Fuchs, Klaus, 208
Function of the Orgasm, The (Reich), 4–5, 19, 31, 32, 35, 36, 74, 78, 81, 82, 89, 91, 93, 114, 126–27, 161, 194, 214, 218, 230–31, 242

Gaasland, Gertrude, 181, 189, 194
Galileo, 6, 151, 214, 230
Gardner, Martin, 1, 2–3, 4, 204, 209, 233, 235
Genêt, Jean, 138
Genital consciousness, 110–11
Genital (libido) theory, 97, 113, 150–51; *See also* Libido theory
Georget, E. J., 41
German Association for Proletarian Sexual Politics, 136
German Psychoanalytic Association, 157–58
Gerst, Richard, 31
God, Reich's concept of, 213
God That Failed, The (Koestler), 134
Goering, Hermann, 144
Goethe, Johann Wolfgang von, 17, 124
Grad, Bernard, 196
Greene, Graham, 110
Greenfield, Jerome, 200, 201, 217, 220, 230
Griesinger, Wilhelm, 39
Groddeck, George, 133–34

Guevara, Che, 231
Gulliver's Travels (Swift), 198
Gurdjieff, 167

Handel, George Frederick, 110
Hapsburg family, 23
Harnik (psychotic), 154
Harper's (magazine), 200
Harris, Frank, 137
Hartmann, Eduard von, 46
Head consciousness, 110–11
Heiberg, Edvard, 153
Hesse, Hermann, 231
Higgins, Mary Boyd, vi–vii, 230
Hindenburg, Paul von, 144
Hinduism, 91
Hippocratic oath, 94
Hiroshima, atomic bombing of, 207
Hirschfeld, Dr. Magnus, 31, 32,
   135–36, 140, 162
History of Medical Psychology
   (Zilboorg), 5
Hitler, Adolf, 7, 10, 141, 142–43,
   144, 153
Hitschmann, Eduard, 70–71, 86
Hoel, Nic, *see* Waal, Nic (Hoel)
Hoel, Sigurd, 157, 175, 178
Hölderlin, Friedrich, 84
Holliday (FBI agent), 225
Homosexuality, 32, 60, 128, 138, 163
Hoover, J. Edgar, 221
Hoppe, Dr., 204
Horney, Karen, 57
Houston, Jean, 52
Human aura, 8–9, 195
Husserl, Edmund, 192
Hypnotherapy, 41
Hypnotism, 40–41, 42, 64, 244–45
Hysteria, 42, 45, 127, 244, 246; simi-
   larity between hypnosis and, 43

Ibsen, Henrik, 75–76, 178
"Ibsen's Peer Gynt, Libido Conflicts
   and Hallucinations" (Reich), 74–
   76
Id, 85, 97, 99, 106
Immaturity (Shaw), 64
Infeld, Leopold, 19
Inhibitions, Symptoms, Anxiety
   (Freud), 93
Inquisition, 213

Institute for Sex-Economic Life-
   Investigation, 169
Institute of Sexual Science, 32
Interference mechanism, 103–4
Internationale Zeitschrift, 70
*International Journal of Psycho-
   analysis,* 147–48
*International Journal of Sex-
   Economy and Orgone Research,*
   193, 194
International Psychoanalytic Asso-
   ciation, 154, 158
International Psychoanalytic Con-
   gress of 1922, 85
*Invasion of the Compulsory Sex-
   Morality, The* (Reich), 119
Invisible Writing, The (Koestler),
   134
Israfel (Allen), 18

Jackson, Hughlings, 104
James, William, 54, 111
Janet, Pierre, 244–46, 248
Jesuits, *see* Society of Jesus
Jesus Christ, 6, 15, 230
Jews, 25, 65, 149, 177
John of the Cross, St., 142
Jones, Ernest, 5, 34, 37, 54, 55, 56,
   57, 61, 71, 76, 94, 122, 154, 158
Jonson, Ben, 17
*Journal for Political Psychology and
   Sex Economy,* 157
Jung, Carl Gustav, 5, 31, 37, 57, 69,
   70, 71, 73, 90, 91, 116, 121, 151,
   236; Freud and, 52–53, 63–64,
   93; interest in alchemy, 72
Jupiter Symphony (Mozart), 124

Kammerer, Paul, 35, 36, 73, 237;
   suicide of, 172
Kantorowicz, Alfred, 134–35
Karrer, Aurora, 227, 230, 240
Keats, John, 17, 199
Kelley, Dr. Charles, 212, 217
Keyhoe, Major Donald, 216
Kilner, Dr. Walter J., 8, 195
Kipling, Rudyard, 82
Kirlian, Semyon, 8–9
Klein, Melanie, 57, 134
Kleist, Heinrich von, 84
Klimt, Gustav, 31

Koestler, Arthur, 134, 135, 156
Kokoschka, Oskar, 31
Kolbenhoff, Walter, 152
Krafft-Ebing, Richard von, 31–32, 33, 150
Kraus, Friedrich, 159
Kraus, Karl, 65, 66
Krishnamurti, 15, 178

Lange, August and Lizzi, 175
Langley Porter Neuropsychiatric Institute, 104
Lapique, Dr. Louis, 171, 235
Last Supper, The (da Vinci), 110
Lawrence, D. H., 21, 102–3, 109, 110, 249
Leibniz, Gottfried Wilhelm von, 45–46, 48
Lenin, Nikolai, 151
Lennach, J. H., 156
Léonie (peasant woman), 244–45
Lermontov, Mikhail, 63
Lewis, Sinclair, 75
Lewisburg Penitentiary, 229, 230
Liberalism, 214
Liberal Party (Austria), 122
Libido deficiency, 192
Libido theory, 33–34, 53, 89, 93, 95, 150, 159, 160, 161, 169, 186, 191, 192, 243; Freud's abandonment of, 150; laboratory isolation of (by Reich), 179; Reich's version of, 120–21
Liébault, Auguste, 41, 42
Liebeck, Lotte, 156
L-fields, 243
"Life and Death of Wilhelm Reich, The" (Kelley), 217
Life and Work of Wilhelm Reich, The (Cattier), 159
Life of Freud (Jones), 5, 61–62
Lincoln, Abraham, 218
Lindenberg, Elsa, 7–8, 14, 144, 149, 154, 156, 158–59, 172, 173, 177, 178, 239
Listen, Little Man! (Reich), 16, 197–99, 204
Little Hans case, 20, 57–59, 64
Lives of a Bengal Lancer (motion picture), 164
Lives of the Saints, 15

Loos, Adolf, 31
Lubbe, Marinus van der, 144
Lucie (patient), 245

McCullough, Bob, 223, 224
McDonald, A., 196
Maguire, Joseph, 228
Malicious animal magnetism (MAM), 2
Malinowski, Bronislaw, 118, 137, 141, 153, 154, 175, 176, 182, 194
Mangravite, Thomas, 228
Man in the Trap (Baker), 166
Mann, Thomas, 65, 87
Mantell, Captain Thomas F., 215
Mao Tse-tung, 7
Marx, Karl, 1, 7, 115, 116, 117, 151, 173, 193
Marxists, see Communism
Marxist Workers' Center (Berlin), 134
Maslow, Abraham, 51, 129, 130, 162, 248
Masochism, 32, 161–63; Reich's theory of, 161–63
Mass Psychology of Fascism, The (Reich), 142, 143, 153, 155
Masturbation, 32, 80, 81, 176, 203
Me and the Orgone (Bean), 164
Meditation, 49
Memories, Dreams, Reflections (Jung), 52–53
Memory-trace, unconscious, 61
Mendel, Gregor, 236
Mesmer, Franz Anton, 8
Mesmerism, 41
Messiah (Handel), 110
Meynert, Theodor, 39
Miller, Henry, 14
Mind Possessed, The (Sargant), 167
Mocigeno, 213, 214
Moise, Bill, 211, 221, 222–23, 226
Monadology (Leibniz), 45–46
Mount Catalina, 223, 224
Mozart, Wolfgang Amadeus, 17
Mueller-Braunschweig, Carl, 158
Munch, Edvard, 175
Murder of Christ, The (Reich), 15, 16, 213, 214, 218
Muscular therapy, 165–66, 193
Musil, Robert, 30

Mussolini, Benito, 141, 142
Mysticism, 72, 103

Nagasaki, atomic bombing of, 207
"Nancy school" of hypnotherapy, 41
Nassauer, Rudi, 11
National Theatre (Norway), 175
Nazi Party, 135, 141, 142, 145, 149, 176–77, 188
Neergard, Sigurd, 153
Neill, A. S., 6, 7, 13, 14, 15, 16, 19, 155, 168, 196, 199, 204, 213
Neue Freie Presse, 66
Neurasthenia, 39–40, 79
Neurological and Psychiatric Clinic (University of Vienna), 82
Neuropathic Institute (Moscow), 122
Neurosis, 123, 126–27, 249; and anxiety, 101–2, 119; basic mechanism of, 46, 101–2, 108–9; Beard's theory, 39–40; blocked orgone energy and, 192–93; brain and, 104–12; cause of, 162, 186; development of, 50; feedback mechanism of, 53, 112; Freud's theory of, 97–99, 100; negative feedback, 53–54
"New Cult of Sex and Anarchy, The" (Brady), 200
New Jersey State Hospital, 203
New Method of Weather Control, A (Kelley), 212
New Republic, The (publication), 200
New School for Social Research, 178, 181, 182, 189
Newton, Sir Isaac, 4, 34
New York *Times,* The, 210
Nietzsche, Friedrich, 65, 66, 87, 230
Ninth Symphony (Beethoven), 124
Norway Psychiatric Institute, 175
Noyes, John Humphrey, 201
Nuclear radiation, 210
Nunberg, Hermann, 71, 86, 88

Occult, The (Wilson), 8
Occultism, 41, 64
Ode on Intimations of Immortality (Wordsworth), 50
Odic force, 8, 195

Oedipus complex, 37, 56, 66, 67, 127, 128
Oeverland, Arnulf, 175
Ollendorff, Ilse, *see* Reich, Ilse
Ollendorff, Mrs. Kirstie, 9–10
Ollendorff, Robert, 9–10, 11, 12, 16
Oneida Community, 201
Oranur (orgone antinuclear) experiment, 208–10, 216, 222
Organicism, 39
Orgasm Reflex, Muscular Posture and Bodily Expression (Reich), 175
"Orgasm Reflex, The" (Reich), 175
Orgasm theory of sexuality, 36–37; Freud on, 88; Reich's investigations of, 159–61
Orgone Accumulator, 2, 9–10, 187, 191, 193–94, 201–3, 217, 219, 225, 226, 244; cost of, 202; discovery of, 183–86; FDA destruction of, 229; genital excitement in, 185; rental of, 202, 222, 228; suspension over running water, 211; treatments, 185–86
Orgone energy, 2, 5, 8, 184–85, 187, 192, 197, 208, 211, 217, 220, 229, 234, 235, 239, 243; and atomic radiation, 207–8; bion cultures, 10; "force" from, 207; meaning of, 2; naming of, 179; neurosis and, 192–93; Oranur (antinuclear) experiment, 208–10, 216, 222; photographed, 195; scientific cosmology based on, 213
Orgone Institute, 229
Orgone Institute Press, 200
Orgone Journal, 194, 201
Orgone Operation Emotional Plague (OROP-EP), 220
Orgone pressure, 210
Orgone radiation, 182–83
Orgone therapy, 9, 89, 93, 117, 126, 159, 168–70; lack of organization and control in, 243
Orgonon (laboratory), 195, 197, 199, 201–3, 204, 209, 211, 216, 217, 220, 224, 226, 229
Ornstein, Robert, 21, 104

OROP Desert (Orgone Energy
  Operation in the Desert), 222–23,
  227
Oslo Bacteriological Institute, 176

PA bions, 171–72, 182
Pappenheim, Bertha ("Anna O"),
  44–45, 46, 47, 54–55, 57, 79, 100,
  245
Paranormal phenomena, 53
Pasteur, Louis, 169
Paul, St., 213
Pavlov, Ivan, 163
Peer Gynt (Ibsen), 76
Philipson, Dr. Tage, 149, 156, 157,
  167, 178
Philosophy of the Unconscious, The
  (Hartmann), 46
Physiological Institute (England),
  154
Physiological Laboratory
  (Sorbonne), 171
Pietroni, Raymond and Jennifer, 9
Pink, Annie, 82, 239
Plan (magazine), 152, 153
Pleasure principle, 89, 99
Poe, Edgar Allan, 18, 119
Polanyi, Michael, 103
Poltergeist effect, 53, 237
Possessed, The (Dostoevsky), 60
Pragmatism, 35, 212
Premarital chastity, 117–18
Principia (Newton), 4
*Problems of Mysticism and Its Sym-
  bols* (Silberer), 72
Project Blue Book, 215, 222
"Project for a Scientific Psychology"
  (Freud), 34
Proust, Marcel, 111
Psychiatric Clinic (Vienna), 64, 70
"Psychic Contact and Vegetative
  Current" (Reich), 158
Psychic energy, 243
Psychoanalysis: aim of, 99; history
  of, 39–68; sexual theory, 54–64;
  unconscious theory, 43–57; *See
  also* names of psychoanalysts
Psychoanalytic Association, 7, 120,
  122, 148–49, 151, 168
Psychoanalytic Polyclinic (Vienna),
  85–86, 120, 187

Psychoanalytic Press, 148
"Psychoanalytic Quackery," 176
Psychokinesis, 53
Psychological Institute (Oslo Uni-
  versity), 157
Psychological tension, distinction
  between force and, 246–47
Psychology of Human Drives, The
  (Santlus), 31
Psychopathia Sexualis (Krafft-Ebing),
  31–32, 33
Psychotronics, 235
Puységur, Marquis de, 40

"Quantity of excitation" energy, 34
Question of Lay Analysis, The
  (Freud), 97–98

Race, Victor, 40
Radetsky March (Roth), 25
Radiation sickness, 208
Radioactive Phosphorus-32, 208
Rado, Sandor, 77, 133, 143, 152, 182
Raimann, Professor, 64
Raknes, Ola, 7, 11, 14, 157, 167, 191,
  204
Rank, Otto, 5, 66, 71, 72, 121
Ravel, Maurice, 175
Reality principle, 99
Red Help (communist organization),
  152
"Red Revue," 175
Reductionism, 4, 20, 72, 110, 116,
  150, 191, 243
Reich, Annie, 91, 92, 114, 133, 143,
  145, 148, 149, 155, 181, 182
Reich, Frau Cecile, 23, 26, 28–29;
  suicide of, 29
Reich, Eva, 86, 208, 209, 223, 230
Reich, Ilse, 5–6, 7, 8, 10–13, 16, 19,
  25–26, 28, 29, 76, 82, 91, 116, 117,
  122, 134, 136–37, 143, 181, 182,
  183, 186, 188, 189, 194–96, 204,
  208, 209, 214–15, 223, 227–28,
  229, 230, 239–40
Reich, Leon, 25–26, 27, 28; death of,
  29
Reich, Peter, 14, 196, 209, 223, 224,
  227, 230
Reich, Robert, 26, 29, 30, 31; death
  of, 86

Reich, Wilhelm: agitator reputation, 132, 148; army life, 29; arrested, 194, 228; attempts at personal analysis, 76–77; Berlin period, 133–45, 147, 155, 161; bion research, 170–72, 176, 178–79, 182, 191, 194, 195–96, 234–35; birth of, 25; break with Freud, 74, 89, 90–91, 112, 123–25, 132, 133; character analysis technique, 163–64, 244; childhood of, 26–28; "cloudbuster" experiments, 210–12, 220–21, 222, 224–26, 239; communism and, 115–18, 120–22, 125, 133–37, 149; conversion to Freudianism, 34; Danish smear campaign, 153; in the Davos Sanitarium, 91–92, 94, 95, 113; death of, 1, 2, 230; in Denmark, 149, 152–54, 157, 163; depths of insight, 250–51, 252; divorced, 181; education of, 29–30, 82–83; Einstein episode, 186–90, 240–41; in England, 154–55, 172–73; European tour (1933), 154–56; explanation of Freud's hostility, 37; expulsion from Communist Party and Psychoanalytic Association, 122, 151–52, 153, 158; first meeting with Freud, 69–70, 72; Freudian theory and, 77–82; imprisoned, 229–30; insights into processes of madness, 83–84; introduction to, 1–22; jealousy of, 8, 204; last visit with Freud, 133; leftist sympathies, 114–15, 151; life-work and fallacy, 97–112; literal-mindedness of, 78–79; marriages, 5–6, 82, 181; Moscow trip (1929), 122, 123; New England trip (1940), 183; new psychoanalytical techniques (in Norway), 163–67; in Norway, 159–79, 183, 201; notion of "character armor," 36; nudism article, 152, 153; obsessive character of, 194; paranoia of, 15, 17, 37, 149, 159, 163, 177, 213, 214, 226, 229, 233; Party membership (Communist Party), 120, 151; patient sent by Freud (1919), 77–80; Peer Gynt paper, 74–76, 219; persecution mania, 14, 36, 154, 199, 219, 220; on premarital chastity, 117–18; pseudonyms, 157, 227; at Psychoanalytic Polyclinic (Vienna), 85–86; psychoanalytic practice and techniques (1920s), 113, 120, 126–29; relationship with Freud, 36–37, 68, 69–70, 72, 73–74, 87–95, 147–48, 242; Schattendorf killings, 113–14; scientific attitude toward (in 1970s), 235; sexual politics, 117–19, 132–33, 136–43; sterile hay experiment, 169–70; Swedish period, 154, 156–57, 159; temperament of, 73, 79, 168, 173–74, 202; trial of, 227–29; UFO phase, 215–17, 222–24, 227, 231, 236; in the United States, 181–231; Vienna circle, 69–95

Reichenbach, Baron Karl von, 8
Reich family, 25
Reichian therapy, 11–12, 162, 192–93, 203, 215, 222, 230; vital energy hypothesis, 10
Reich Speaks of Freud, 36–37
Reichstag fire of 1933, 144, 156
Reik, Theodor, 71
Reisman, David, 116
Reitschüle (Vienna), 30
Renouvier, Charles, 54
Repression, 81, 99–100, 121, 126
Resistances, 126–27
"Response" (Reich), 218
Reverse effort, law of, 101
Revolutions of 1848, 25
"Right Man" theory, 6, 8, 9, 13, 14, 25, 29, 90, 95, 213, 240; Reich's childhood and, 26–28; and suicide, 28
Rite of Spring, The (Stravinsky), 236
Roazen, Paul, 37, 66–67, 69, 70, 71, 72, 73, 85, 86, 122
Roerich, Nicholas, 236
Rolfe, Frederick (Baron Corvo), 17
Roman Catholic Church, 118, 120, 135, 136
Roman Catholic confession, 99
Roniger (grandmother), 26
Rooth-Tracey, Constance, 11, 16
Roth, Joseph, 25
Rousseau, Jean-Jacques, 84, 118

Ruppelt, Edward J., 215

Sachs, Hanns, 71, 133
Sade, Marquis de, 138
Sadger, Isidore, 76
Sadism, 32
Sagan, Carl, 106
Samadhi, 91
Sar.tlus, Jacob, 31
SAPA (sand packet) bions, 179
Sargant, William, 167
Satori, 91
Savonarola, 230
Scharfenberg, Johann, 179
Schattendorf, killings at, 113–14
Schiele, Egon, 31
Schilder, Paul, 83
Schizophrenia, 75
Schjelderup, Harald, 157, 160, 167
Schneider, 136, 141
Schönberg, Arnold, 31
Schönberg Society, 82
Schopenhauer, Arthur, 46, 65, 87
Schroeder, Max, 134, 153
Schumann, Robert, 84
Seipel, Ignaz, 113, 114
Self-consciousness, 103
Self-esteem, 7, 94, 162, 189
Self-observation, 167
Semmelweis, Ignaz, 84, 236
Sexual Crisis, The (Reich), 141
Sexual electricity, 159
Sexual freedom, 117–18; Reich's
    views on, 137, 138–39
Sexual Question, The (Forel), 34–35
Sexual Revolution, The (Reich), 153,
    229
Sexual Struggle of Youth, The
    (Reich), 141, 144
Sexual theory, 20, 54–64, 72, 77–82,
    83, 87–88, 99–100, 123–24, 140,
    191; abandonment of (by Freud),
    125; Little Hans case, 20, 57–59,
    64; Reich's life work and, 97–112;
    Wolf Man case, 20, 59–63, 64,
    242; *See also* Unconscious, theory
    of
Shakespeare, William, 17
Sharaf, Myron, 214–15
Shaw, George Bernard, 3–4, 64, 159,
    249–50

Shelley, Mary, 191
Shelley, Percy Bysshe, 137
Silberer, Herbert, 71, 90, 150;
    Freud's rejection of, 72–73
Silverman, J., 108
Silvert, Dr. Michael, 224, 225, 226,
    228, 229, 230
Smith, Dr. Anne, vi
Social Democrats (Austria), 113–14,
    132
Social Democrats (Germany), 135
Socialist Society for Sex Consulta-
    tion and Sexological Research, 120
Society of Jesus, 148, 149
Socrates, 52, 230
Somnambulism, 42, 45
Sorbonne University, 171
South, Mary Ann, 41
Spartacist revolution (1919), 114
Sperry, Roger, 21, 104, 106, 109
Split-brain experiment, 105–6
Sportsman's Sketches (Turgenev), 26
Stalin, Joseph, 7, 14, 155, 214
"Stasis," 124, 185
Steinach, Eugen, 36, 73
Steiner, Rudolph, 35
Stekel, Wilhelm, 36, 70, 73, 81
Sterile hay experiment, 169–70
"Strange Case of Wilhelm Reich,
    The," 200
Stravinsky, Igor, 236
Strindberg, August, 17, 156
"Struggle for Psychoanalysis, The"
    (lecture), 153
Studies in Hysteria (Breuer and
    Freud), 46, 54, 55
Studies in the Psychology of Sex
    (Ellis), 32
Suicide, 29, 37, 50, 62, 153; Right
    Man theory and, 28
Summa Theologica (Aquinas),
    115–16
Superego, 85
Swann's Way (Proust), 111
Sweeney, George C., 228
Swift, Jonathan, 84, 198
Synchronicity, 237, 238

Table Talk (Hitler), 142–43
Tausk, Viktor, 37, 66–68, 69, 70, 73,
    90, 91, 150; suicide of, 67–68

T-bacilli, 4, 171–72, 182, 209
Templeton, Clista, 202
Thanatos theory, *see* Death-instinct theory
Third Congress of the World League for Sexual Reform, 135–36
Thirteenth International Congress of Psychoanalysis, 157–58
Thjotta, Professor, 176
Tillich, Paul, 137
Tolkien, J. R. R., 231
Tolstoy, Leo, 30, 110
Tone, Franchot, 164
Transference, 55
Trotsky, Leon, 155
Trotskyists, 155
Turgenev, Aleksandr, 26

Ufologists, 216
Unconscious, theory of, 21, 32, 43–57, 75, 80, 87–88, 101, 106, 109, 121, 242, 248–49; anxiety and, 132; chief role of, 50; energy supply, 49–50; feedback mechanism, 48, 50, 51, 53, 56; functions of, 49; Jungian concepts, 52–53; learned knowledge in, 48–49; poltergeist effect, 53, 237; repression and, 56; *See also* Sexual theory
Under the Banner of Marxism (Reich), 122
Unidentified Flying Objects (UFOs), 215–17, 222–24, 227, 231, 236
United States Air Force, 212, 215, 222, 224, 225, 241
United States Constitution, 218
United States Immigration and Naturalization Service, 204
United States Weather Bureau, 220, 221
University of Oslo, 157, 160, 176
University of Vienna, 30, 31

Van Gogh, Vincent, 84
Van Vogt, A. E., 6–7, 13, 28
Varieties of Religious Experience (James), 111
Vegetotherapy, 176, 193, 195
Verlag für Sexualpolitik, 141
Vienna Psychoanalytic Society, 66, 74, 76

Vienna University Hospital, 82
Vietnam War, 231
Vital energy, 3–4, 10, 12, 35, 89, 115, 150, 161
Vogt, Ragnar, 175
Volkischer Beobachter, 145
Volta, Count Alessandro, 237
Voltaire, 198
Von Reichenbach, 195

Waal, Nic (Hoel), 7, 157, 167, 168, 169, 178
Wagner-Jauregg, 82–83
War and Peace (Tolstoy), 110
Wertenbaker, Colonel, 222
Wessel, Horst, 141
What Is Class-Consciousness? (Reich), 155–56, 157
Whitehead, Alfred North, 3
Whitman, Walt, 249
Wilhelm Reich: A Personal Biography, 5, 6
Wilhelm Reich, Life Force Explorer (Wyckoff), 136
Wilhelm Reich and Orgonomy (Raknes), 199
Wilhelm Reich Foundation, 229
Wilhelm Reich—The Evolution of His Work (Boadella), 16, 122, 167
Wilhelm Reich Vs. the U.S.A. (Greenfield), 200, 217
Wilhelm II, Kaiser, 156
Wittels, Fritz, 66
Wittgenstein, Ludwig, 31
Wolfe, Dr. Theodore P., 178
Wolf Man and Sigmund Freud, The, 61
Wolf Man case, 20, 59–63, 64, 242
Wood, Charles, 202
Wordsworth, William, 50
"Wordsworth effect," 50
Workers' Help (organization), 120
World Almanac, 19
World League for Sexual Reform, 140
World War I, 23, 30, 67
World War II, 51, 197
Wright, Sir Almroth, 154, 159, 234
Wyckoff, James, 136

Yates, Frances, 214

Yearbook of Sexual Deviations (Hirschfeld), 32
Yiddish language, 26
Yin and yang, 17, 106, 199
Young Communist League, 137

Zadig (Voltaire), 198

Zahle (Danish Minister of Justice), 153
Zen Buddhism, 91
Zentralblatt (psychoanalytic journal), 70
Zilboorg, Gregory, 5